Trekking in  Mountains

THE KAÇKAR

by

KATE CLOW

and

TERRY RICHARDSON

This book is dedicated to Recep Akyürek for his devoted work for the preservation of Yusufeli.

1st Edition, English, February 2008: THE KAÇKAR - Trekking in Turkey's Black Sea Mountains
ISBN: 978-0-9639218-5-0
Research and editing: Theresa Day
Photograph editor: Metin Tekeroğlu
Publisher: Upcountry (Turkey) Ltd. 3, Kinnesswood, Palace Road, Buxton SK17 6AF, UK
   www.trekkinginturkey.com
Printed by: Grafiksanatlar Tasarım Hiz. Şti., Istanbul +90-212 219 3400
Copyright: Kate Clow. All rights reserved.
Map copyright: ifj Zsiga György. All rights reserved.

Thanks..............

Without the help of the following people, writing this guide would have been a more time-consuming task. Our grateful thanks to them all.

Aytekin Şeker of Terra Anatolia introduced Kate to the Kaçkar, and Şerif Büyüktaş of Seb-tours encouraged her with in-depth information. Atıl Ulas Cuce, Kerim Karaerkek and Erdoğan Türkyılmaz of Middle Earth Travel shared Kate's first trek there and helped with this project. İbrahim Türgüt, Egemen Çakır, Meidan Vishinski and Özkan Yaşar gave route advice. Özkan Şahin, based in Yusufeli, and Cemil Albayrak, of the pension in Tekkale, supplied local advice.

Ahmet of Barhal and his horse Şimşek (Lightning) took Kate and Jane over the Kırmızı, Hevek and Kavron passes. Fevzi Arslan guided Kate and Tim over the Babur pass in snow and mist. Gökhan and his horse Pascal led Kate and friends over the pass at Okuz Gölü.

Jane Hopton, Tim Salmon and Lem Kenny provided good company while trekking and gave impartial advice about routes and much else.

Brothers İsmail and Naim Altınay of the Çamyuva Pension in Yaylalar were generous with their time, food and accommodation. İsmail Altınay, who also drives the local minibus, got us to remote places and was a mine of information about village paths, customs, old names and history as well as trekking routes. Nadir Demirci, of the Kardelen pension in Ayder, contributed information, lifts, and excellent food. Mehmet of the Karahan Pension in Barhal, Mustafa at the Barhal Pension, the other İsmail Altınay at Olgunlar and the people at the Doğa Hotel also helped.

Özlem Kobal from Başyayla and Hemşin put Kate up for a night, as did Fethi Tamyürek from Bahar Yaylası and Dereiçi. Many people in Davali Yaylası and Sırakonaklar, especially poet Süleyman Kumbasar and his family, looked after Kate. İsmail, the bull-keeper from İspir, took us over the pass near Soğanlı Dağı in a rainstorm and Luman Korucu from Tekkale accommodated Kate during the festival. Cemil took Kate and Jane to Zil Kale in his minibus; Ekrem Demirci of Pokut Yaylası gave them a lift in his Lada; Tezcan Akay of Çat showed Kate around in his jeep and many others gave lifts.

Başak Güner and Terry Underhill gave invaluable help understanding the flora. Özgür Ozarslan and his staff at the Ministry of Culture and Tourism in Ankara gave general support, as did the staff at the Ministry of Culture and Tourism in Artvin. Hasan in Erzurum returned Kate's backpack to Antalya and Alon Robacha at the Taufic Mountain Lodge provided GPS points and maps.

Thanks to the following for fighting to protect the fragile environment of the Kaçkar: the UNDP Çoruh project, the Doğa Derneği (nature society); TEMA (anti-erosion society); Neşe Karahan (of the Cennet Pastanesi), Erol Çağ and Ertuğrul Gazihan of the Yeşil Artvin Derneği. Thanks to those opposing the Yusufeli dam: lawyer Recep Akyürek, Prof. İlyas Yılmazer, Sirali Aydın, Maria Zeiser, Christine Eberlein (www.evb.ch) and Christoph Scheuermann (www.khrp.org, www.ern.org).

Thanks to those who helped to produce the book: George Zsiga for his hard work on the map; Theresa Day for scrupulous editing and Metin Tekeroğlu for layout and printing. Special thanks to Serhan Keser who selflessly gives his own time to keep our website updated and newsletters flowing.

To all at tent manufacturers Saunders (UK) for the Spacepacker lightweight tent; it stood up effortlessly to the rigours of mountain sun, rain and snow.

seb-tours

Aktivreisen für Geniesser und Individualisten

Wander-, Trekking- und Mountainbike-Touren in kleinen Gruppen

KAÇKAR
Almwandern, Trekking
Schneeschuh- und Skitouren
Kombitouren Kaçkar + Ararat

WESTTÜRKEI
Kulturwandern am Bafa See
Trekking und Eselwandern
im Latmos Gebirge

LYKIEN
Genusswandern und Lodgetrekking auf dem Lykischen Weg
Mountainbike Lykienrundfahrt

Kleine Hotels und Pensionen für Ihren Wanderurlaub. Infos und weitere Angebote auf unserer Webseite.

Şerif Büyüktaş   **www.seb-tours.de**
Heßstrasse 72   **80798 München**   +49 89 54290538   info@seb-tours.de

About the team

Kate Clow moved to Turkey in 1989 to sell computer systems in Istanbul. In 1992 she moved to Antalya and started to explore the ancient roads which linked cities of the Greek and Roman periods. From 1995, she connected a series of paths to make Turkey's first long distance walking route. The Lycian Way was opened in 1999 and was followed in 2004 by the St Paul Trail. Kate also writes freelance and leads trekking and bird and flower tours. She first walked in the Kaçkar in 1997, and dreams of life on a self-sufficient yayla in the mountains.

Terry Richardson has a degree in Ancient History and began his travels in Turkey back in 1978. In addition to his work on the Lycian Way, St Paul Trail and Kaçkar guidebooks, he is an author of The Rough Guide to Turkey and a regular contributor to an English-language, daily newspaper in Turkey, Today's Zaman. He has contributed to the Footprint: Turkey and Eyewitness: Turkey guidebooks. Terry leads archaeological tours to various parts of the country and now lives in south-western Turkey.

George Zsiga - who has just turned 28 - studied cartography, geography and law at university then, rather than do an office job, decided to be a freelance cartographer and travel writer. In the past few years, he has travelled around more than fifty countries in four continents, writing over six guidebooks and drawing countless maps for other guide books, including the St. Paul Trail and Lycian Way. When not on the road, he likes to spend his spare time with girls and at the poker tables.

Other trekking guides available from Kate Clow, Terry Richardson and George Zsiga

The Lycian Way. The official guidebook and map to Turkey's first long distance walking trail. The route was pioneered by Kate, and waymarked to Grande Randonnée standards by Kate, Terry and team of volunteers. Winding for over 500 km through coastal Mediterranean Turkey, the trail runs through cedar-forested mountains, past deserted beaches and many rarely-visited ancient sites. The Sunday Times called it 'one of the world's ten best walks', and it now attracts enough trekkers to revitalise the local rural economy.
The Lycian Way (ISBN 0-9539218-1-6) is also available in German: Der Lykische Pfad (0-9539218-3-2)

The St Paul Trail. Turkey's second long-distance trail follows the missionary St Paul on his route north from Roman Perge, over the formidable Toros mountains, to Antioch in Pisidia. Sections of Roman road, nomadic trails, inter-village footpaths and paved Ottoman tracks form this picturesque trail. Deep gorges, dense pine forest, beautiful Lake Eğirdir, a number of remote ancient sites and traditional village hospitality delight the walker. The book includes route descriptions, GPS points, a map and fascinating background information.
St Paul Trail (ISBN 0-9539218-1-6) is also available in Turkish: St Paul Yolu (0-9539218-4-0)

All these books are available from www.trekkinginturkey.com

MUHTEMELEN BU DAĞLARIN EN İYİ TURU

www.bukla.com

Setüstü, 55/6 Kabataş İstanbul Türkiye +90 212 245 0635 bukla@bukla.com

MUHTEMELEN BU DAĞLARIN EN İYİ OTELİ

www.buklaoberj.com

Ayder Yaylası, Çamlıhemşin Rize Türkiye. +90464 657 20 55 oberj@bukla.com

CONTENTS

1. Introduction 11
2. Before you start 12
3. What to bring and wear 19
4. Getting to Turkey and travelling in the Kaçkar 25
5. Local supplies and shopping 28
6. Looking after yourself 32
7. A brief history of the Pontic region and its peoples 35
8. What to look for 44
9. National parks, flora and fauna 50
10. Routes around Tekkale, the Güngörmez Dağları and Zıtlop Sırtı 55
    10.1 Dört Kilise, Bayır Kilise, Elasume Mezrası 55
    10.2 Çubulikar, Doles Mezrası, Çubulikar (or Barhal) 57
    10.3 Bölükbaşı Mezrası, Salent Yaylası (Güngörmez Geçiti, Modut) .58
    10.4 Demirdöven, Solerun, Duruklu, Güzelce, Kışladamları 61
    10.5 Kışladamları, Karbasan, Gravat Yaylası, Sura, Taşkıran, Sarıgöl 65
    10.6 Tekkale, Bölükbaşı, Aşağı Gurp Yaylası, Bahar, Dereiçi 68
11. Routes around Barhal and the Altıparmak Dağları 73
    11.1 Barhal, Amanesket, Naznara, Karagöl (or Satibe Campsite) 73
    11.2 Amanesket Yaylası, Sakser, Bahgat (and Karagöl) 75
    11.3 Kurdat road, Pişenkaya Yaylası, Libler Gölü 77
    11.4 Pişenkaya, Büyükaho Tepesi, Zekarat, Sarnaven Deresi, İrat, Demirdöven 79
    11.5 Barhal, Sarıbulut, Binektaşı, Norsel, Pişenkaya, Okuz Gölü, Satelef, Yaylalar 83
12. Routes around Yaylalar, Olgunlar and the Kaçkar range 88
    12.1 Olgunlar, Yaylalar 88
    12.2 Yaylalar, (Aksav Deresi), Modut Yaylası, Mikelis 90
    12.3 Yaylalar, Karamolla, Sabahde Geçiti, (Tüzpir Y), Sulamenta, Veknal, Demirdöven 92
    12.4 Yaylalar, Olgunlar, Dilberdüzü Campsite, Deniz Gölü, Kaçkar summit and Dilberdüzü 95
    12.5 Olgunlar, Dibe Yaylası, Naletleme Geçiti, Yukarı Kavron (or Yukarı Çaymakçur) 98
    12.6 Yaylalar, Karamolla, Körahmet, Satelef, Babur Geçiti, Palakçur, Kaler Düzü 101
    12.7 Dilberdüzü, Hevek Geçiti, Davaliaşıtı, Apivanak, Karmık, Tirovit 105
    12.8 Olgunlar, Kanucar Geçiti, Dargit, Yüncüler 110
13. North of the range - Ayder and the Kaçkar National Park 112
    13.1 Ayder, Huzur, Ayder 112
    13.2 Ayder, Hazındak, Pokut, Sal 113
    13.3 Yukarı Kavron, Aşağı Kavron, Aşağı Çaymakçur, Palakçur, Avusor 116

Terra Anatolia

Trekking Specialists of Turkey

We like to use our boots!!
Even the old ones..

Sincerely,
Terra Anatolia Team

www.terra-anatolia.com

13.4 Ayder, Aşağı Çaymakçur, Yukarı Çaymakçur, Körahmet Geçiti, Bulut Deresi, Satelef, Körahmet, Karamolla, Yaylalar 119
13.5 Ayder, Avusor, Kırmızı Geçiti, Pişenkaya, Barhal 123
13.6 Yukarı Kavron, Derebaşı Gölü, Kavron Geçiti, Davali, Taşbaşı, Sırakonaklar, Soğanlı, Hevek Geçiti, Dilberdüzü, Olgunlar 127
13.7 Ayder, Aşağı Kavron, Samistal, Amlakit, Palovit, Tirovit, Elevit130
14. Routes in the Fırtına Deresi and Tatos Dağları 134
14.1 Fırtına Deresi, Ortam, Fırtına Deresi 135
14.2 Çat, Çat Yaylası (Vanski) 135
14.3 Elevit, Karunç, church ruins 136
14.4 Tirovit, Karmık, Yıldızlı Gölü (Hacıvanak) 137
14.5 Çat, Kaleköy, Baş Yayla, Kale Geçiti, Hacıvanak, Hodacur Geçiti, Davali, Taşbaşı, Sırakonaklar 138
14.6 Kaleköy, Tatos Gölları, Tatos Geçiti, Yedigöl 144

Appendices:
A. Setting up and using your GPS 147
B. Useful information 149
C. Turkish for trekkers 154
D. Glossary - mountaineering terms 157
E. Photographs 158

Çam Yuva Pansiyon

Yaylalar

15 en-suite rooms, dormitory
4 family bungalows
Restaurant, bakery and shop
Group minibus transport
 to/from Erzurum airport
Guides, mules & drivers arranged

Open all year for trekking, flowers, birdwatching, mountaineering, snowshoeing and skiing.

Hoş Geldiniz

Naim & İsmail Altınay
Tel/fax: (90) 466 832 2001
e-mail: info@middleearthtravel.com

✓tempotour
Since 1980

Tours to the Black Sea, Kaçkar Mountains, South-East and East Anatolia
Holidays in Kaş, Kalkan, Fethiye and Ölüdeniz
Daily Hiking and Cultural Tours from Ankara

Binnaz Sokak No 1/4, Kavaklıdere, Ankara
Tel: (90) 312 428 2096 Fax: 426 1670
www.tempotur.com.tr

Chapter 1 **INTRODUCTION**

Turkey is a land rich in mountains. They include the magnificent Toros chain running parallel to the Mediterranean in the south, the remote Cilo-Sat range on the Iraq/Iran borders, and the chain of Anatolian volcanic outcrops starting on the eastern frontier and finishing at the western Mediterranean. Biblical Mount Ararat, on the Iranian/Armenian frontier, rises to over 5000 m. Wonderful though these mountains are, Turkey's Kaçkar range offers the very best walking and trekking in this vast, mountainous country.

Kaçkar (pronounced Katchkar) probably derives from the Armenian word for a monumental stone; the literal Turkish meaning of kaç kar is 'how much snow?'. Both meanings are appropriate for a massive granite range topped with permanent snow. Situated in the far north-east of Turkey, the Kaçkar rise dramatically above the Black Sea, close to the Georgian frontier. Part of a larger range known historically as the Pontic Alps, they boast exquisite alpine lakes, verdant, flower-studded meadows, glaciers, towering granite peaks with views of the Pontus/Black Sea, richly forested valleys and a wealth of unique and beautiful flora. This compact region is a trekkers' paradise. If you are still in doubt, the region's vibrant yayla/high pasture culture, easy access, good local transport, cheap food and friendly accommodation should convince you that the Kaçkar mountains are well worth a visit. The central part of the range is a national park, and protected accordingly (see www.kackarlar.org for the managing authorities and information about park planning).

We have just spent several sunburned years establishing two marked long-distance walking trails in the Toros mountains (the Lycian Way and St Paul Trail). As a contrast, we opted for the cooler climate of the Kaçkar mountains in Turkey's temperate north-east. The range is snow-blanketed from November through April and snow covers the higher passes well into June making maintenance of a marked trail impossible. Instead, we have described the finest treks in the area. By including lower level routes, we have extended the trekking season into the spring and autumn. By exploring unused high passes, we have opened up new routes and campsites which are not used by organised groups on their 'set' routes.

This area of Turkey is fast losing its culturally diverse peoples; villagers who once won a good living from their mountain pastures are now defeated by falling livestock prices, school closures and lack of winter employment. Almost en masse, from necessity and much against their will, they are moving their families to the towns. We hope this guide will encourage the expansion of environmentally-responsible tourism and help locals to earn a living by providing accommodation, services and food to visitors. The people are the mountains most precious asset.

This comprehensive guide includes background information and colour photos illustrating the landscape, history, culture and nature of the region. We have made it easy to use by including a new, detailed map, GPS data and a 'Turkish for trekkers' quick guide. With 32 routes, from 2.5 hr walks to cross-range adventures lasting several days, this is the most comprehensive guide available to Turkey's most beautiful mountain range.

Chapter 2 **BEFORE YOU START**

Turkey is modernising at a ferocious rate. Swathes of concrete apartment blocks ring nearly every Turkish city and the Black Sea littoral. New motorways (including the motorway stretching all the way from Istanbul to Georgia) push remorselessly across the land. McDonalds and Pizza Hut pepper city centres and affluent suburbs. Multi-screen cinemas show the latest Hollywood movies and young Turks fritter their newly acquired wealth on mobile phones and designer clothing.

But that's in the cities. Rural Turkey remains much as it was - traditional, remote and timeless. The Kaçkar may be reminiscent of the Swiss Alps scenically, but its villages and their inhabitants are a world apart. There are tea-houses/kahve in place of bars or pubs. The shop (if there is one) sells basic commodities such as tea, sugar and soap rather than skiing accessories or handicrafts. Life is tough in these isolated uplands, with little opportunity for Western-style leisure pursuits. Most locals struggle to understand why a clearly wealthy foreigner would chose to visit their region in the first place, let alone tramp across it bearing a 'mule-load' of a backpack on his or her back.

The nearest hospital is far away, mountain rescue rudimentary and locals who can speak a foreign language a rarity. In other words, you need to be reasonably experienced to consider independent trekking in these mountains. The ability to use a map and compass (and preferably a GPS) is essential. To trek the higher, longer routes you will need to carry a tent, stove, food and extra clothing and be prepared for heavy rain and thick mist.

Fortunately, since the 1980's local Turkish trekking companies and loose organisations of pension owners have supported groups and individual trekkers. Several options are now available: self-sufficient backpacking; hiring a mule and its driver to carry your backpack; forming your own guided trekking group; joining a commercial fully-supported trek. For further information, look at the website which supports this book, www.trekkinginturkey.com.

Whichever option you choose, local people will go out of their way to help you. As a visitor to 'their' mountains, they will feel honour bound to try and ensure that you come to no harm.

Which trailhead?

The approach to the Kaçkar mountains is from the north-west (via Trabzon airport or bus garage/otogar), the south (via Erzurum airport, otogar or train station) or from the north-east (via Batumi airport). If you approach from Trabzon, you can visit two important Greek Orthodox religious buildings - Aya Sofya church in Trabzon, and the nearby Sumela Monastery. You also benefit from more frequent connections to Istanbul and to the trailheads. If you choose Erzurum, the city has an impressive range of Islamic buildings and a medieval castle. Both are described in detail in all the independent travellers' guide books, so are outside the scope of this book.

The gateway cities are more or less equidistant from their trailheads. These are (from Trabzon) Ayder, Yukarı Kavron, Çat and Elevit in the north, and (from Erzurum and Batumi) Tekkale, Barhal, Yaylalar and Olgunlar in the south. Ayder, Barhal and Yaylalar/Olgunlar are the important trailheads as they have most accommodation and services for trekkers.

The Kaçkar

On the north side, Ayder (see Chapter 13, page 112) is the gateway to the Kaçkar National Park and as such has benefited from much inward investment in accommodation, renovation of the hot spring/hamam, quality roads, etc. However, it lies, at 1500 m, well below the alpine zone, the focus of most trekkers' interest. As a centre of Turkish tourism, it has over 50 pensions and hotels, many at the expensive end of the market and, compared with the southern side, is often overpriced. Yukarı Kavron, at 2100 m and 15 km closer to the alpine zone, is the usual start point for organised treks into the high peaks. Unfortunately, Yukarı Kavron is largely spoiled by unregulated development and hordes of day trippers, so we recommend starting your treks from other nearby summer villages/yaylas. Çat (1200 m) and Elevit (1600 m) (see Chapter 14, page 134) are reached by the Fırtına Deresi road, which is one of the most beautiful in Turkey. Both are smaller, with limited accommodation and transport links, but have far more charm.

On the south side, the lowest trailhead is only 7 km from Yusufeli at Tekkale (700 m, see Chapter 10, page 55), a small but scenic village on the banks of the Çoruh. It's long walk or a hitchhiked ride from here to Bölükbaşı, the starting point for most walks. The other trailheads are on the single-track road which follows the Barhal/Hevek Deresi to the heart of the Kaçkar. Barhal (1200 m, see Chapter 11, page 73), has a noted Georgian church, three pensions and several shops. Higher up the valley, Yaylalar (1800 m) and Olgunlar (2000 m) are only 10 mins drive or 30 mins walk apart (see Chapter 12, page 88). Between them they have four large pensions and several shops and Yaylalar has a campsite. Yaylalar is also the centre for organised treks, mule hire and (rudimentary) mountain rescue services.

You can read more information about the regions and the trailheads at the start of chapters 10 - 14.

Maps / harita

High quality, detailed maps of Turkey are still not available (maps are the prerogative of the Turkish Military). We have included a detailed plan (backed up by GPS data) which provides more than enough information for safe trekking. As elsewhere in Turkey, many place names (including those of mountains) have been changed in the last thirty years. Locals, influenced by their Armenian, Georgian, Laz as well as Turkish roots, have largely ignored the changes. When trying to ask the way or showing a local the map, this can lead to confusion. We have tried to use the names the locals themselves use and give alternative or 'official' names for some yaylas in the text.

Please check our website for updates to the routes described. We welcome any additional information and GPS points you may collect.

GPS data

We have collected several hundred GPS points with altitude measurements for the routes described in the guide. These help ensure easy navigation in mist or rain, which is common on the north side of the range, and compensate for the relatively small scale of the map. Over most of the routes, with the exception of the thickly forested areas, satellite reception is good and the points are often accurate to within 10 m. If you don't have a GPS, you can use an altimeter as well as a compass to help navigate. The route section of this book lists waypoints and shows altitude profiles; the GPS points are also available to download direct from the website.

Route descriptions and grading

Each route description includes an introductory paragraph summarising the trek. We give an overall time (based on the time we took, but not allowing for stops for meals, etc). There is a GPS point list (including altitudes) and an altitude profile diagram. The summary points out any hazards, seasonal considerations, special equipment requirement and linked or alternative routes. On the map routes suitable for mules are show in a different line. We haven't, however, graded the routes, as grades depend on snow cover and vary during the season.

From this information you can assess which routes and/or alternatives are suitable for you.

We use the following abbreviations in the text:

WP - waypoint	m - metres	GPS - global positioning system
Alt - Altitude	km - kilometre(s)	N - north
TL - Turkish Lira	kg - kilogram(s)	S - south
Est - Estimated	g - grams	E - east
Av - Average	l - litres	W - west
hr, hrs - hour(s)	Lat - Latitude	NNW - north-north-west, etc.
mins - minute(s)	Long - Longitude	° - degrees Centigrade

We also use the following Turkish or local words or suffixes, often as part of place names:

aşağı - lower	kale - castle, fort or tower
-aşıt(ı) - paved route, usually over a pass	kilise(si) - church, chapel, monastery
-başı - head or top,	kışla - winter quarters
bakkal - a small shop selling everything	köprü(sü) - bridge
barınak - small stone hut at altitude	köy(ü) - village
-çat - juction of rivers	-ler/lar - plural endings
çeşme - tap or piped spring	mahalle(si) - administrative district
-çur - Laz for yayla	mezra(sı) - village used in spring and autumn
dağ(ı) - mountain; dağlar(ı) - mountains	nehir(i) - major river
dere(si) - valley with stream and tributaries	oluk - gutter or ditch carrying water
-dibi - lower, at the foot of	otogar - a bus garage or terminus
dolmuş(u) - minibus running on a set route	pınar - natural spring
düz(ü) - high-level flat grassy area	sırt(ı) - ridge or spur off a main ridge
-evit/ovit - Hemşinli for yayla	tepe(si) - summit or hill
geçit(i) - pass over mountains	-vank, vanak - Hemşinli for monastery
göl(ü), deniz(i) - natural lake	yayla(sı) - summer pasture with buildings
kahve(si) - village tea shop / general store	yukarı - upper

When to walk - climate / iklim

The latitude of the Kaçkar (around 40 degrees N, roughly the same as the Alps) give the range a temperate, alpine climate. Climate and weather patterns are very different on each side of the range The north-western, Black Sea facing slopes are wet and mild. In the lower zones, tea is a major cash-crop, the plantations giving way to hazelnut plantations, then chestnut, spruce and beech; higher up are dense fir or pine forests and finally, above 2100 m, a true alpine zone of flower carpeted meadows, petering out into bare rock, permanent snow patches and even glaciers. During the summer months, dense mists can (and do) sweep up these seaward-facing slopes to altitudes of up to 3000 m, making navigation difficult. By contrast, the south-western slopes, sloping to the parched Anatolian plateau, are generally dry and sunny in the summer months. They are less well forested and verdant than the northern slopes but have beautiful alpine meadows and working yaylas.

So, when to walk? July and August have, by tradition, been the most popular months to trek: they are the warmest, the days are long and the snow-pack has receded from even the highest passes. The upland pastures or yayla are inhabited, wild flowers bloom and you are most likely to find walking companions. There are distinct advantages to trekking at other times of the year. In July and August the most popular routes and campsites may be crowded with other trekkers - especially organised groups - and the mists churning up from the Black Sea are thicker during these months. Lower altitude treks on the southern side of the range are free of snow from May onwards. If you are experienced in using an ice-axe (and possibly crampons), May and June are good months in which to trek at higher altitudes as well. Both the foothills and the mountains proper are almost deserted, awkward scree is still snow-covered, vibrant alpine flowers are just emerging from the retreating snows and the call of the snow cock reverberates from the high cirques. September and the first half of October are also excellent, as the villagers gather the last hay and firewood and settle in their winter abodes. Again, there are few trekkers, and the high passes remain snow-free. Perhaps most importantly, the afternoon mists rising from the seaward side of the mountains abate and stable weather conditions usually prevail, especially in the Tatos / Verçenik area. The downside of both May-June and September-October is that the yayla are either just beginning to be occupied, or they are emptying, according to altitude and a well-established tradition.

Snow usually begins in earnest in November, and lasts through until April (though you'll find snow patches at high altitudes and ice bridges in north-facing valleys virtually year round). The only infrastructure for winter mountain activities are the pensions in Ayder and Yaylalar which are kept open to support heli-skiing (starting from Ayder). If you base yourself in Yaylalar, the possibilities for ski-touring and snow-shoeing are endless. You need to be experienced and self-sufficient, but a few guides do take people into the mountains in winter.

Temperature and rainfall chart

This is the best rainfall and temperature information we can find for Yusufeli (south-east of the range) and Rize (north-west):

	Jan	Feb	Mar	April	May	June	July	Aug	Sept	Oct	Nov	Dec
	\multicolumn{12}{c}{Yusufeli - south-east}
Rain mm	20.1	19.9	23	33.8	36.2	40.2	23.4	15.6	12.5	24.3	31.0	29.4
Av °C at 500 m	1.1	3	8.3	14.9	19.1	22.7	25.8	25.8	22.2	16	8.5	2.7
Est Av °C at 2500 m	-12.9	-11	-5.7	0.9	5.1	8.7	11.8	11.8	8.2	2	-5.5	-11.3
	\multicolumn{12}{c}{Rize - north-west}
Rain mm	220	155	116	108	97	135	132	180	259	233	264	249
Av °C at 0 m	5.6	6.7	8	11.8	15.9	20	22.3	22	19.4	15.6	11.4	7.6
Est Av°C at 2500m	-11.9	-10.8	-9.5	-5.7	-1.6	2.5	4.8	4.5	1.9	-1.9	-6.1	-9.9

The estimated figures for the 2500 m contour south and north of the range are based on an average drop in temperatures of 7° C for each 1000 m rise in altitude above Yusufeli or Rize. They cannot be verified as there's no recording equipment at this altitude.

How to walk - independently or mule-supported

Throughout the Kaçkar mountains, villagers have traditionally made a living from their mules. Before the 1950's, when the roads were built, pack animals were essential to carry produce to markets and to bring supplies back. In addition, mule and horse trains carrying Black Sea produce (tea, timber, dried fish, nuts, etc) plus the essential paraffin and salt traversed the mountains. Travel was mainly limited to the summer season and the mules had to be maintained indoors or in the lowlands during the winter. Now the practice of guiding and supporting trekking groups has partly replaced this traditional work. Many mule and horse drivers work for trekking companies, carrying gear to and from base camps. Others work on the longer routes, taking their mules over high passes and rocky terrain.

If you are planning a long trek, especially if it is your first time in the Kaçkar, then it may make sense to use a mule/horse driver. They can be hired through the pension owners at Yukarı Kavron, Barhal and Yaylalar and the drivers are paid a standard rate per day. This is agreed (informally) between the drivers at the start of each season, and at the time of writing was 35 euros. One mule is adequate for 3-4 people or about 40-50 kg; a horse can take a little more baggage, but is less nimble in snow or on a difficult pass.

The driver has his own tent and sleeping bag, usually a kettle and stove, and sacks or panniers for your backpacks. The hirer provides food for the driver and supplementary food (if required) for the mule. The drivers don't usually speak any foreign language so you must allow time for an initial conversation through an interpreter (for example, your pension owner) and cover such points as animal food, supplies, cooker and fuel, etc. It's also wise to take your driver when you shop for food - that way you know he will eat what you buy and he can suggest necessary items.

Of course, you should show the driver in advance which route you want to take and he will know (or easily be able to find out) whether your planned passes are open and problem free. Mules can tackle snow up to a foot or so in depth provided that the path below is not littered with rocks. They can handle deeper snow if the surface is hard enough for them not to sink (ie. on north facing slopes) and the gradient is not too steep. Over rocks, they need to be able to see where they are walking. Provided that more snow doesn't fall, the first mule of the season over any particular pass will leave a trail which subsequent animals can follow. Remember that the mule is its owner's livelihood; do not push the driver too hard and be prepared to help unload the animal and carry packs over any really difficult sections.

In camp, the driver will first have to attend to his animal so will probably leave the cooking to you. As he gets to know you, he may help to cook and certainly make tea the way he likes it! Each night, agree a starting time for the next morning so he can saddle the mule and strike his camp. The mule and his driver don't necessarily walk with you - they may have to take an easier path or want to go ahead to an agreed campsite to let the animal graze.

Remember that, if you intend trekking with a mule, you will need a decent day-sack to comfortably carry the stuff you need during the day - waterproof, fleece, sun-cream, hat, gloves, guide, notebook, camera etc.

Mule hire - points for and against
For:
1. You only need to carry a daysack, the mule carries your main pack
2. The driver knows the route; you can't easily get lost
3. The driver can help with jobs around the camp
4. The driver can give you an introduction to village/yayla families who can provide you with extra food
5. The driver will know the closest shelter in case of sudden storms
6. The driver knows how to deal with bulls or curious cows
7. A mule may be able to carry an injured person or the driver can summon help
8. Increases the number of days you can trek without re-supplying
9. Makes it easier to trek with children

Against:
1. Hiring a mule increases the cost of your trek
2. A driver has a personality - you may or may not get on with him
3. Lack of privacy - some of every day/night is spent in his company
4. The driver may control how many hours you walk per day
5. Less flexibility about campsites - mules need grazing overnight
6. Mules attract flies
7. Drivers tend to be conservative - they may be unwilling to try new routes

Animal hazards

The dogs you're likely to meet (often at least part Kangal, a famously huge breed of Anatolian sheepdog) are used to guard people and their animals against bears and wolves, mainly at night. A few dogs are also used to guard the flocks of sheep kept in the southern part of the range. A dog-scaring whistle could thus prove useful. Alternatively, stop walking, pick up some stones, show them to the dog, stand your ground and throw the stones if necessary.

Domestic bulls (and cows) are a different matter and, if they feel that you (or your tent) are in their territory, they may charge. Cows are gathered in every evening for milking so you may encounter them when they are walking to or from their grazing grounds in the early morning or evening, often with a child in attendance. They are incredibly curious and like to take a look at anything new on their territory. If they approach too close to your tent, a small stone thrown at their ribs may be a sufficient deterrent. Bulls, however, are often left out to graze on high ground for the whole summer in herds that can number up to 100 animals. They scatter over the hillside during the day but move downhill to a gathering and watering point in the evening. Such a herd will usually have a guardian but on Fridays the herdsmen frequently go down to the nearest village and mosque to pray, gossip, see their families and collect stores. Try to avoid unattended animals where possible by skirting around them and, if they approach, don't make any sudden movements. Often they are impelled by curiosity and, having examined you, will get bored and amble away. If they don't, banging a rock with a trekking pole may be a sufficient warning to them. If you have to make an escape, remember that they will not follow you onto scree slopes or rocks as they could break a leg on the uneven ground.

Bears are fairly common in the Kaçkar but only at the lower, forested altitudes. If you do some of the lower level treks/walks described in this guide, you may well comes across their droppings, brightly coloured by the fruit on which they live. They are mainly nocturnal but you may be lucky enough to see one at dawn or dusk, returning to or emerging from its den. Provided it has heard your approach, it is unlikely to do you any harm. The locals tell stories about their intelligence and would certainly rather be raided by a bear than a wolf. They have been known to take beehives from the centre of a village and usually choose the heaviest hive from a row. Around Ayder, hives are hung in trees so bears can't reach them; near Çamlıhemşin and on Ovit Dağı, they are racked on an inaccessible cliff wall and reached by a (removable) ladder.

Language

Although Turkish is a difficult language to master, it is comparatively easy to learn a few basic words and phrases. Refer to the Turkish for Trekkers section on page 154 and try to learn a few words every day. The locals you meet will much appreciate your efforts; they will likely earn you far more credit than you deserve in the local village or yayla! Few Turks in rural areas such as the Kaçkar can speak a foreign language but you may come across 'returnees' who do. These are Turks who have lived and worked abroad (usually in Germany) and have returned, either for the summer or permanently, to their home village.

Local accents can be very strong so even if you speak some Turkish you may not be able to understand what the villagers are saying. This is compounded by the fact that the local speech is peppered with Laz and/or Hemşin words and phrases.

Chapter 3 WHAT TO BRING AND WEAR

What to bring and wear depends on the season you chose to walk, the altitudes you intend walking to, and your own special interests (photography, bird-watching, etc). The suggestions made below should cover your needs for trekking from June to October (and longer for the lower altitude walks).

Compass / pusula

Even if you are an expert GPS user (see below) a compass (and the ability to use it properly!) is an essential item. The afternoon mists, for which the Kaçkar are notorious, can obscure the clearest path in seconds, leaving the walker confused, disoriented and damp.

GPS

We recommend you use a GPS, preferably one that calculates altitude. Even people who are not technically minded can master one and they give an element of safety, especially to a lone or inexperienced walker. The advantages of using a GPS are as follows:
- it's almost impossible to get lost; the GPS will give you a distance and bearing to the next GPS point on your chosen route, so that even if you wander off the path you can find your way back.
- you can measure your distance and therefore estimate your time from your target or any other point.
- you're not totally dependent on the map and book; if you lose them, you can still continue
- in emergencies, you can phone for help, give a GPS location and know someone can find you.
- you can mark any problem areas or interesting finds for future users of the trail (and for us!)

However, like any other electronic device, they can malfunction, be lost or fall in a river! Don't rely on one completely. It is essential that you learn how to use your GPS before you arrive in the Kaçkar. Remember to bring sufficient spare batteries and the instruction book. For technical information about setting up your GPS, loading the routes etc, see Appendix A, page 147.

Mobile phones / cep telefonu

Until 2007, mobiles hardly worked in this area. But, in the summer of 2007, mobile phone masts were erected in Barhal and Yaylalar and were due to be commissioned in October 2007. It is likely that by 2008 things will have changed dramatically and that you'll be able to get reception from most higher points and larger villages; check the website for information. It may well be worthwhile buying a local SIM card. Should you decide to do so, the most reliable network with the widest coverage is Turkcell. Just take your phone into one of the many specialist shops in one of the 'gateway towns' (see page 25). They will unlock your phone if necessary, fit the SIM card and 'top-up' your phone with 100 or 250 prepaid units. The cost for the card, registration and the initial 100 units is around 12 euros; they may require a photocopy of the relevant page of your passport to do this. Transferring to the Turkish network will increase coverage and save you money (a one minute call to Europe costs around 0.50 euros).

THE KAÇKAR

Camera / fotoğraf makinası

The 'gateway' cities to the region, Erzurum and Trabzon, have specialist photography shops where you can stock up on print film or cfc cards, have your films developed and/or put onto a CD. In Yusufeli and Ayder, internet cafes will allow you to upload your digital images and burn them onto a CD. If you use slide film (especially specialist films such as Fuji Provia), you must stock up at home - slide film is now very hard to obtain outside of Istanbul and finding a developer even trickier. Prices for film are similar to the rest of Europe, processing generally a little cheaper. Bring adequate spare batteries and the camera cable.

When you are on the trail, make sure that your camera is well protected from the elements (particularly grit and rain) and yourself (most damage to cameras is caused by people dropping them!). If you want to take photos while carrying a pack, we recommend a padded camera case that straps around your waist. It's also a good idea to have a soft cloth and brush to clean your camera, and foil to protect film from the sun and the x-ray machine at airports.

The Kaçkar mountains are very beautiful - a photographer's dream. Granite summits, snow-choked cirques, ice-rimmed lakes, meadows a riot of multi-hued alpine flowers and local people (particularly women) wearing their traditional dress. If you wish to photograph local people, please use your discretion. If the photographer is male, women (particularly the younger ones) may well take offence. Make your intentions clear - smile, point at your camera and then at them - they will soon make it clear if they don't wish to be photographed. With the majority of local men, the problem is not that they don't wish to be photographed (most love it!) but that they will adopt a formal 'studio' pose. For more natural pictures, use as a telephoto lens and try to photograph them while they are working.

Local dress codes and customs

The inhabitants of the Kaçkar mountains are generally traditionally minded and overwhelmingly Muslim. It is advisable to observe the local dress codes and dress conservatively. When approaching a village or yayla, catching a local bus or talking to a cow- or goat-herd, make sure that your shoulders, chest and knees are covered. If you choose to walk in shorts, it is a good idea to have long trousers handy to cover-up when approaching habitation.

You are certain, at some point of your trek, to be invited into a village/yayla house for a glass of tea, a cool ayran (a salty but refreshing mix of yoghurt and water) or even a meal. Take off your boots/shoes where indicated - you'll see a pile of them - and enter the living area in socks or bare feet. Should hospitality extend further to the offer of a bed for the night, it will probably be in a spare yayla house.

A tiny percentage of the men of the northern slopes are, unusually for rural Turkey, heavy drinkers. Groups of male day trippers can also drink to excess with their barbecues or picnics, which are usually eaten by the side of their cars. Women walkers should avoid such groups. Dress sensibly, act conservatively and there'll be no problem.

Boots and socks / ayakkabı ve çorap

Many of the treks described in this book lay wholly or partly in the alpine zone. In the main trekking season, conditions underfoot will be largely rock and scree, with gushing streams and snow patches to cross. You should wear decent mountain

THE KAÇKAR

walking boots with thick soles, good ankle support and a sewn-in tongue to prevent water penetration. Take some trekking sandals or lightweight shoes to wear around the camp or while your boots are drying. For winter and spring trekking, your boots should have a sole rigid enough to take crampons. Gaiters are also useful above the snowline and help keep your boots dry while crossing bogs and streams or if you get caught out in heavy rain. Take at least two pairs of thick, good-quality walking socks to protect and insulate your feet, absorb sweat and (most importantly) help prevent blisters.

Clothing / giyim

Although the Kaçkar have a temperate climate, temperatures still vary enormously depending on the time of day, amount of sun or shade and altitude. Layered clothing enables you to cope with these climatic extremes. Wear a thermal vest or T-shirt made from polypropylene or a similar 'breathable' and quick drying fabric. A fleece jacket or pullover is best for the mid-wear layer, as it is both light and quick drying. The outer (shell) layer should be both windproof and waterproof - a breathable (gortex or similar) fabric jacket with a hood is best. For the northern side of the range, a waterproof poncho that covers both you and your pack is a good addition to a thin waterproof jacket.

A pair of thermal (polypropylene) or silk long johns are essential for early summer/autumn treks at higher altitude, and are a useful 'back-up' even in summer. Specialist trekking/walking trousers (made from a suitable material such as polyamide) are advisable, as they are lightweight, quick drying, durable, and have useful zipped pockets. A pair of lightweight overtrousers (preferably made from a breathable fabric) will provide protection against heavy rain and snow. If you intend camping or walking in the alpine zone (above 3000 m), a warm pair of gloves and a hat are advisable.

If you come to these mountains in the spring, autumn or in winter, you will need to 'beef-up' the above clothing with a down/fibre jacket, fleece-lined gortex (or similar fabric) gloves and a balaklava.

Sunglasses / guneş gözlüğü and sun protection / güneş kremi

The sun, particularly on the south-western slopes and in the alpine zone, is fierce. Fair skinned people should take a sunhat with a wide brim, to protect their neck and prevent sunburn. Even if you're dark skinned, take a cotton scarf; you can use it to stop sweat trickling into your eyes. Sunglasses are essential items. Those designed for skiing or mountaineering are best (and more expensive!). They have better quality lenses and filter more damaging rays; plus they are less likely to break when dropped or sat on than normal sunglasses. Bring a cheaper pair as back-up.

Everyone should use sun block for lips and noses, ears and the backs of their hands, backed up with sunscreen. If you do get burnt, blister cream will help relieve the discomfort.

It's possible to swim in the small mountain lakes in July and August, so you could bring swimwear. Be very careful - some of the lakes are deep; the water is icy cold so cramp is a possibility.

Tent / çadır

If you intend camping, take a lightweight, free-standing backpacking or mountaineering tent. It should be quick and easy to erect (models where the fly is pitched first are best for rain as the inner tent can be kept dry) and as light as possible (unless a mule is carrying it), preferably under 2 kg. It should have sufficient space between the inner and outer tent to allow you to cook if it is raining (or snowing) outside.

Backpack / sırt cantası

For anything other than day or mule-supported hikes, you need a durable, internal frame backpack with a capacity of 65-75 l. It should have a padded hip belt and a chest strap joining the two shoulder straps; these will help redistribute the load and lessen the strain on your back and shoulders. A pack specifically designed for mountaineering has the advantage of a narrow profile, making it easier to balance when moving over rocky terrain and less likely to snag on the lower, forested routes described in this guide. Use a heavy-duty liner to keep your things dry. Indeed, given the likelihood of encountering a day or two of torrential rain, an external pack-cover or a poncho that covers you and your pack is also a good idea. No matter how good it is, if you pack it incorrectly it will be uncomfortable, so try to keep heavy items as close to your back as possible and items you are likely to want during the day in an easily accessible place.

Walking poles / direk

Walking poles take some strain off the knee joints and lower back and help maintain balance on scree, snow slopes and stream crossings. They also give you a feeling of security if challenged by a sheepdog or a bull. If you are backpacking, we really do recommend them. On the negative side, they are yet another thing to carry, break or lose.

Sleeping bag / uyku tulumu and mat / mat

Take the lightest, best quality 3-4 season sleeping bag that you can afford. Down bags are less bulky, lighter and provide better insulation than (admittedly cheaper) synthetic bags. However, they are more difficult to dry and lose their 'loft' if they get wet. An inner silk liner helps to keep your bag clean and provides extra insulation.

Self-inflating sleeping mats provide better insulation and are more comfortable than foam mats but are heavier, more expensive and puncture easily, so you should take a repair kit.

Waistsack or daysack

If you are backpacking, you need a separate waistsack or daysack for anything you may want handy, such as cash, this book, a compass, penknife, notebook, sunglasses, watch, sunscreen and lip salve or vaseline. This can be stuffed in your backpack much of the time. Passport, large amounts of money, credit cards etc. are better in either a concealed body belt or in a secure place in your backpack.

A daysack is useful if you intend leaving your backpack while peakbagging. You can also pack it full of unwanted gear and leave it at a pension or send it by bus to one of the trailhead towns/villages. On the downside, it weighs more then a waistsack. Some type of small sack is essential if you are planning to trek with mules.

Cooking / pişirme

Butane or petrol stoves are the only two real options but it's forbidden to bring butane cartridges or petrol in by air. Both have their advantages and disadvantages. Butane stoves are simpler and cleaner to use but they do not burn well at altitude.

It is easy (and cheap) to buy butane stoves, of the type that pierces a hole in the cylinder, around the Kaçkar. There are 2 sizes, taking either 190 g EN 417 cylinders or 500 g cylinders. At the time of writing, stoves and cylinders are available in the gateway cities of Trabzon and Erzurum. Yusufeli, Barhal and Yaylalar, en route to the southern side of the range, all have stockists. On the northern approaches, they are available in Pazar, Çamlıhemşin, Ayder, and Elevit. Stores in other villages may stock them - it's worth asking if you're desperate - but don't rely on this.

Petrol stoves are expensive to buy, more complicated to use, dirtier and more dangerous. On the other hand, they perform well at high altitudes, burn hotter and are cheaper to run. Petrol stoves are not available in the area and petrol is quite hard to find in the Kaçkar range proper. Trabzon and Pazar have petrol stations and there is one 1 km south of Çamlıhemşin. Some village stores (eg. in Elevit) also have petrol in jerrycans. On the south side of the range only Erzurum and Yusufeli have petrol stations, although petrol may be available at the village store in Yaylalar. Bearing this in mind, stock up with plenty of fuel before heading into the mountains proper - you can always leave a bottle at one of the pensions while you trek.

Methylated spirits for priming petrol stoves or for Trangia-type stoves is available in Erzurum and Trabzon and hardware stores in Yusufeli and Çamlıhemşin.

Take a lightweight, all-purpose, non-stick pan, a kettle (much more efficient than a pan for heating water for drinks), a spoon, fork, knife, bowl and mug. Don't forget matches and a lighter.

Water / su

Due to a combination of hot, dry summers and porous limestone rock, in many of Turkey's mountains water is in short supply. The Kaçkar range, with its high rainfall and largely granite geological structure, has plenty. Streams and mountain lakes abound. The water from high-level streams is safe to drink without purification but do not drink from streams below a village or yayla, as these may be contaminated by animal and/or human waste. Be wary of drinking from lakes as the apparently crystal waters may be slightly polluted (the banks of lakes are favoured campsites). Take water purification tablets or iodine.

Dehydration is possible even in these alpine mountains - summer days are hot, the air is dry and the exertion of long days on the trail will ensure you lose plenty of water through sweating! Carry a full water bottle (minimum 1 l) or a Platypus/Camelbak-style drinking system and drink frequently. Near Yusufeli, water is less freely available so you should check the route notes and ensure that you carry enough.

When you sweat, you lose essential salts as well as water and you should replace these by eating salty snacks and adding re-hydration salts to your water. We recommend adding rehydration salts to your second bottle of water every day. The Turkish brand, GE-oral, used for re-hydrating children with diahorrea, is available at most chemists.

Other useful equipment

A torch (preferably a head torch) is invaluable for pitching/striking your tent in the dark, finding items in your bag/tent at night, if you are caught out after dark on the trail or for pre-dawn ascents. It can also be used as a signalling device.

A Swiss Army knife or Leatherman tool can prove useful for everything from cooking and tent maintenance to prising open the lock on an empty yayla house!

A lightweight nylon cord can be used as a washing line or an extra guy-line in a storm. You also need a selection of small plastic bottles or containers with good caps/lids to store cooking oil, salt/spices, matches, etc.

Presents / hediye

If you are shown kindness (and this is almost certain to happen) it is nice to be able to offer something in return. If you are a guest in a village or yayla, a handful of sweets or a pen for your hosts' children will be most appreciated. If you have something from your home country (a postcard, photographs of your family, etc.) show it/them around - rural Turks are always interested in life outside of their own communities and are obsessed by families! If you have digital camera, take photos of your hosts (make sure they consent first) and show them the results on the display screen. Follow this up by taking their name and address and promise to send them the printed result.

It is not a good idea to hand out sweets or pens to groups of unsupervised children as in some popular areas this has resulted in hordes of youngsters surrounding visitors and demanding sweets and even money.

Test before you start

It shouldn't be necessary to say this but, before a long trip, a test run is a good idea. The easiest way to test if you have packed too much gear is to load up your backpack, including daysack or waistsack, food and half-full water bottles and weigh it. We recommend keeping the weight of your pack down to less than 15 kg, less for women, though this depends on your strength and endurance! Now put on the pack and walk steadily and slowly uphill at a gradient of 25% for an hour. If you can carry on comfortably with a 10-minute rest every hour, the pack is not too heavy. If it is, you'll find that even removing 1-2 kg makes a huge difference. Check for chafing, uneven distribution of weight and uncomfortable straps and buckles. Make sure your boots are comfortable. Also test the pack going downhill and, finally, make sure you can unpack essentials in the dark (make sure the torch is readily available!)

Stowing gear

It is possible to store unwanted items at any of the pensions. This means you can arrive in the region with excess gear (for example ice-axe and crampons which you may need on a June ascent of Kaçkar peak) and store them in a pension whilst you do some lower-level trekking routes. Of course, if you use mules, you can carry more gear anyway.

THE KAÇKAR

Chapter 4 **GETTING TO TURKEY AND TRAVELLING IN THE KAÇKAR**

For reasons of time, most walkers will arrive in Turkey by air but we also give information about travel by bus and rail. Once within the area, your choice is between bus, dolmuş and taxi.

Getting to the region by air

Turkey's largest city, Istanbul, is the logical entry point. The national carrier, Turkish Airlines /Turk Hava Yolları/THY, has frequent flights from most European capitals, and good services from both North America and Australia/New Zealand. Booking with THY is more convenient as your return flight from your home country to either Erzurum or Trabzon (gateway airports to the Kaçkar) is, in effect, one ticket. The domestic leg is discounted and, for a small extra fee, you can stop over for a night or two in Istanbul. Batumi, Georgia flights (summer only) count as Turkish; you travel on a closed bus to the Turkish border and pass through Turkish, not Georgian, Customs.

If saving money is more important than saving time, find a budget flight into Istanbul (easyJet now fly Luton - Istanbul; Condor, German Wings and Sunexpress fly from various German/Austrian and Dutch airports) then fly on to either Erzurum or Trabzon with one of Turkey's new private airlines. These airlines are now expanding their routes to Europe, so you may find that Onur Air, Pegasus or Sunexpress, in season, offer direct scheduled flights from Europe to Trabzon and possibly Erzurum, targeted at Turkish returnees. Israeli trekkers may find budget charters to Antalya, which connect with scheduled Sunexpress or Pegasus flights to either Trabzon and Erzurum.

If you fly via Istanbul, remember that there are 2 airports, Atatürk and Sabiha Gökçen, and the transfer between them is not quick or easy. Havaş (www.havas.com.tr) has connecting shuttle buses.

The following domestic airlines have English-language websites and offer online and/or phone booking:
Turkish Airlines - www.thy.com
Atlas Jet - www.atlasjet.com
Onur Air - www.onurair.com.tr
Sunexpress - www.sunexpress.com.tr or www.sunexpress.de
Fly Air - www.flyair.com.tr
Pegasus - www.flypgs.com

Getting to the region by bus or train

The bus ride from Istanbul to either Trabzon or Erzurum takes around 18 hrs and from Antalya about the same. This may seem a poor alternative to flying but has the advantage of allowing you to see something of the country en route, is a little cheaper and the coaches are modern and comfortable. Tea, coffee and cake are served on board and there are regular stops at service stations. The price of a ticket on the best bus companies, which use new, air-conditioned Mercedes coaches, is around 2/3 of the price of the cheapest tickets on budget airlines. Istanbul buses depart from Harem otogar on the Asian side of the Bosphorus or Esenler on the European side. There are ticket offices for these inter-city buses in many areas of the city and service buses (free if you buy a ticket) ply between city centre booking offices and the otogars. Advanced booking is only essential at major holiday times, particularly the two Islamic religious festivals of Kurban and Şeker Bayram.

If time is not crucial (allow at least 35 hrs), the cheapest way to reach Erzurum is by train. TCDD/Turkish State Railways is not known for its speed but a train journey will allow you to see a lot of the country (the lines in Turkey are very circuitous) and meet the locals. Pullman seats are the cheapest; a bed in a sleeping compartment is a little over double the cost of a Pullman seat. Seats often book up well in advance and though the online booking system is not easy to use, you should try to book seats in advance. Check out the TCDD website www.tcdd.gov.tr or phone 90 216 336 0475 or 2063 or use one of the agencies listed on the website under Acentalar. Trains depart from Haydarpaşa station on the Asian side of the Bosphorus at 8 am or from Ankara railway station at 15.25 and 18.45 pm. From Erzurum they return at 12 noon and 1.30 pm.

Getting to the southern trailheads - Yusufeli, Tekkale, Barhal and Yaylalar

If you plan to stay the night in Erzurum, you can reach the city centre using the Havaş airport service bus. However, buses for Yusufeli leave from the Gölbaşı Semt Garajı, not the main otogar, around 1 km north-east of the city centre. There are 3 buses daily starting at 6 am and the journey takes about 3 hrs. As most flights into Erzurum arrive at midday, you should take a taxi straight to Gölbaşı otogar to connect with the last Yusufeli bus, which leaves at 1 pm. If you miss this bus, you could take an Artvin bus (from the same otogar) to the junction with the Yusufeli road and then hitch-hike or take a taxi to Yusufeli. Local dolmuşes are timed to leave Yusufeli after the last Erzurum and Artvin buses arrive; if you give your destination to the ticket office at Erzurum, they will ensure a connection.

Yusufeli - Barhal dolmuşes run from the Yusufeli otogar to Barhal daily; in season 2-3 buses depart during the afternoon; the journey takes about 2 hrs.

Yusufeli - Yaylalar dolmuşes run from the same otogar. In season 2 or more dolmuşes run on this route, leaving Olgunlar and Yaylalar early in the morning (6 or 6.30 am) and returning during the afternoon; the journey takes about 3 hrs.

Both these journeys are currently being affected by road works involving diversions and road closures on the Yusufeli - Yaylalar road, so journey times can be longer. The road, which is narrow and, in places, dangerous can be closed by landslides in winter; normally these are cleared almost immediately, because schoolchildren have to use the route daily.

Yusufeli - Tekkale - Kılıçkaya or Güngören dolmuşes depart several times a day from the otogar. Tekkale is only 7 km from Yusufeli.

Currently the taxi-fare from Erzurum airport to Yusufeli is about $100, possibly less if you bargain. If you are travelling in a group, your pension owner can arrange a minibus airport transfer. For 4 people or over, this is the most economic and reliable way of reaching Barhal, Yaylalar or Olgunlar. See the accommodation page on the website for links to the pensions.

Getting to the northern trailheads - Ayder, Yukarı Kavron, Çat and Elevit

Trabzon airport is on the main coastal road; walk out of the airport, turn eastwards and cross the road at a roundabout/underpass. Here you'll find a Prenskale company bus office, where you can buy a ticket on a large, comfortable bus to Pazar, a scruffy town on the coast some 1.5 hrs east of Trabzon - buses run every 30 mins (see www.prenskale.com/hareket.htm for departure times). There is also a stop opposite the airport exit (under the underpass) where Pazar-bound dolmuşes stop.

Pazar - Çamlıhemşin - Ayder dolmuşes run 4-5 times per day in season, infrequently in winter. The journey takes about 2 hrs and the road is good. The signed bus stop is on the south side of the road 100 m before the market place and bridge. Locals will point you in the right direction. Later dolmuşes may terminate in Çamlıhemşin, where there are one or two scruffy hotels.

Çamlıhemşin - Ayder dolmuşes run frequently in season and for a TL or two will drop you at your hotel. After the last bus has gone, you can take a taxi from the rank on the left at the entrance to Çamlıhemşin for the 22 km to Ayder. Negotiate the fare before you start.

Çamlıhemşin - Çat - Elevit - Tirovit dolmuşes run early but unreliably from an office opposite the taxi-rank and return mainly from mid-afternoon onwards. Alternatively, you could take a taxi.

Ayder - Kaler Düzü - Yukarı Kavron dolmuşes run from Ayder centre, just below the baths, several times a day according to demand - the first runs at 9 am (sometimes 8 am). In high-season, either be there in good time or buy your ticket the night before. The last return is usually at 5 pm.

Pazar - Avusor dolmuşes pass through Ayder at around 9 am, but often don't stop unless the driver knows in advance that he has customers. Ask your pension owner or the central dolmuş office to phone. They return from Avusor at 3 pm.

The dolmuş drivers of central Ayder will quote special rates for group trips to such places as Zil Kale, Palançur, Yukarı Çaymakçur, etc. For 4 or more people, this is an economical and quick way of getting to your destination. These are sample prices from summer 2007: Zil Kale, wait and return, 80 TL; Avusor, wait and return, 60 TL.

Travelling from south to north of the range

By bus there are two ways around the range - via Artvin to the east or via İspir to the west. The Artvin route is much easier. From Yusufeli, long-distance buses go to Pazar via Artvin, Borçka and Hopa; you could also change buses at Artvin. From Pazar you take a dolmuş to your chosen trailhead. There are also occasional buses between Yusufeli and İspir but they are infrequent except in winter. From İspir, buses run over Ovit Geçiti to Trabzon otogar. If you want to visit Ovit Dağı (which is beautiful and has possibilities for trekking towards Verçenik) or İkizdere, you could try this route; there is hotel and chalet accommodation just north of the pass and chalet accommodation at İkizdere.

In summer, with a few days notice, it's often possible to have your baggage taken from the pension at Yaylalar to Ayder.

Hitchhiking/otostop

Hitchhiking in Turkey is rather different from the US or Europe. In rural Turkey, people hitch a ride on routes where there is no public transport, rather than to save money (public transport is fairly cheap anyway). On some unsurfaced roads, eg. from Tekkale to Bölükbaşı, it's normal to hail a ride on pick-up trucks, lorries, tractors or anything else going your way. Some drivers may expect a contribution to the journey cost, most simply see it as another form of hospitality to travellers.

Chapter 5 **LOCAL SUPPLIES AND SHOPPING**

The Kaçkar mountains are remote and almost uninhabited; once you reach the trailhead villages, shopping opportunities are few. You should stock up on major items in either Erzurum or Trabzon, the gateway cities for the Kaçkar. These cities have everything from supermarkets and daily fruit and vegetable markets through to chemists, cobblers and photography shops.

On the north, Black Sea Coast side of the Kaçkar is Pazar, 2 hours north of the trailhead village of Ayder. This ugly but substantial town has supermarkets, chemists, a choice of smaller food stores, a fruit and vegetable market and banks. En route for Ayder, Çamlıhemşin has butchers, small food markets, greengrocers, a gas shop and restaurants. Ayder itself has several restaurants, a butcher, mini-markets and outlets selling film and gas cylinders. Yukarı Kavron has a much smaller range of packet food, sold from the café near the bridge, and pastries and bread, sold from the upper kahve, which is a good place for breakfast. (Currently, the only spot for mobile phone reception is standing on a large rock outside the kahve). Çat has a bakkal under one of the pensions whilst, further up the valley, Elevit has 3 tiny bakkals which sell small gaz cartridges and other supplies.

Approaching from the Erzurum side of the range, Yusufeli has supermarkets, butchers, bakers, greengrocers and stockists of both gas cylinders and film. Barhal has several small bakkals and a bakery. Further up the valley is Yaylalar, which has 3 bakkals. The most central, opposite the village's only pension, belongs to one of the pension owners (Naim) and has a good range of foods including packet meat, tinned fish, vegetables and fruit, gas cartridges, meths, etc. With a bit of notice, he will refill fuel bottles with petrol. Olgunlar, half-an-hour's walk on from Yusufeli, has a café by the upper bridge and a small bakkal with some basic supplies.

Some of you may be interested to know that beer is available (usually from the pensions) in all of the trailhead villages.

Banks and money / banka ve para

In Trabzon and Erzurum, you can change money in change offices, the Post Office/PTT or banks. Change offices give the worst exchange rate (and some will try to charge you commission) but they are quicker and are open at weekends. Both Trabzon and Erzurum have plenty of banks, which are open between 9 am and 5 pm, usually closed for an hour for lunch, Monday to Friday. The nearest banks to the trailheads are in Çamlıhemşin on the Black Sea side of the range, and Yusufeli on the south; Ziraat Bankası, which gives the best exchange rates, operates in both.

Most banks have ATM's which allow you to debit your home account directly (provided the phone line is functioning). You should bring some foreign currency (euros or dollars are preferred) and change it as you need to, though of course there is no compensation if you lose it.

You need to have sufficient Turkish Lira to last you for your stay in the mountains - that is to cover costs of travel, pensions, mule hire and food, plus some for emergencies.

Post offices / PTT

Town post offices are open between 9 am and 5 pm for changing money, stamps etc. and 24 hours for telephone calls. Public telephones use phone cards available in

30, 60 or 100 units; you can buy them in post offices or at newsagents. Some post offices and newsagents have metered phones where you pay for units used; ask for 'kontorlu telefon'.

Turkey's international dialling code is 90.

Internet

There are many internet cafes in both Trabzon and Erzurum and a few in Yusufeli. Ayder has two internet cafés, and the Karahan Pansiyon in Barhal allows guests to have internet access.

Medicines / ılaç

Most medicines and first aid equipment (including antibiotics) are available over the counter in wide variety but often under unfamiliar trade names. Bring the packet so the chemist can find the nearest equivalent. Tampons are not generally available outside large towns.

Mosquitoes can present a problem in the summer months, particularly on lower altitude treks. It is better to bring a repellent from home as local brands tend to be less effective and contain harsher chemicals, though they have the advantage of being cheaper. More problematic are midges and the savage horse flies associated with cattle.

Rehydration salts purchased at home are more palatable than local brands (which are aimed at babies dehydrated by diarrhoea rather than walkers who have overdone it in the heat!) but both do the job and the Turkish variety (Ge-Oral) is considerably cheaper.

If you get a stomach bug/diarrhoea that lasts more than 24 hrs, it may be worth taking a course of the antibiotic Flagyl. It is available in every pharmacy and is cheap. Eat sensibly, don't drink alcohol and you'll soon be better.

Food shopping

In the last few years, several supermarket chains have sprung up but most Turkish women still shop from local outdoor markets for all except bread, meat and household products. We recommend a visit to a local market at least once in your trek; the variety and cheapness of the food on offer will delight you. Although you can bargain for most goods in Turkey, don't try bargaining for food; prices are fixed by market inspectors.

Bread / ekmek

Corn bread, a speciality of the eastern Black Sea coast, is available in Trabzon, Pazar, Çamlıhemşin and Ayder. Its dense texture means it keeps well and packs in plenty of carbohydrates. The standard Turkish town bread is a white, crusty oval loaf. The price is very low and it is distributed to most remote villages. Delicious when fresh, this light, airy bed quickly turns stale and it is not nutritious. A better choice is pide, a semi-risen flat bread (somewhere between pita and paratha bread in size and texture) available in Ayder, Yusufeli and Barhal. You could buy flour from a village store and 'bake' your own flat bread (dampers) in a frying pan.

Grains, pasta and pulses

Cracked wheat/bulgur is a good trail staple. It is cheap, nutritious, readily available, requires very little cooking and can be flavoured with anything from tomato paste to honey. Rice is an equally popular and easy to obtain staple but takes more cooking than bulgur. Pasta in a variety of shapes is also widely available; look out for the tiny rice-grain sized pasta pellets which are great for hearty soups. Far tastier (albeit more difficult to find) is mantı/Turkish ravioli, small pasta wraps filled with spicy ground beef and usually eaten with a yoghurt sauce. Pulses are much used by the Turks and are cheap but only lentils are suitable for a trail food as (particularly when pre-soaked) they cook quickly. Muesli, cornflakes and other breakfast cereals are only available from supermarkets in Trabzon and Erzurum.

Meat, fish, cheese and yoghurt / Et, balık, peynir, yoğurt

Red meat such as beef and lamb can be found in butchers in towns (but very rarely in village stores). It is expensive by local standards (little cheaper than in Western Europe though often better quality) and doesn't keep well on the trail. Chicken is better value and found in specialist shops (which also sell eggs) in towns and occasionally in villages. Burgers and frankfurter-style sausages are now widely available in grocers' stores. A better bet is salami, sold in plastic wrappers, as it keeps longer. Even better is the traditional Turkish sausage/sucuk, usually sold in a shrink wrapped, horse-shoe shaped package. It is so full of garlic and spices that it lasts ages even after opening; it is usually fried up with eggs for breakfast, though it will add flavour to any kind of stew.

With a temperate climate and cow-rearing culture, this region produces as much cheese from cows' milk as it does from sheep and goats'. The cheese produced from cows' milk is known as kaşar and is not unlike English cheddar. Matured kaşar is more expensive than fresh but is far tastier and keeps better. Locals use copious amounts of full-fat yellow cheese to make the regional speciality, muhlama. A kind of fondue made by mixing corn flour with melted cheese and butter, it is rich, tasty and energy-giving - ideal trekking food! You're sure to come across it in a pension, café or village house. Goats' cheese, or beyaz peynir, is similar to Greek feta. Less common here than elsewhere in Turkey it is, nonetheless, available in most village stores. A cheese powder called lor is useful for flavouring and thickening stews.

Yogurt is a staple food, served sour, not sweet, though there's nothing to prevent you adding jam or fruit. The easiest to carry is suzme yoğurt, a thick, creamy paste which has most of the water sieved out; it can be reconstituted with water, used as a spread or mixed with most other foods; it keeps several days.

Fish is not terribly practical to carry on the trail, though tinned tuna is readily available and a useful standby. Trout is commonly farmed throughout Turkey, and there are trout farms/restaurants between Çamlıhemşin and Ayder.

Fresh fruit / meyve, and vegetables / sebze

Best brought from local outdoor markets, a wide variety of fruit and vegetables are (seasonally) available. Potatoes, aubergines, courgettes, carrots and onions enliven trail stews, whilst tomatoes, cucumbers and peppers are great for picnics. Oranges, apricots, cherries, peaches, apples, pears, plums, water and yellow melons, mulberries and grapes can all be found, very cheaply, in season.

Dried fruit, nuts / kuru yemiş

Dried apricots, figs, mulberries and raisins, available cheaply at markets and shops specializing in dried foodstuffs, make great (and healthy) trail snacks, especially when eaten with local hazelnuts or walnuts. Salted nuts include peanuts, pistachios and almonds. Salted and roasted sunflower and other seeds are even cheaper than nuts, as are the roasted chickpeas known as leblebi.

Pestil, made in this area mainly from mulberries or apricot syrup, is a thin, fruit leather, often studded with nuts. It is chewy, flavoursome, energising and doesn't melt in the heat, so makes a great alternative to chocolate. A sausage-shaped sweet similar to pestil (but threaded onto string) is called tatlı sucuk. Helva (a tahini-based sweet) is available in its plain form or, better, flavoured with cocoa powder or studded with nuts. Less healthy, but also good on the trail, are the many varieties of Turkish delight.

Sweets, chocolate, biscuits and cake / Şeker, çikolata, biskvit, kek

Western-style sweets are becoming more popular in Turkey. Look out for hard-boiled, sour-cherry flavoured Mis Bonbons, chewy 'Starburst'-style Tofitas and imitation Smarties UFO's or Bonibons.

Locally produced chocolate, especially that produced by Ulker, is very good. Their chocolate bars include bitter, milk, hazlenut and pistachio. Metro bars copy the Mars bar, Albeni the Twix and Balmond the Toblerone. Best of the packaged, Western-style biscuits is Ulker's Biskrem, with a shortbread exterior enclosing a chocolate centre preventing the chocolate melting on trail. Dried biscuits, locally baked and sold by the kilo, can be purchased from cake shops in the bigger towns, and are better value than the packaged varieties. A good cake is Eti's Dan Kek, a pre-packaged sponge cake in various flavours; Eti also produce small Pop Keks with soft centres and individual chocolate brownies.

Drinks / içecekler

Although the spring water along the trail is usually delicious, powdered fruit-flavoured drinks encourage you to consume more liquid and provide some sugar, both of which help prevent dehydration. The best brand is Tang, available in lemon, sour cherry, strawberry and orange flavours. Coffee creamer, instant milk powder, teabags (including fruit teas) and instant coffee are available in most markets. Long-life milk is available in towns but once opened won't keep for long. Ayran, a salty drink made from yoghurt and water, is sold in town restaurants or cafés either in plastic tubs or by the glass; it is very refreshing and rehydrating in the heat.

Tea is the national drink in Turkey. It is drunk from tiny, tulip-shaped glasses, black and usually very sweet. In rural areas in particular making a brew is a ritual and can take some time, so try not to be impatient if your schedule is put back whilst some hospitable villager boils the kettle. Tea from village kahve is very cheap and will give you an insight into rural life and the locals the chance to observe at first hand the strange ways of foreigners. Turkish coffee/Türk kahvesi, served in miniature cups and saucers, is available in most kahve.

Locals who like a tipple prefer rakı (an aniseed-based spirit like Greek ouzo or French Pernod). Lager-type beer is available in towns and at pensions; the best brand is Efes Pilsen. Imported lagers are now available in large towns but are more expensive. Although grapes are grown locally in the Çoruh valley, wines are produced further west. Turkish wine is currently variable in quality, although continuously improving; the most reliable buys include Kavaklidere and Dikmen brands. In Turkey, taxation on alcohol is 80%, so wine is expensive - especially when compared to the negligible cost of the raw material, grapes.

Chapter 6 **LOOKING AFTER YOURSELF**

A holiday of this sort is slightly different from the all-inclusive hotel or holiday-village type where, if you are sick, there is a doctor who speaks your language instantly on call. Some of these routes are hardly ever used, so you should tell someone where you are going and when you will return. If you are walking from pension to pension, make sure your target pension knows your intended arrival time and will take action if you do not arrive.

Basic precautions:

1. Buy health insurance which covers emergency rescue services and repatriation. If you plan to walk alone, fax a copy of your insurance and passport to your consulate so that, if you are notified missing, they can initiate rescue operations.
2. Take evidence of your social insurance entitlement in your home country, which will probably entitle you to Turkish hospital treatment under the reciprocal arrangements scheme. You may still have to pay and claim later. (If necessary, obtain and complete the appropriate social insurance form before you come).
3. You will probably be advised that inoculations are required against rabies, cholera and malaria but the most important inoculation is against tetanus. Hepatitis A is the most common contagious disease which could affect you, if your resistance is very low. Malaria and cholera are almost unknown. Rabies is a theoretical possibility, but highly unlikely. If you do get bitten, the nearest state hospital or clinic will give free treatment and a tetanus injection. Normally they won't give anti-rabies injections unless the animal is wild or a vet confirms it's infected. Several injections are needed, so you may have to finish the treatment in your home country.
4. Take a first-aid kit, which need contain no more or less than for any other European country. The important items are: treatment for minor cuts, scratches, blisters and stings, rehydration salts, an effective diahorrea remedy, an insect repellent, cortisone for insect bites, an all-purpose antibiotic for a sudden flare up of a tooth problem or an infected scratch and sunscreen.
5. Check if you are allergic to bee stings and, if necessary, bring an antidote. If you are one of those very rare people who are allergic, a bee sting can stop your heart in 15 minutes. If you are not allergic and don't scratch, a sting may swell and be uncomfortable for an hour or two, but will soon pass.
6. Pamper your feet! Take every opportunity to check and clean them and your boots, change your socks, add or subtract inner soles and use the old climbers' trick of resting with your feet above head height.
7. Be on the alert for dehydration or sunstroke. If you feel dry-mouthed, all your energy drains away, you feel light headed, have a headache and your vision is blurred, you are on the way to collapse. Drink some water with rehydration salts immediately, then get in the shade, cool off by wrapping a wet scarf round your head and rest for an hour or so. It is also possible to dehydrate gradually over a period of several days. Check how much urine you are producing; if it's rather less than normal, you must increase your water and salt intake.
8. Sunburn is a possibility in summer, particularly on the southern slopes and at high altitude. Cover most flesh and use sun-block on the remainder, especially on ears and lips, remembering to reapply it regularly.

THE KAÇKAR

Safety aids

At all times, carry a plastic or foil person-sized emergency survival sack. It will insulate you from cold and rain or you can spread it out to act as a signal for a search party. Bring spares of anything essential to your well-being - contact lenses, glasses, false teeth, etc, plus sufficient prescription medicine. If you have known allergies or health problems, carry the necessary information in your passport so that in an emergency someone will find it.

Health services

Free basic health services are available on demand at health clinics/sağlık ocak in Çamlıhemşin (1 km north on the Çat road), Ayder (behind the thermal baths), Sarıgöl and the hospital at Yusufeli. The clinic at Yaylalar has closed. They will treat minor injuries, stitch wounds, administer injections, etc. and will refer you to a hospital if you need further treatment. There are major hospitals in Rize and Trabzon on the north side of the range, in Artvin to the east and in Erzurum to the south; Yusufeli has a smaller hospital. Doctors in Turkey all theoretically speak English, but their proficiency varies enormously. As a general rule, the more remote the hospital, the less English they know.

Do not worry that Turkish medical services are below European standards. Like other Middle Eastern countries, the nursing care is indeed different, as the system relies on having a relative or friend stay with the patient in hospital to attend to basic needs.

Walking alone

Much of this book was researched by Kate walking with her dogs. But we don't recommend solo walking, especially outside the summer season. If you do walk solo, tell someone responsible exactly where you are going and when you will return or phone in. Make allowances for breakdowns in communication.

As an example, a middle-aged, experienced Israeli couple were caught in mist while crossing the Naletleme pass from Olgunlar to Yukarı Kavron. They expected to catch the last minibus from Yukarı Kavron and were booked into a pension at Ayder. When they didn't arrive, the pension owner rang their starting pension at Yaylalar. Yaylalar rang Yukarı Kavron but the phone was out of order. Since other walkers arriving at Ayder reported that they had seen no-one on the route, everyone assumed that they had missed the last bus and were staying the night at Yukarı Kavron. In fact, they spent a damp, cold but safe night under a rock only 2 hours from Yukarı Kavron.

This sort of problem can arise on the most-used route in the Kaçkar; little-used routes are therefore more risky. In case of an accident, the jandarma (Turkey's rural gendarmerie) will take charge of search and rescue; the problem is deciding if someone is missing and when the jandarma should be called out.

The Turkish Dağcılık Federasiyonu/Mountain Federation has asked İsmail Altınay at the Çamyuva Pensiyon in Yaylalar and Yalçın or Ali Şahin at the Şahin café and pension in Yukarı Kavron to act as co-ordinators for rescues. In other words, they will decide when to call out the jandarma and/or any local guides who may be available. It's better to leave your route details with one of these people. A mountain rescue group is being formed so, before your holiday, check our website for further information.

6. Looking after yourself

If you walk in twos or more then, in case of an accident, one person can go for help. Do NOT walk in the dark, in thick mist or cloud.

Going for help

If you are the one who has to go for help and the injury is serious to the point where rescue or evacuation is required, then your main problem is to make yourself understood. Take some digital photos and use those, plus paper and pencil and the map, to help get your message across. Inform your consulate and insurers as soon as possible; your consulate has to authorize a helicopter, if it's required, because they have to guarantee that it will be paid for in due course.

Emergency phone numbers

Police / emergency 155
Rural gendarmerie (Jandarma) 156
Forest fires 177

Chapter 7 — A BRIEF HISTORY OF THE PONTIC REGION AND ITS PEOPLE

Because of the considerable historical differences, we have considered the north Black Sea coast and the southern slopes separately.

The Black Sea Coast

According to Greek legend, Jason and his Argonauts sailed along the Black Sea coast to Colchis (modern day Georgia) in search of the Golden Fleece. This story no doubt has its basis in the exploration of this part of the world by land-hungry Greeks. During the 8th century BC, many mainland Greek city-states sent out colonists who founded small, independent and largely self-sufficient settlements - including some on the southern shores of the Black Sea. For example, colonists from the Aegean city-state of Miletus founded Trabzon (ancient Trebizond). In 401 BC, following defeat in Mesopotamia, the Greek mercenary general Xenophon decided to take his 10,000 men north to the nearest friendly Greek city-states on the south-eastern coast of the Black Sea.

Towards the end of the 3rd century BC, the Hellenised (but non-Greek) kingdom of Pontus expanded and took over the Pontic Greek city-states. In 64 BC, the Romans (under Pompey) defeated Mithridates of Pontus. The Romans (who had been established in Asia Minor since 133 BC) encouraged the establishment of a new Pontic client-kingdom; in AD 64, they annexed this as their north-easterly border province of Pontus. Trabzon, positioned strategically at the north end of the important Zigana pass, became the headquarters of the Roman Empire's Black Sea fleet. During this entire period, the land between the Kaçkar watershed and the coastal plain remained tribal; the Romans had difficulty exacting tribute from these troublesome inhabitants on the north-eastern borders of their empire.

During the Byzantine era, the coastal areas as far as modern Rize continued to be inhabited by Greek-speaking Christians, whilst further east and in the mountainous hinterland pagan tribes resisted the local representatives of Constantinople. The tribes formed a useful, if unreliable, buffer zone between the Byzantine Empire and the Sassanid Persians to the east.

During the 7th and 8th centuries Muslim Arab incursions into Byzantine areas didn't penetrate the Pontic mountain chain to the Black Sea coastline. Free of conflict, the coastline prospered and by the 10th century Trebizond (Trabzon) had become a major trading centre. The current ethnic population mix, which make this remote corner of modern Turkey so interesting, originated in this period of Arab wars. The Laz (see page 41) and the Hemşin (see page 42), both at least nominally Christian people from further south-east fleeing Arab raids, first reached the Black Sea coast at this time.

In 1071, another group of Muslims, the Selçuk Turks, entered Anatolia (Asia Minor) and defeated the Byzantine army at Malazgirt (just north of Lake Van). Again, the barrier of mountains prevented the invaders reaching the north-east Black Sea coast. In 1204, Constantinople fell to the armies of the Third Crusade and branches of the Byzantine imperial family, the Kommenos, went into exile in three separate kingdoms. One of them, Alexios Kommenos, had been educated and protected by Queen Tamara of Georgia; after the fall of Constantinople, her armies secured Trebizond for Alexios. He returned there from Constantinople and soon after proclaimed himself the legitimate Byzantine emperor; Trebizond became the capital of a small empire which, in 1214, was further reduced when the two major ports of Sinope and Samsun fell to the Selçuks.

In 1243, Selçuk hopes of pushing east from Sinope were ended by their defeat by the newly-arrived Mongols at the battle of Köse, near Erzincan. Although Trebizond became a virtual vassal of the Ilkhan Mongols, it was left pretty much to its own devices. The Mongol incursions to the west had caused Silk Road traffic to divert north through Tabriz, Erzurum and over the Pontic Alps to Trebizond, which boomed. The pragmatic Genoese, and later the Venetians, quickly cornered the transport of the spoils of the Silk Road to the markets of the west; along with prosperity they brought Western ideas to this Byzantine outpost of the Christian world. The Mongols were replaced by Turcoman emirs who were in continual dispute with each other over much of eastern Anatolia. Wisely, the Kommenos family coped by using diplomacy rather than warfare; this mainly involved marrying off their famously beautiful princesses to various emirs.

In 1263, the Byzantines had recaptured Constantinople from the Crusaders. In 1453, it fell to a leading emirate, the Ottoman Turks, led by Mehmet the Conqueror. Secure behind the Pontic barrier, it wasn't until 1461 that Trebizond surrendered to Mehmet's army and the last of the Kommenos family went into exile in Constantinople. Even during the heyday of the empire of Trebizond, it's likely that the authority of the Kommenos did not extend to the coast east of Rize (inhabited largely by Laz), or into the foothills (where the Hemşin lived). With an Ottoman governor in Trebizond, the allegiance of these tribes switched from Georgia to the Ottoman Empire. Their religious allegiances were not changed by Muslim rule; Greek Orthodox monasteries continued to flourish around Trebizond and, although there is less evidence, Armenian ones probably continued to flourish in the mountains.

Trebizond maintained its importance in the early years of Ottoman rule - indeed one of the governors of the vilayet/province of Trebizond was the future Sultan Selim the Grim. His son (later known as Suleyman the Magnificent or, in Turkish, Kanuni/law-giver) was born and lived in the city until becoming sultan in 1520. From the mid-18th to the early 19th centuries the governors lost control of outlying castles to petty barons/derebeys and Trebizond's importance declined. From 1840, the fortunes of the region changed (briefly) for the better. The western powers and Russia were gaining great influence over the 'sick man of Europe', as the moribund Ottoman empire had become known. In Trebizond, European consulates opened up, missionaries became established and once again trade flowed down from Tabriz via Erzurum. The population, especially Greek-speaking and/or Christian families prospered through trade or by working in Russia; the high number of churches and private villas of this period testify to their wealth.

In the early 20th century, this came to an end. Although still nominally ruled by the sultan, a triumvirate of Turkish nationalists - Enver Paşa, Cemal Paşa and Talat Paşa took over the government of Ottoman Empire's shrinking domains. At the outset of the First World War, this trio took Turkey into the war on the side of the Germans. From the west, the British and later the Greeks and, from the east, the Russians attacked the badly-defended Ottoman Empire; Trabzon fell to the Russians in 1916. Perhaps justifiably, the triumvirate saw the Christian minorities of the empire as at best unreliable, at worst treacherous. The majority of the Pontic Greeks were either forced out or voluntarily departed a land which had been under Greek cultural influence since 700 BC. In 1923, after the Turkish War of Independence, the new Republican government signed the Treaty of Lausanne, which stipulated a population exchange between Greece and the new Turkish Republic; the remaining Greeks were exchanged for Turks from Greece.

The Anatolian side of the Pontic Alps

Then 'sunny side' of the Pontic Alps has a markedly different history to that facing the Black Sea. The Greeks of the classical era did not settle in the region, though no doubt some, besides the retreating Xenophon and his 10,000, did explore it. The Persians, arch enemy of the Greeks, exerted the greatest influence over the region's mainly Armenian population. During the rule of the Achaemenid dynasty, Persia became the mightiest empire in the world. In 546 BC, the high Armenian homelands became a province of Persia and prospered. Xenophon, who passed through the province en route to the Black Sea in 401 BC, commented on the quality of the wines and sumptuousness of the banquets arranged for himself and his men by his gracious Armenian hosts.

In 331 BC, at Arbela, the Macedonian king Alexander the Great defeated the Achaemenid Persians. Armenia became a part of his empire, the Hellenistic world, which stretched from Greece to the Punjab and from Afghanistan to Egypt.

Under the Seleucid successors to Alexander, Armenia became more urbanised and wealthier, partly because it lay on the great Silk Road trade route from China and India to the Mediterranean. Influenced by both Persian and Greek culture, and nominally subject to the Seleucids, Armenia nonetheless continued to develop in its own distinctive way.

As Seleucid power waned, the Armenians began to assert more independence and, under Tigranes the Great (95-55 BC), it expanded westward. This, however, brought it into conflict with the Romans, who were pushing the frontier of their empire eastwards. Tigranes was forced to give up his conquests and Armenia became a vassal of Rome. Though it was dominated first by the Roman and then Byzantine empires, from AD 53 to 428 a Parthian (Persian) dynasty ruled in Armenia. In 301, Armenia was converted to Christianity, giving the Armenians a good claim to being the first Christian nation (though this is disputed by the Syrian Orthodox Church). Around 405, an Armenian churchman, Mesrop, in order to translate the bible into his people's native language, developed a distinctive Armenian alphabet. Christianity also developed independently; the Armenian church adopted the monophysite creed (the belief that Christ had a single, divine nature). However, in 451, at the Council of Chalcedon, the Byzantine Orthodox view, which held that Christ had 2 co-mingled natures - divine and human - was adopted as official Byzantine state policy. The Armenian church, which clung to its traditional religious beliefs, was declared heretical but still commanded the allegiance of the Armenian people. (The Nestorian church, centred in Mesopotamia, which believed Christ had a dual but predominantly human nature, was also excommunicated).

In the 7th and 8th centuries, in response to the Muslim Arab invasion, powerful Armenian dynasties began to emerge, challenging both the Arabs and the Byzantines. The Bagratid dynasty held Theodosiopolis/Erzurum until it was taken by a Byzantine force in 949. Between the 8th and 11th centuries, income from trade plus the Armenians' distinctive skills in architecture, stonework, frescoes and metalwork allowed the construction of many glorious religious buildings. In 1064, the invading Selçuk Turks ended this Armenian resurgence by capturing the Bagratid capital, Ani; the variety of architectural achievements can be seen in the wealth of churches still remaining. Although the Kaçkar lie outside the borders of historical Armenia proper, the plethora of Armenian place names and remains of monastic churches prove that Armenian communities continued to flourish there for many centuries.

The Georgians, whose medieval churches still scatter the remote valleys to the north-east, east and south of the Kaçkar mountain range, developed politically more slowly than their Armenian neighbours. In ancient Greek legend, the proto-Georgian kingdom of Colchis was home to the famed Golden Fleece. From the 7th century BC, the Greek colonies of the Black Sea influenced the tribal groupings and mini-kingdoms of Georgia. The Georgians sided with the Armenians, led by Tigranes the Great, in his westward expansion. Facing Roman opposition, they were forced to become clients and allies of Rome. They were never conquered by their other powerful neighbours, the Parthians, but in this period were much influenced by the culture of the East.

Georgia and Armenia continued to 'run in parallel' with the conversion of Georgia to Christianity in AD 330, just 20 years after that of Armenia. Both 'nations' began to shed the influences of Zoroastrian Persian culture and moved towards Byzantine Orthodox Christianity. In the 7th century, however, the area which forms the modern state of Georgia briefly fell to the Arabs then to the Bagratids. Already linked by geographical proximity, history, culture and Christianity, as the Bagratid dynasty ruled both, the fortunes of the southern part of Georgia and Armenia further converged. This dynasty, originating from İspir and Bayburt (on the Anatolian side of the Pontic Alps) provided able rulers for both Armenia and parts of Georgia. Not surprisingly, Georgian and Armenian church architecture, particularly of the period AD 836 - 1045 but also afterwards, shows many similarities.

Until 1064, when the Selçuk Turks took Ani, the southern marches of old Georgia (known as the Tao-Klarjeti) were under Bagratid control. Fortunately for the Georgians, Selçuk power was diluted in three ways. Firstly, they had invaded Anatolia 'by accident' en route to richer pickings in Egypt and consequently had little interest in north-east Anatolia. Secondly, the waning but still powerful Byzantine presence in Anatolia prevented total Selçuk domination. Thirdly, the Crusaders, who crossed Anatolia for the first time in 1097 en route to the Holy Land, were a constant thorn in the Selçuk side. After the end of the Bagratid dynasty, united Georgia reached its apogee between 1122 and 1213. Under rulers such as King David Magisterium and Queen Tamara, the kingdom, centred on Tiblisi (still the capital of the modern Georgian state), stretched from the Pontic Alps in the south-west to the Caspian in the east. The arrival of the Mongols in the 13th century put an end to Georgian power, but, with its strong feudal system and distinctive Georgian Orthodox Church, its national identity has been able to survive until today.

The vacuum left in eastern Anatolia by the end of the short-lived Mongol Ilkhanate (1256-1335) and the declining Selçuk Empire was filled by competing Turcoman tribal groupings, notably the Akkoyunlu (White Sheep) and Karakoyunlu (Black Sheep). One such tribal group, the Osmans, who became known to the West as the Ottomans, eventually gained control of most of Anatolia. Georgian and Armenian lands became (as they had been under the Romans and Byzantines) buffer zones between the Turkish Ottoman Empire, Persia and, later, the expanding Russian Empire. The Georgian kingdom, already in decline, suffered greatly from the rampaging forces of Tamerlane (a Turkic warlord) and began to shrink; ethnic Georgians either fled north-east to gain Russian protection in the territory of the modern Georgian state or converted to Islam and sought protection in the Ottoman Empire. The Armenians had became a part of the Ottoman 'millet' system; that is a recognised minority group, inferior in status to the Muslim inhabitants of the empire, but pretty much free to follow their own devices - including freedom of worship; the Georgians never acquired this status.

Tsarist Russia was to figure largely in the history of the region in the 18th, 19th and early 20th centuries. With the Ottoman Empire in terminal decline, Russia advanced south and west from the Caucasus, absorbing parts of Georgia and Armenia into its own empire. The Russians claimed to be protecting the interests of the Ottoman Empire's Christian minorities as an excuse to extend their territory. The Young Turk triumvirate, then in charge of the collapsing Ottoman Empire, accused the Armenians of being fifth columnists for the Russians. From 1915, most of the Armenian population were moved away from the border areas under Ottoman control. Until 1917, the cities of Kars and Erzurum, as well as large swathes of what is now north-east Turkey, were held by the Russians, when the upheaval caused by the Bolshevik revolution allowed Ottoman forces to retake much of the lost land. In 1918, the collapse of the Ottoman Empire created further chaos; the borders constantly changed and whole populations were on the move. In December 1920, the boundary between independent Armenia and the Turkish Republic was fixed. In 1921, under the treaty of Kars, the Turkish nationalists under Kemal Atatürk and the recently-formed Soviet Union fixed the modern boundaries, incorporating modern Armenia and Georgia into the USSR and dividing both Armenia and Georgia's historical lands.

A brief history of exploration

Prior to the 19th century, when the idea of mountains as 'playgrounds' began to develop amongst Europe's wealthy elite, they were simply obstacles - separating cultures and diverting trade routes. In 400 BC, retreating from Mesopotamia following an attempt to overthrow the Persian king, Xenophon and his 10,000 Greek mercenaries battled their way north and over the Pontic Alps. Their goal was the Black Sea coast, where there were numerous Greek colonies.

> When the men in front reached the summit and caught sight of the sea there was a great shouting. Xenophon and the rearguard heard it and thought that there were some more enemies attacking in front...so they rode forward to give support and heard the soldiers shouting "The sea! The sea!" and passing word down the column. When they all got to the top, the soldiers, with tears in their eyes, embraced each other and their generals and captains.
> - Xenophon, The Persian Expedition

In all probability, Xenophon used the Zigana Pass, still the main link between the Anatolian plateau and the eastern Black Sea coast. Several 19th century travellers have left vivid accounts of crossing the Zigana, including Robert Curzon and Isabella Bird. The doughty Bird crossed in early December, and reported snow to a depth of 9 feet, though on emerging on the seaward side of the pass said:

I was astonished with the magnificence of the scenery, and with the vast pine forests which clothe the mountainsides....an uplifted snow world of ceaseless surprises under a blue sky full of light make one fancy oneself in Switzerland, till a long train of decorated camels or a turbanned party of armed travellers dissipates the dream.

Curzon, making the same journey some years earlier but later in the same month, describes his approach to the Pontic range from Erzurum thus:

About twenty attendants accompanied me, besides a certain levy from every village I passed, who were to march to the next village every day to clear the roads, move the snow, pick us out of it when we tumbled in, etc.

HFB Lynch, the last of the great British Victorian adventurers in Turkey, had the following advice for travellers intent on crossing from the Anatolian Plateau to the eastern Black Sea coast:

But to the traveller who is in search of romantic scenery one may confidently recommend the summer road which we adopted. The passage of the first barrier will afford him a near view of the beautiful peak of the Jejen; while the later journey lies among the summits of the Pontic Alps and among some of their wildest glens.

It was not, however, until the 1960's that the Kaçkar massif was explored by mountaineers and walkers. Denis Cecil Hill, an inveterate British teacher/mountain wayfarer/historian, crossed the range from south to north, taking in the summit en route. His Turkish companion, Muzzafer, was so enamoured of the Kaçkar that he exclaimed 'Why go to Switzerland when we have all this at our doorstep?'.

Several British mountaineering expeditions (in 1963; 1969; 1977 and 1980) added to the general sum of knowledge of the Kaçkar. Following one of these expeditions Sidney Nowill commented:

But the splendour of the great rain forest through which the voyager passes on his way to the upper ranges; the verdant lushness of the tea gardens on the sub-tropical littoral below; and the high world of glaciers and snow fields above, to which the traveller finally penetrates, are surely enough to compensate for the rigours of the climate.

During this period the Swiss, Germans and the Turks themselves began to explore the area. It was not, however, until the mid 1980's that the Kaçkar began to attract numbers of walkers and climbers. In 1988, the first commonly available map was drawn, and in 1989 Lonely Planet's 'Trekking in Turkey' was published. In their introduction to Turkey's mountain ranges, joint authors Marc Dubin and Enver Lucas declared :

In terms of our own personal preferences, we were most taken with the Kaçkar range on the Black Sea, where the trekking compares favourably to that in Nepal.

Karl Smith was similarly enthusiastic in his book 'The Mountains of Turkey' published by Cicerone Press in 1992. Most independent travellers guides to Turkey, including the Rough Guide, Lonely Planet and Footprint, now include a short section on trekking in the Kaçkar.

An ethnic mosaic

Although for millennia seafarers have used the aptly named waters of the Black Sea, until the 20th century the Black Sea mountains resisted the encroachment of imposed government. For centuries, there has been a tradition of men working away from home, but the population movements of the early 1900's caused rapid depopulation and disruption to the remaining people. In the 1930's, tea growing was introduced to stem outward migration and prevent the drain on foreign currency for the purchase of imported coffee. However, the men continued to work away and the women were left to run the tea plantations in addition to their other work. On the south side of the range, the Çoruh valley was and is an important source of crops which cannot be grown elsewhere in the region - olives, rice, grapes, maize, vegetables and fruits. It also supported many head of cattle during the winter, but the decline in cattle farming, import of food from the south and the threat of the Yusufeli Dam has here, too, decreased self-sufficiency and encouraged outward migration.

Apart from links formed by seasonal trade and migration, valleys often remained culturally separate, with their inhabitants living a seasonally mobile life, moving between winter and summer homes, but having little contact with their neighbours in adjoining valleys. Since the 1960's, entire families have migrated to Turkish and foreign cities, where they form their own local sub-cultures which cling to their traditions. In order to keep their culture, traditions and languages alive, they visit their relatives and yaylas every year. A few families are even permanently re-settling in their traditional homeland.

The Laz

The Laz inhabit a small but well-defined area of Turkey's eastern Black Sea coast, at the foot of the eastern Kaçkar between the main ridge and the sea. Except for the plain between Pazar and Ardeşen, the mountains plunge straight into the sea. Traditionally seafarers and boat-builders, the hamsi/anchovy has long provided them with an income and staple foodstuff. The Laz are a Caucasian race, and many of them have blue or green eyes and red or blonde hair. Their native tongue is closely related to Georgian, but they all speak Turkish as well. So many ethnic Laz live outside their homeland - in western parts of Turkey, northern Europe and even the USA - that the Laz language is in danger of extinction. In 1999, a Laz from Pazar named İsmail Avcı Bucaklışı produced a Laz-Turkish dictionary - a brave attempt to preserve this threatened south-western Caucasian tongue.

For centuries, the Laz lands formed part of the buffer between the Romans/Byzantines and the Persians. In 522, the Laz ruler adopted Christianity. The people followed his lead, and Laz nobility intermarried with their Byzantine Greek counterparts. Up to the Arab incursions of the 7th century, Laz-ruled territory extended east and north to the Rioni river in modern Georgia. After this, the kingdom shrank to its present geographic limits. Well protected by the highest peaks of the Kaçkar to the south, and by a forbidding stretch of the Black Sea to the north, the Laz were able to retain their independence until the 16th century, when they were conquered by the Ottomans and converted to Islam.

The Laz are often the butt of jokes (very similar to Polish jokes in the USA and Irish jokes in England); they are stereotyped as an extrovert race of hamsi-eating horon dancers with a penchant for unworkable scams. The reality belies the image - Laz families control much of Turkey's shipping, and the far-flung Laz diaspora has produced thousands of successful businesses in Turkey and abroad.

The Hemşin

Much less well-known than the Laz, their close neighbours the Hemşin comprise a small but distinct ethnic group. They inhabit a compact region on the northern, Black-Sea-facing slopes of the Kaçkar range inland from Pazar and Ardeşen. Their origins are obscure, but it seems likely that the present day Hemşin are descended from Armenians who arrived in this region from Armenia proper in the 9th century AD. There is evidence dating to the 15th century that points to the existence of an independent 'neo-Armenian' kingdom, centred on the twin castles of Zil Kale and Kale-i-Bala (see page 49) in the upper Fırtına valley. The Spanish traveller Clavijo, who passed through these wild mountains in 1405, described the natives thus:

> and the people are of a barbarous race. As we passed through we were in some danger from them, for although they are Armenians and profess to be Christian all are robbers and brigands.

Isolated in their rugged, forest-cloaked and rain-soaked mountain terrain, the Hemşin were able to maintain their independence from the empire of Trebizond /Trabzon in the Middle Ages, and were only nominally under Ottoman control from 1461 (the fall of Trebizond) until the formation of the republic in 1923. Thus they were able to maintain their own language (derived from Armenian) and identity, based on seasonal migration with their cattle. Although Hemşin men have adopted the 'Western' dress code introduced by Atatürk, the women still wear a distinctive headscarf. Worn turban-style, these brilliantly-hued (yellow, red and black) scarves are actually of Indian origin, and in historical times were imported via Tabriz, Erzurum and Trebizond, along a branch of the Silk Route.

Although the Hemşin converted to Islam early in the 19th century, they are not particularly pious. Some men are quite heavy drinkers, which can be blamed on either their Christian origins or their often rain-soaked forest environment. The difficulty of earning a living in the mountains has driven many Hemşin to work in other parts of Turkey. The men are noted pastry-chefs, and run some of the best pastane (sweet/pudding shops) in the country.

The Georgians

Ethnic Georgians, survivors of a once-powerful medieval Georgian kingdom centred around the Çoruh valley, still live in the mountains north and east of the Kaçkar proper. Their medieval forebears left several splendid churches in these isolated valleys, and two, Dörtkilise (see page 47) and Parhali (see page 48), fall within the area covered by this book. Once fervent Orthodox Christians, Turkey's Georgian population converted to Islam in Ottoman times. A few scattered Georgian speakers remain but probably the best place in Turkey to hear Georgian spoken is at the Kafkasör festival, where Georgian-speaking Turks and their ethnic kin from modern Georgia make merry in the hills above Artvin.

The Pontic Greeks

The terms of the Treaty of Lausanne (1923) included the compulsory exchange of populations between the new Republic of Turkey and Greece. The entire Greek Orthodox Christian population of present-day Turkey excepting Istanbul (estimated at some 1.5 million) was transferred to Greece and the Muslim population of Greece excepting Thrace was relocated to Anatolia. The Orthodox Christians of the Black Sea region, who were known as Pontic Greeks, were forced to pack up and leave their ancestral homeland to start a new life in a Greek state to which they owed little allegiance and with which, culturally, they had little in common.

The decision to relocate was made on the basis of religion, not language. For many years, some of the population who had converted to Islam during the Ottoman era continued to speak Greek; with the coming of universal education in Turkish most gradually lost their traditional language. A small group of Greek-speaking Muslims still live around the pious town of Of, west of Rize.

THE KAÇKAR

Chapter 8 WHAT TO LOOK FOR

Here are some things to look out for while you are in the area:

Local festivals

The culture of extended families plus the annual return of the diaspora has encouraged a vibrant folk-culture to survive into the 21st century. The number and variety of traditional festivals are just one manifestation of this. The majority take place in late spring, summer and early autumn on the yaylas and provide an opportunity for local people to 'let their hair down' and enjoy a weekend's entertainment. Many festivals feature wrestling competitions, traditional dance troupes decked-out in local costume and folk music concerts. The more spirited make their own entertainment (far more likely to be alcohol fuelled than in most other parts of Turkey) with impromptu folk dancing - often to the strains of the tulum/ a type of bagpipes and kemence/violin.

On the Anatolian side of the Kaçkar range, festivals most likely to be of interest are: the Tekkale Yayla Festival held on the last weekend of July; the Barhal Nature and Culture Festival held on the second weekend in August and, in Yusufeli, the Karakucak Wrestling Festival on the first weekend of October.

Most interesting of all (and a little way out of the area of this book) is the Kafkasör Bullfighting Festival (last weekend in June) which takes place in a pretty yayla above the provincial capital of Artvin. Although hard-line animal rights activists may take exception to this traditional 'sport', it bears no resemblance to the cruel and macho posturing of Spanish bull fighting. For a start, the bulls are pitted against each other, not against an armed matador and, although the bulls lock horns, push and shove each other and kick up clouds of dust, they do not seriously damage each other (the pride of the 'losing' bull aside!). The spectators crowding around the scrapping beasts are at greater risk; they are forced to scatter in panic as one or more bulls careers away from the battleground.

The origin of bull wrestling lies in yayla culture. Having been kept in barns all winter, the bulls were let out on the high pastures each spring. Full of pent up aggression following months of confinement and sexual excitement at the onset of the spring mating season, the bulls would battle each other for dominance, sometimes resulting in a valuable bull being pushed to its death over a rocky precipice. To avert this, the locals cleverly hit on the idea of allowing the bulls to battle each other on a flat area and in the process unwittingly created a grand excuse for a festival.

At least as interesting as the sparring bulls is the audience, many of them Turkish citizens of Georgian origin, with a liberal sprinkling of their ethnic kin from over the border in Georgia. Everyone is out for a good time, with some consuming copious amounts of alcohol, all eating much barbequed meat and the line-dance known as the horon breaking out impromptu day and night.

The Friday of the Kafkasör is given over to poetry recitals and Georgian folk-dancing; the second day sees wresting taking centre stage, followed by a concert; the Sunday is saved for the main event - the bullfighting. The springy grass of the yayla makes for excellent (and free) camping, but don't count on getting to sleep early!

The Black Sea slopes of the Kaçkar have an equally vibrant yayla culture and the festivals to go with it. Naturally these festivals reflect the ethnic make-up of this verdant region, with Laz and Hemşin (see pages 41 and 42) culture proudly on display. The festival at Ayder, held the first week in June, is the best, and includes bullfighting as well as music and dancing. The second week in August sees attention focus on Palovit Yaylası. Of a rather different nature is the festival at Elevit Yaylası, which sees evenings given over to folk dancing (particularly the horon) between August 15th and September 5th.

Trade routes

The bulk of the Kaçkar has never stopped trade between the coast, the mountains and the interior, although snow restricted the season. The Black Sea coast has traded dried fish, salt, spirit for lighting, maize and, more recently, tea, in exchange for wool, milk products and meat. Higher up, forestry products included honey, shingles for roofing and timber. The low-lying market gardens along the Çoruh produce rice, fruit and fruit syrups (sugar substitutes) and vegetables for sale to the coast and yaylas. In addition, for centuries Trabzon was the terminus of the Silk Route, and many more diverse products came via this route, including metal goods, spices and silks. Defence and administrative needs led to certain routes gaining importance. The Çoruh river was the most important trade route; fleets of boats drifting on the fast current carried crops to the coast for export and returned upstream, sailing against the current, with imported goods.

Goods were carried overland on mule trains, which operated in relays across the range. The best-established route was from the coast to İspir via Çamlıhemşin, past the two castles of Zil Kale and Kale-i-Bala and over the passes of the Verçenik massif. The paved mule road over the Davaliaşıtı was used for official correspondence from Istanbul and Erzurum and sheeps cheeses destined for Rize. Pazar (known in pre-Republican times as Atina) was the starting point for the trade in salt and lighting gas. The Korahmet Geçiti was used to bring pekmez/fruit syrup from the south side of the range to the north in exchange for roofing shingles for yayla houses, whilst the Kavron Geçiti was used to bring grapes from the Çoruh valley to the Black Sea side of the mountains. The Güngörmez Geçiti was a short but difficult route used to supply the yaylas with fresh fruit from Yusufeli.

Until the 1960's the roads and tracks were built by local labour of local stone. In summer, each headman/muhtar supplied one able-bodied man from every 10 in his district to build or repair the roads. A labourer worked for a week or so before being replaced by another. Thus the network of mule trails was cheap to construct and maintain; it still exists in many areas and makes for very pleasant walking.

Vernacular housing

One of the delights of trekking in the Kaçkar range is to be found in the traditional houses in the villages and yaylas. Nearly all are built on steep slopes, against the hillside, so may have 1-2 more storeys at the front than at the back; each storey has a separate purpose and may be reached by ramps or stairs according to the lie of the ground. Buildings are often isolated, taking advantage of any available suitable ground and positioned to enjoy the view and natural lighting. Constructed of a mixture of wood or stone, usually with pitched roofs, they bear more resemblance to traditional mountain houses in Northern Europe (eg. the Alps) than to the more Middle Eastern flat or domed-roofed houses of central and southern Anatolia.

Families may have 3 houses, which are in use at different seasons of the year. The village or town house is in use throughout the winter. Animals are wintered there so

8. What to look for

byre or stable accommodation plus hay storage is incorporated in the house and rising heat from the animals keeps the people warm. Dereiçi is a typical village with this type of accommodation. A mezra house is used in spring and autumn and generally has vegetable gardens, hay barns and facilities for making cheese. The house usually has 2 or more storeys and the hay barn may be separate, often with animal accommodation below. A yayla house, which doesn't require hay storage, is only used for 2-3 months in summer when the weather is usually warm. Normally above the treeline, the houses are stone-built with flat sod or shallow-pitched shingled roofs. Not all the family moved up to the yaylas - pregnant women, young children, old people and some of the men stayed at lower levels, tended the vegetable gardens and took the produce of the yaylas to market.

Nowadays, as migration has left so many houses empty, families don't need to move their flocks or herds to the highest yaylas so many are neglected and empty, trails unused and grazing wasted. Mezras and yaylas with road access, such as Pokut or Korahmet, are often well-used for 2-3 months in summer, not only for pasturing cattle, but by returnees who bring their children to their traditional homes for the summer holidays.

In the foothills of the northern side of the range, between Pazar and Çamlıhemşin, there are numerous mansion houses/ konak. Most of these date back to the 19th century, when the more entrepreneurial locals (who had made fortunes running businesses in Czarist Russia) displayed their newly-won wealth through these ostentatious mansions. The ground floor is usually dressed stone. The upper front of these houses is often a wooden-frame in-filled with small stones and plaster, giving a charming chequer-board effect. Otherwise, the upper floors of these houses are mainly stone. The quality and intricacy of the (often painted) carved relief work on doors, window frames, cupboards and fire surrounds is astonishing. Çağlayan (near Fındıklı, on the coast north and east of Ardeşen) has some fine examples, but those around Çamlıhemşin are more likely to be of interest to those heading for the Kaçkar. Peeking out from verdant woodlands high above the Fırtına river, some are still only accessible by mule, on foot or via an electric cable lift. The houses of the southern slopes are less grand, but still impressive. Some have Armenian inscriptions or crosses which show that the residents were once Christians. Wonderful examples can be seen in Sırakonaklar (the name means rows of mansions); Yaylalar, Barhal and Karbasan have simpler houses.

The higher one progresses, the simpler the architecture becomes. Houses in mezra tend to be made of a timber upper storey on a stone base or stone first storey, with pitched roofs to shed the heavy winter snows. The stone is normally dressed and neatly laid, often with decorative lintels over windows. The upper walls and gables of these houses are generally constructed of thick, hand-sawn planks reinforced with stout, load-bearing uprights. Heavy wooden shutters help keep draughts out and can be locked shut in winter, when the houses are left unoccupied. Traditionally, roughly sawn oak shingles were used as the roofing material but, on most inhabited houses, these have been replaced by corrugated iron.

Yayla houses are built of readily available materials. In some yaylas, entire houses may be constructed from sizeable tree-trunks (eg. at Pişenkaya). More commonly, as in the Çaymakçurs or Hacıvanak, sawn timber is used. In others, such as Davali, stone is preferred; the floor is paved and even the gaps between the buildings are paved and guttered. In some yaylas, such as Dibe, spring water can be directed over the paving to wash away animal waste. Often, the roof can be removed and stored inside the building during the winter - corrugated iron does not stand up to strong winds or the weight of snow. In the high northern yaylas like Avusor and Başkale, sod roofs, laid on a wooden base, provide excellent insulation and stand up to winter snows. In Avusor, the houses are partly set below ground level, to provide extra protection from the winds. Timber is rarely carved or decorated but some stones have crudely cut patterns - crosses and pictograms.

The more substantial houses often feature at least some external decoration, such as carved moon-and-stars motifs or arabic inscriptions on gable ends or above doors and windows. Many have hoists to raise hay to the top storey. Buildings can occasionally be dated by an inscription over a doorway or on a keystone. The large iron hinges used on doors and shutters are often decorative in themselves, the surface beaten by blacksmiths until dimpled, and the 'tails' wrought into sinuous curves.

Unless you know the history of a particular village, mezra or yayla it is very difficult to date domestic housing. The vast majority of dwellings you are likely to see date from the period between the beginning of the 19th century and about 1980. It was then that steel-and-concrete framed houses began to appear in some villages. In the National Park, traditional building materials have now become mandatory.

Historical remains - churches

The two major Georgian churches which lie within the scope of this book are virtually identical to each other (the church at Barhal was based on the earlier Dört Kilise) but are quite different to the majority of the churches surviving from the medieval Georgian principality of Tao-Klarjeti. Whilst Barhal, Dört Kilise, Bayır Kilise and the chapel opposite Barhal are basilica-style churches, the others largely conform to the cruciform plan with a dome over the transept.

Dört Kilise (Othta Eklesia) is well worth visiting. It stands on a low hill above the Güngörmez Deresi and is reached from the small village of Tekkale (see page 55). In both Turkish and Georgian its name means 'Four Churches'. From the evidence of inscriptions, it was established as a monastery church by David Magisterium (David the Great) between 961 and 965. Overall the monastery, with the remains of a mortuary chapel, a refectory and seminary building, is crumbling beneath dense stands of walnut, mulberry and other fruit trees, but the main church is in surprisingly good condition.

In both plan and size it is very similar to the church at Barhal (see page 73), with a length of 28.5 m, width of 22 m and height of 22 m. The interior comprises 3 aisles, with the central nave separated from the narrower side aisles by rows of arched piers. The semi-circular apse at the east end of the nave is broken into 5 bands or registers of frescoes, including an enthroned Christ and Virgin Mary, bishops, prophets and angels. Unfortunately these have been damaged by age, damp and smoke, and it is very difficult to make out what is what unless you know exactly what to look for. At the rear of the church, an upper gallery is supported by more pillars and arches and an arched passage connected the church with the cloisters and other monastery buildings.

Externally and internally, the most impressive feature of the church is the sense of height. This was achieved by building the church as high as it is wide and giving it a steeply pitched (and, unusually, tiled) roof over the nave, and lower pitched side roofs over the aisles. The blankness of the walls over the side-roofs is broken by a band of blind arcades, with pilasters and colonnettes between them. There are 5 blind arcades on the west front. A Maltese cross, with an (now illegible) inscription honouring David Magisterium, can be seen on the eastern gable of the church.

Bayır Kilise/church on a hill, much higher on the same slope as Dört Kilise, is spectacularly set on a rock platform below a semi-circular pinnacled ridge. Only 12 m long, with a single aisle, it is more chapel than church. The 3 arches at the west end of the church once supported a raised gallery (now collapsed). Opposite this, in the apse, a single window admits light and looks out over the wooded valley. Openings either side of the apse presumably held stairs leading to the roof. The stone roof is badly damaged, which has no doubt accelerated the deterioration of the now barely-discernible frescoes, and small trees have taken root above the door. The situation is very picturesque, with the church silhouetted against a backdrop of dark firs, but the church itself is desperately in need of stabilisation if it is not to crumble away entirely.

Parhali/Barhal Kilisesi is just a short walk above the village of Barhal. Like Dört Kilise, Parhali was also established by David Magisterium, and its design is clearly based on that of its predecessor. The proportions of the church are similar to Dört Kilise, with a length of 28.5 m, and a height of 22 m, but this height is exaggerated by the width of the church being only 18 m (as opposed to the 22 m width of Dört Kilise). From the visitor's point of view, however, the major difference is that whilst long-abandoned Dört Kilise is crumbling into ruin, because Parhali has been converted into the village mosque, it has been preserved . A mihrab (prayer niche facing Mecca) has been set in what was the south doorway of the church and the once-frescoed walls are now whitewashed. The 3-aisled interior does, however, have more decorative carving than Dört Kilise, with relief carvings of flowers and figures (including angels) embellishing pilasters and capitals.

The overall impression of the exterior is one of simplicity. However, as at Dört Kilise, rows of blind arcades divided by pilasters and colonnettes decorate the walls over the side aisle roofs. The smooth stone walls are punctured by small windows with decorative arches. A sense of depth is achieved by the use of well-proportioned and stepped blind arches on the end walls. A closer look reveals some quite intricate carving; parts of the north and west façades sport animal, bird and human figures, whilst sections of the east, south and west facades are given over to stylised flower and plant motifs, combined with geometric patterns. Unlike Dört Kilise, the roof is made of huge stone slabs and is still mainly sound.

On the hill opposite the church at Barhal is a small ruined chapel, built of squared blocks and once roofed in stone. It's smaller than the similar Bayır Kilise, but probably once had similar spiral staircases to the roof. It's difficult to tell what the original height was, or to determine if there was a gallery.

Historical remains - castles

The major routes across the Pontic chain are to the west of the scope of this book: the Ovitdağı Geçiti links Rize with İspir and Erzurum; the more famous Zigana Pass connects Trabzon with Erzurum via Gümüşhane and Bayburt.

THE KAÇKAR

However, from the Middle Ages to the 19th century, the passage over the western Kaçkar, from Pazar to İspir, was clearly of some importance. 4 castles (from north to south at Pazar, Cıhar (near Yücehisar), Zil and Varoş castles), were built to control passage along this valley route between the Black Sea and İspir and thence Bayburt/Erzurum (there are also unidentified ruins south of Kale-i-Bala, on the same route). Who first built these castles is uncertain (Byzantine, Genoese?) but they were certainly occupied by the pre-Ottoman Beylik lords and the Ottomans themselves. Only Zil and Varoş/Kale-i-Bala are described, as the remains of the other 2 are outside our area.

Zil Kalesi/castle of the bell is visited more for a spectacular position than its history. Set on a crag high above the Fırtına Deresi, its most notable feature is its tall and slender keep. With a giant-sized Turkish flag fluttering atop, mist swirling all around and the forest-blanketed slopes towering behind, photographing Zil Kalesi is irresistible.

Exploration is less rewarding but if you do potter about the crumbling keep and battlements, remember: local lore has it that the castle (not finally abandoned until the 1840's) is still inhabited by the ghosts of its former guardians. Apparently, on certain nights, the sound of their horses neighing and crowing of their cockerels still echo out from the castle across the valley!

Kale-i-Bala or Varoş Kalesi is 30 km upstream from Zil Kalesi at around 2000 m above sea level. The castle sits atop a spur above the village of Kaleköy, where the upper reaches of the Hemşin Deresi meet. Its location is even more remote and spectacular than that of Zil Kalesi but it's far more difficult to photograph. Reached by a path from the north-west, the castle is 70 m long by 40 m wide. The interior is very ruinous, though traces of a monumental doorway and barbican can be seen. There is a Muslim village cemetery just outside the castle walls.

Chapter 9 **NATIONAL PARKS, FLORA AND FAUNA**

The Kaçkar mountains are part of Turkey's important flora and fauna area number DKD005. This is the largest contiguous classified area in Turkey, comprising 1728 square km. Encircled by Trabzon, Rize, the Georgian frontier, Artvin, the Çoruh Valley, Bayburt, Gumuşhane and the coast west of Trabzon, this area contains numerous rare and threatened species. 125 plant species, 7 bird species, 4 mammals, 7 amphibian and lizard species, 3 fish and 20 butterflies and dragonflies appear on the International Union for the Conservation of Nature Red List or the Turkish Red List of endangered species. The whole area is rated as deteriorating badly; habitat is being lost or damaged throughout. The region is also classified by Birdlife International as (Important Bird Area) IBA060.

The major threat to the environment is the planned construction of the massive Yusufeli Dam, last in the series of huge dams currently being constructed on the Çoruh river. This dam will drown Yusufeli town and 17 villages, displacing several thousand people. Mining, especially in the Çoruh area and the Hatila Valley National Park above Artvin, is a potentially serious pollutant and forestry-related activities such as logging are ongoing threats. Tourism is beginning to be a problem too. New access roads, the often unregulated construction of restaurants and hotels and the lack of proper waste disposal are all putting pressure on the environment.

Many of the Red Book species are endemic - ie. they are not found in any other country; many are known only from this region. Some species of birds have been reduced to very low numbers; for example, the Caucasian black grouse is estimated at about 100 pairs, and the Doğa Derneği (Nature Society) has a protection programme in place.

Within the general boundary of the area are a National Park, Nature Conservation Areas, Nature Parks, Natural Monuments, Wildlife Breeding Areas, Special Nature Conservation Area, Natural Sites, and Archaeological Sites. These are classifications of the Turkish Ministry of Forestry and Environment and some of the lower classifications are, on the ground, not visible.

In 1994, 515 square km of the highest part of the Kaçkar, Altıparmak and Verçenik ranges was designated as the Kaçkar Mountains National Park. It contains the range's most dramatic peaks, glaciers and lakes, and its boundary is marked on the smaller map. It includes the Fırtına Deresi above Şenköy, the Kavron Deresi above Ayder and the Hevek Deresi above Olgunlar, with their villages and yaylas. The main gateway to the National Park is at Ayder - as you approach the village you will see a checkpoint manned by the National Park administration, which gives them the facility to charge a entry fee, although currently this is not levied. Other entry points near Çamlıhemşin and Olgunlar are unmanned.

The National Parks Administration is mandated to produce a management, improvement and tourism plan for the parks in its custody but the plan for the Kaçkar Mountains National Park has not yet been published. The administration is well aware of problems within the National Park (rubbish, water pollution, concentration of visitors in certain areas, illegal construction, hunting, etc), and appears to have every intention of taking action but as yet has done next to nothing. It has, however, become an important local employer and a pensioned job with the National Parks or Forestry is regarded as an enviable asset.

Meanwhile, residents within the park, especially those in Ayder, find their lives hedged around with restrictions as they have to apply for permission to build or alter their properties both to the local and park authorities. In many areas, title deeds have not been issued, so occupiers are concerned that ownership could be given to the park. (Property is regarded as a family heritage and very rarely sold.) Another problem identified by the locals is the increase in the number of bears. Since hunting was banned, bears have become bolder, helping themselves to honey or fruit from even the lower villages. There is no compensation scheme for loss of beehives or fruit to the bears but locals aren't allowed to hunt them, even those continuously causing damage. Because of these factors, there is a certain tension between villagers and the National Parks administration.

The National Parks service currently does very little to publicise or visibly manage the Park - there are no leaflets, maps, information booths, rangers, rescue services or other aids to visitors of the sort which you would find in a National Park in more developed countries. Information on the web is also difficult to find; www.kackarlar.org (a site set up by the Doğa Derneği) is probably the best site. The official site, www.milliparklar.gov.tr is only in Turkish, concentrates heavily on hunting and the links to the National Parks don't produce much result.

If you are interested in plants and wildlife, please check the Bibliography in Appendix B; you can get books on Turkish flora and fauna more easily from outside the country before you arrive. If you are a birdwatcher, do bring a pair of binoculars (also good for spotting mountain goats, bears, etc). A spotting scope is probably too heavy to carry up to the peaks but would be a great thing to have for shorter walks. It is also worth considering a guided nature holiday - check the links on the website for tour specialists.

The region divides naturally into areas below and above the treeline but there are also seasonal considerations. Plant spotting is most definitely seasonal and naturally follows the melting snow up the valleys - a carpet of miniature alpines unfurl themselves as the snow retreats and is followed by gentians and orchids, then later, as the meadows dry a little, by colourful annuals and perennials. Autumn brings a flush of colour to the trees; as families return to winter quarters, beautiful displays of colchicum and crocus decorate the meadows. Birds are easiest to spot and identify just after the migration (June) when they are searching for a mate or on the autumn return migration. In late summer there are plenty of juveniles around in various stages of plumage, which makes birds easy to see but identification hard work! Below, we have described some habitats and indicated what you may find in each area.

Peaks and the alpine zone (3000 m upwards)

The granite ridges of the Kackar once stood above several major glaciers. Eroded by ice into saw-edged ridges and peaks, they offer an inhospitable environment for flora and fauna. A few remnants of glaciers remain and some snow patches are perennial. Moraine dropped by retreating glaciers dams small and, sometimes, deep cirque lakes. This area is home to the larger raptors - lammergeiers and other vultures and golden eagles. Smaller birds include occasional wallcreepers, alpine accentors and water pipits in abundance, snow finches, shore larks and choughs which wheel and call around the cliffs. Tiny alpines, such as draba, viola, gentiana verna, cyclamen parviflorum and veronicas, are the usual plants; bulbs include colchicum, muscari and fritillaries. You may see chamois and mountain goat prints in mud or snow and hear them rolling rocks down the slopes but they are difficult to see.

Above the treeline between 1800 and 3000 m

This zone was once glaciated and the characteristic scenery is huge U-shaped valleys divided by spurs of the main ranges. Hanging valleys abut the main valleys and piles of moraine dropped by retreating glaciers often hold back small lakes. Piles of boulders, rounded by the ice, are piled up in some valleys.

Above the full-sized trees there is a variety of vegetation. On the northern slopes, up to about 2200 m, is rhododendron scrub growing up to a height of about a metre. On the southern slopes are dwarf birches and spindly pines. Parts of this area, especially around Yusufeli, are much dryer and springs are scarce; plants include vetches, daisies and geraniums. Many yaylas are situated in the valley bottoms as the meadows düzlük give good grazing.

The best flowers are in these damper areas - primulas, the white anemone, the dactylarhiza orchids and taller gentians. Early spring flowers, mainly on the slopes, include fritillaries, drabas, saxifrages, polygala vulgaris and geraniums. Bulbs include lavish displays of autumn crocuses and colchicums. The Caucasian black grouse breeds in rhododendron bushes and the Caspian snowcock on rocky areas. Wheatears, black redstarts, white and grey wagtails and pipits abound and are easy to see; kestrels are common too. Bats may live in the empty dwellings of abandoned yaylas. Bears hibernate in caves in this zone and you may be lucky to see one return from a night's hunting further down the valley. On the dryer hillsides, herds of wild horses graze above the treeline and you may see wild goats too.

Evergreen forest between 900 m and 2000 m

Oriental spruce, starting at 900 m and continuing to the tree line, is common throughout the region on north-facing slopes. Pines grow on dryer slopes, from the same altitude, and continue to about 2000 m on the southern slopes, lower on the northern. Some of these trees are massive and shut the light off from the understorey, so there is very little growth below them. In clearings there are beeches and on rocky areas the creeping juniper spreads. Look out for crossbills, kreuper's nuthatches, goldcrests and greenfinches, groups of tits, including long-tailed and sombre tits. The squirrels are the Persian variety, and the rare marbled pine marten lives here too. Along the streams are dippers and grey wagtails and buzzards sometimes nest. Flowers are less common, but include the yellow azalea, honeysuckles, wild raspberries and viburnums.

Meadows, terraces and grazing lands below 2000 m

Mainly on the southern slopes, tree cover is not general and the hillsides around the mezras have been terraced for crops. These are often no longer cultivated but grazed by cattle; the stone retaining walls form natural rock gardens, with sedums, saxifrage and sempervivums. Meadowside trees include neglected fruit trees such as plums or apples, rowans and maples and dwarf willows along streams. Blackberries raspberries and strawberries grow in hedges or at the edge of forest. Helleborines dactylorhizas and pyramidal orchid are common but there are many rarer orchids to be found in this zone, including several varieties of bee orchid. The bulbs are mostly over before the trekking season starts, but you may see wild onions, bellevalias the star of Bethlehem and wild gladiolus. Cornflowers, bellflowers, flowering peas, thistles and geraniums collect clouds of butterflies. Rosefinches, larks, cuckoos, corn and other buntings, various shrikes and many warblers make their summer homes around the houses and deserted buildings may house owls and bats. Endemic red-spotted trout live in the streams.

Broad-leaved forest

Below the glaciated levels, especially in wetter areas, erosion has deepened the valleys, forming very steep, wooded slopes. These beautiful forests are mostly found above the hazelnut and tea plantations on the north slopes, between 700 and 1700 m altitude. Mainly of sweet chestnut and oak trees, they also have oriental beech and hornbeam and an understorey of rhododendrons, brambles, hawthorn, etc. Box forest grows in the Fırtına valley. More level areas have been used for cultivation or building; some of the meadows around old houses have a good variety of plants. With high rainfall and waterfalls hurtling down cliffs between the trees, the humidity is high and paths through the forest soon become overgrown. Look out for beehives hanging in the treetops, bear droppings on the paths and scratched trees where they have sharpened their claws. Woodpeckers, chaffinches, willow, wood and green warblers and mountain chiffchaffs are all found in this zone.

Butterflies

The main butterfly season is in August, when the muddy puddles swarm with blues. Yellow and black swallowtails are real beauties; parnassius apollo - a huge delicate silver-white butterfly with orange dots on the wings - is also gorgeous and quite common; parnassius nordmanii is a much rarer relative. The best place to see them is around Olgunlar where huge quantities of dead butterflies are trapped in the roof of the café near the bridge. See Appendix B for Dr Ahmet Baytaş's new book on the subject and a link to his checklist of butterfly species.

Bird migration

Unless it's held up by storms, the spring migration moves through north-east Turkey at the beginning of June. The larger birds arrive first - vultures, buzzards, the Levent Sparrowhawk and falcons. Many ruddy shelducks pass through, mainly to the east of the Kackar. Bee-eaters and rollers colonise the Çoruh valley, where they join orioles, rose-coloured starlings and flycatchers. The passerines include buntings (black-headed and ortolan), rosefinches, shrikes, serins and at higher levels stonechats, blue and ordinary rock thrushes. Two beautiful birds to look out for are the blue-throated and white-throated robins. The autumn migration continues from September to October and is also a good time to spot birds. See the website for a link to a checklist of birds.

This brief summary may encourage you to observe the flora and fauna around you; if you see anything especially noteworthy, please let us know.

Chapter 10 ROUTES AROUND TEKKALE, THE GÜNGÖRMEZ DAĞLARI AND ZITLOP SIRTI

The foothills of the Kaçkar in the area bounded by the Hevek, Barhal and Çoruh valleys form an excellent early- and late-season trekking area. The mountains are mainly of softer sedimentary rock, so they are more rounded than the central Kaçkar, the climate is drier and the altitude lower. The area is dominated and divided by a steep-sided grassy ridge, which strikes N from the E end of the Güngörmez Dağları and terminates just S of Barhal. Below the ridgeline are steep forested slopes, mainly pine, leading down to the fast-flowing valley bottom streams, where farming villages occupy the more level areas. You could walk the length of the ridge or explore the 4 pretty, well-farmed valleys which descend its eastern flank towards Yusufeli. Tekkale is at the mouth of the southernmost valley, on the banks of the Çoruh Nehri and is the starting point for some treks. It has a pension, kahves, several bakkals and a dolmuş service to Yusufeli, only about 10 km away. It's a base for rafting on the Çoruh Nehri, which is a leading white water rafting and canoeing venue. Rafters start near Ispir and take three days to reach Tekkale, then continue beyond into the gorge of the Çoruh. The peak season for the tough stuff is from May to July but less energetic rafting continues all summer. The Tekkale wrestling festival is held on the second Saturday in July, on meadows 9 km up the valley, just before Bölükbaşı Mahallesi. The day before the festival, cows are slaughtered and the meat prepared - the villagers carry on feasting for several days. Approaching Tekkale from Yusufeli, there are good views of a medieval castle and chapel perched on an insurmountable crag.

Sarıgöl/Sarikevi is the main shopping and agricultural centre on the road from Yusufeli to the mountains. It has a small range of shops, a rather seedy pension/hotel, bakery, schools and clinic. The wide main street acts as a transport hub and locals will advise you on transport and organise tea and food while you wait. The Barhal Deresi between Sarıgöl and Yusufeli is used for a more relaxed type of rafting - it's shallower and flows more slowly than the Çoruh.

Some treks in this area start from the Sarıgöl-Yaylalar road between Barhal and Mikelis but finish in the other valleys E of the ridge. Transport from Yusufeli, Barhal or Yaylalar can get you to the start of these treks.

10.1 Dört Kilise, Bayır Kilise, Elasume Mezrası and return (or Kusara Mezrası and route 10.3) (5 hrs 40 mins)

This is a walk to 2 churches and their associated monastery buildings, in the Güngörmez Deresi which flows down to the Çoruh Nehri at Tekkale. The first church, now known as Dört Kilise, which means 4 churches, is a large monastery complex situated just above the road in the valley bottom. It's 7 km NW up the road from Tekkale, so taking a taxi or hitching a lift is a good option. The second church, Bayır Kilise, is only 1.2 km from Dört Kilise, but high above it on the hillside. The climb between is a stiff one over indistinct path, so take poles. The return route is via the lovely old mezra of Elasume, linked to the upper church via a pretty, horizontal path and the long valley-bottom road (again, try to hitch a lift). We also describe an alternative link from Elasume to route 10.3 to Salent Yaylası.

This trek starts from the church at Dört Kilise; if you want to walk, see route 10.3 on page 58. Otherwise, take a taxi or hitch a lift to the church.

About 7km NW of Tekkale, just after the 3rd river bridge, on the W of the Güngörmez Deresi is the church of Dört Kilise, hidden by walnut trees on a small hill top. Continue on the road for 50 m to the stream bed and turn up towards the church here (5 mins, A167). Flocks graze around and fenced vegetable gardens adjoin the east wall. The church is unrestored and the frescoes all but invisible but extensive remains of the monastery complex and baptistery still stand (see page 47).

To reach Bayır Kilise, continue along the dirt road for about 500 m, to a bridge leading to a mahalle on the W side of the stream (10 mins). Turn L/SW up a muletrack through forest, which rises and crosses the stream leading down to the church. Turn R/upwards on the narrow path on the S side of the streambed; it climbs the valley just below the trees then bends R across the stream and climbs to Bayır Kilise (1 hr 10 mins, A154). The church is on a high buttress N/above the streambed, with a semi-circle of steep cliffs on the southern side (see page 48).

To continue from the church, climb the narrow path NE through bushes to a second roofless building, tucked under a overhang. Continue up the path, make a hairpin over rocks and climb to an open spur over the valley. Turn the corner, descending on a lovely cool path into firs and across a stream bed (20 mins). Here, a pınar runs into a hollow log and beyond is a second pınar. Climb again to another headland, passing over a scree patch and descending again into firs. There is then a gentle climb to another, mainly bare spur, with short, bushy spurge (euphorbia) and scattered pines. After this, the firs resume again.

Walk amongst tall firs on good path across small rock falls and damp patches, then emerge into the open. The path climbs over rocks, with some built-up sections, to a final spur, Çobankaya Sırtı. From here you have views over the valley below and to the final building of Elasume Mezrası positioned in a beautiful situation on a level hill-top plateau to the NW (30 mins).

On this grassy and pine clad spur, the route divides. Ignore the faint path going up the spur and take the better path which drops NW down the far side, again entering woods. The path soon levels and is fenced on the lower side. Ignore paths leading R and L and walk along the water channel to the houses ahead (5 mins, A163).

WP	Lat (N)	Long (E)	Alt (m)
A167	40.81403	41.47103	1144
A042	40.82227	41.46782	1197
A150	40.81400	41.46352	1300
A149	40.81012	41.46285	1360
A154	40.81425	41.45716	1658
A152	40.81704	41.45961	1713
A156	40.82004	41.45592	1646
A158	40.82329	41.45766	1673
A161	40.82756	41.45626	1634
A163	40.83158	41.45270	1598
A165	40.83278	41.46005	1338
A042	40.82227	41.46782	1197
A167	40.81403	41.47103	1144

10.1 Dört Kilise, Bayır Kilise, Elasume Mezrası

> **Elasume Mezrası** is perched above the Güngörmez Deresi and is accessed by a steep zigzag road. It's inhabited from April to November, as the grazing is good and there are vegetable gardens just below the 20-30 densely packed, tall wood-and-stone houses. Electricity and phones are connected. The residents used to move up to Sagule Yaylası but now the number of cattle has decreased, there is enough grazing and hay locally.

Walk almost level between the houses to the çeşme in the centre of the mezra.

Alternative route: Continue level and leave the mezra by good path which rises over a low ridge then descends slightly around a valley. Approaching the deserted mezraa of Kusara, the path has been eroded. It passes a spring and between a few houses. Bear L in front of more houses to find a good, level path which continues to the lower edge of a sloping field. Here, turn R/down for 50m to join the dirt road rising from Bölükbaşı. To your R the road leads down to the main valley floor. To your L the road immediately crosses a low col on the route to Salent Yaylası. **End.**

Here, turn R/down then immediately L on a horizontal path across fields. Turn R along the edge of a field, following a well-used path with a ditch and fence running alongside. Bear R and, on the end of the plateau overlooking the valley, meet the dirt track (15 mins).

The route continues down the zigzagging, sandy but driveable track to the junction with the valley-bottom road (30 mins). Under some walnut trees, turn R onto the unsurfaced road and walk down it to Dört Kilise church (1 hr 30 mins, A167). It's a long and fairly boring walk from here back to Tekkale, so if you are offered a lift, accept it (1 hr 40 mins, A180).

10.2 Çubulikar, Doles Mezrası and return (or by road to Barhal) (3 hrs 5 mins)

This is a short but steep walk past a mill to a mezra perched on the shoulder of the wooded ridge SW of Barhal. There are views over the Barhal valley and the lower ridges of the valley; the mezra itself has substantial old houses. As an alternative, you could return the long way, down the dirt road which wanders along the N facing slopes, passing above the mahalles of Börekli, Köseler and Şabangil before descending to Barhal. Take poles to aid the short, steep climb up scree.

Walk or drive S out of Barhal for about 1 km on the Yaylalar road, until you come to a wooden bridge on metal girders, leading to the small mahalle of Çubulikar (20 mins, A185).

Cross the bridge, pass a house on the L and find an unused path just to the L of the stream. It starts on the L bank, crosses to the R then back to the L. The path rises SE into a steep-sided valley, and passes under 2 mulberry trees on the L bank, then climbs higher and away from the river, until it reaches an old mill, in very good condition with the mechanism still intact and almost unused (30 mins, A187).

At the mill, the path doubles back L/N and climbs slippery hairpins to the ridgetop (20 mins) Here, turn R/SE again and zigzag up the ridge, passing large fir trees on the R side. Above/L, on the skyline, is a telegraph post that marks the edge of the mahalle. The track climbs diagonally R then turns back L into oak scrub. This is the final leg of the hairpins as the path turns into woodland around the head of a valley; there is a hedge and beyond that fields on the R (20 mins, A190).

Cross the upper trickle of the valley stream and continue to climb up/N towards

WP	Lat (N)	Long (E)	Alt (m)
A185	40.96102	41.38351	1207
A187	40.95803	41.38972	1355
A188	40.95921	41.38965	1409
A190	40.95938	41.39247	1522
A191	40.96013	41.39237	1546
A192	40.95830	41.39492	1622
A186	40.96046	41.38506	1250
A185	40.96102	41.38351	1207
A030	40.79001	41.49262	805

the mezra. This path meets a better path at a diagonal; turn R and continue climbing less steeply towards the lower houses. Climb a steep path between the houses and turn R to continue on a path leading to a çeşme (15 min, A192).

> Doles/Dökyüz/Deykuz Mezrası is one of the medium-level mezra (about 1600 m) on steep, W facing slopes to the E of the Hevek Deresi. It has about 20 substantial stone houses, mostly with 3 storeys, log barns and good hayfields. Now sadly underused, a few families live there for 2-3 months each year. It's surrounded by a beautiful fir forest, and accessed by a long but well-maintained road; electricity and telephones are connected. Some of the houses are being repaired and renovated and the vegetable gardens are in use. There are 2 çeşmes; from the one on the S side, a path rises upwards, probably towards Aho Yaylası. The spectacular views from the yayla are over the Barhal valley, towards the steep-sided ridges and the Altıparmak Dağları beyond.

To descend by the quickest route, leave the yayla by the way you came in but instead of turning L onto the difficult track, continue NW on good track to the telegraph post at the head of the ridge. This track continues in zigzags down the ridge, following telegraph posts and the pylons supplying the telephone tower and arrives at the houses close to the bridge.

The views from this track are spectacular (1 hr, A185). Cross the bridge and turn R to return to Barhal (20 mins).

10.3 Bölükbaşı Mezrası, Salent Yaylası and return (or Güngörmez Geçiti and Modut) (6 hrs 5 mins)

This route follows part of the old mule trail from Yusufeli and Tekkale to Modut, Mikelis and Yaylalar in the Hevek Deresi. The pass was once used by mules carrying fruit and vegetables from the fertile valley of the Çoruh to markets in Yaylalar but, due to the height of the pass, was probably only open for 2-3 months per year. The walk described below is a day-walk from Bölükbaşı to Salent Yaylası; you will need to hitchhike to Bölükbaşı from Tekkale (there is transport on the route, especially during July and August) or take your own transport there and walk back. Alternatively, you could walk up the dirt road, taking sleeping bags and food, and sleep in the yayla, returning next day.

Additionally, we have added notes to help you attempt the pass but we haven't done it ourselves; mist prevented us from crossing it. Don't underestimate the difficulties; remember that there will be snow until August and the path disappears into scree as you cross to the Modut side. Turn back if there is mist and take compass bearings at the top, for you risk descending S into the wrong valley. It may be easier under snow, provided you have an ice-axe and good boots.

2 km after the church of Dört Kilise (see 10.1), as the valley broadens out again, there are houses on the outskirts of Bölükbaşı and open fields where the annual wrestling festival is held. At a final river bridge above the festival ground, the road divides (10 mins, A029). Stay on the L of the Güngörmez Deresi, on a tractor track which becomes stonier. Pass an uphill turn on your R, and about 200 m beyond, cross the stream on your L via a shallow ford, onto the opposite bank (25 mins). Walk W up the track, which is lined with wild strawberry plants, on rising zigzags through forest with occasional meadows (15 mins, A006). The path from Elasume Mezra joins just before a low col.

After the col, the track has been damaged and in places becomes a narrow path. Descend SW to another sidestream and cross (5 mins); on your R a path runs down to the Güngörmez Deresi. Our track continues past the sidestream with the Güngörmez Deresi on the R/N - bulldozing has damaged many trees along this section. Further along, the track turns L and rises over a bluff away from the stream, then rejoins it. Soon after, it again leaves the stream, climbs up in a hairpin and ends abruptly at the base of a gully (25 mins). The gradient of the hillside is now steep, so the route continues on the old mulepath. The badly eroded path rises W from the L side of the track about 50 m before its end point and runs upwards among small pine trees, keeping to the L bank of the gully.

The first few bends of the path are hard work, as the ground is soft, but after that the path zigzags into trees and becomes clearer and easier, sometimes splitting into 2.

WP	Lat (N)	Long (E)	Alt (m)
A029	40.83706	41.45789	1358
A005	40.83857	41.45581	1381
A006	40.83736	41.44679	1485
A145	40.83416	41.44296	1620
A007	40.83411	41.44162	1656
A009	40.83583	41.43526	1742
A010	40.83672	41.43086	1851
A011	40.83773	41.42865	1895
A012	40.83634	41.42744	1984
A013	40.83690	41.42622	2015
A014	40.83684	41.42310	2102
A015	40.83731	41.42010	2185
A016	40.83753	41.41733	2264
A017	40.83761	41.41358	2378
A018	40.83812	41.40428	2477
A181	40.82921	41.39121	2890
A182	40.82398	41.37607	3320
A183	40.82781	41.36696	2940
A184	40.84093	41.34390	2335

alternative route

10.3 Bölükbaşı Mezrası, Salent Yaylası and return

The main path turns R and crosses the gully, dipping slightly, then turns uphill with the gully on the L. Ahead is a waterfall and wooded crags. The path reaches the top of a rise, where there is a fallen tree on a grassy bank (50 mins). The path continues straight, climbing less steeply, then passes close to a large pine tree with the lower branches lopped. (40 mins, A015).

Past this last tree, the forest is replaced by a wide scree bank sloping from L to R. The path crosses the scree on good path and continues up the hillside, passing scattered pine saplings. Salent Yaylası comes into sight ahead/W, on a slope between 2 streams but still some distance away. Contour along the valley side, with the stream on the R, then descend to meet and cross it on stepping-stones. Walk diagonally R up the bank and turn L to walk along a grassy ridge to the yayla, on the way crossing a trickle which supplies the houses with water (45 mins, A018).

Looking back from the yayla, you can see, on the far side of the valley below, perched on a grassy ridge just above the forest, the yayla of Bavut. Below you is the deep tree-filled valley leading down to Bölükbaşı and around are meadows, which would pasture many cattle.

> **Salent/Güngörmez Yaylası** is well-named - Güngörmez means 'that which doesn't see the sun' - it often lies in mist in the huge basin of the upper E-flowing Güngörmez Deresi. On either side and in front are forests of fir trees and above it are 2 lakes - Büyük and Küçük Göl (big and little lake). This yayla consists of about 60 sawn timber houses with barns below arranged neatly in rows facing E at an altitude of 2200 m. It is on the once-important mule route between Yusufeli and the Hevek Deresi via the Güngörmez Geçiti, also known as the Naletleme or Pas Geçiti. Most of the houses are still in good condition; some have had their timber roofs replaced with corrugated iron. Nearly all are locked and are surrounded by a sea of nettles and weeds but, with perseverance, it's possible to find an unlocked house to stay in. Most haven't been used for several years but occasionally hunters stay in the yayla.

Alternative route to Güngörmez Geçiti and Modut: The onward path rises diagonally R above the yayla and bears L around a bluff, then bends back to cut upwards across the slope, with the stream on the L, towards Küçük Göl. It rises in zigzags above cliffs, then runs L/N towards and above the lake.

To continue, aim up the valley at the pass to the WSW, following the R slope of the valley towards a needle-shaped rock perched on the valley side. At the rock (you can pass either below or above it) cut across to the L side of valley and climb the slope diagonally R to the lower ridge on your L. Then turn R/NW and continue on faint path to the top of Güngörmez Geçiti, above the Mikelis Deresi. There is a second path rising from the Cevizli Dere to the L/SE, which meets our route just before the pass. The descent is to the NW, down the Mikelis Deresi and it's here that you will encounter scree and maybe rockfalls which have obscured the path.

After the initial 15 mins, the route becomes easier as you continue down the N side of the Mikelis Deresi. After it passes a wide cirque on the L, with the lake of Poso Gölü, the route crosses the stream. Where a sidestream enters the Mikelis stream, there is a deserted yayla, Nabadere Yaylası and, from there, a well-used path contours L/NW, away from the Mikelis Deresi, to Modut (6 hrs). The descent from

Modut to Mikelis is described in route 13.2. End.
Return down the valley to the area of the sidestream, just before Bölükbaşı (1 hr 30 mins, A013). Turn L, descend across boulders to the water and cross the Güngörmez Deresi. There are 2 crossing places: one for the cows and, below it, another where people can jump from rock to rock. The track on the opposite bank runs R and descends slightly. As the bank becomes wider and less steep, walnut orchards are planted above and below the clear path; a tree below the path is impressively huge. The path continues at the base of rocks on the L, then descends slightly and crosses a water channel; it runs with the channel for about 10 m then continues below it. A few metres further on, turn R and descend diagonally through meadows with more walnut trees.

Cross a large water channel onto an open meadow (15 mins, A027). A white house is just ahead; keep L of it and follow the water channel along the top edge of an orchard of fruit trees and walnuts, passing a barn.

> Bölükbaşı Mezrası is now a name given to a group of mezra at the junction of the 2 streams named as Güngörmez Deresi. On lush green sloping or valley-bottom land, surrounded by hills with plenty of timber, the tall houses and barns are still well-used by summer returnees and cattle farmers. All summer, hay is transported down the valley to fill barns at Tekkale, where the cattle overwinter; formerly some would stay in the mezra all winter long as the altitude is only about 1400 m. Walnuts and honey are the other produce.

Immediately before you reach more houses, turn down on a winding path, which passes a çeşme and meets a wider path. Turn R onto this and continue between houses, taking the lower of 2 paths and continue to a cluster of mills fed by the water channels. The path is now wider and has a wall on the R. It descends to meet a road; continue down this and come to the main valley bottom road, just above the bridge and fork (15 mins, A005).

10.4 Demirdöven, Solerun Mezrası, Duruklu Mezrası, Güzelce Mezrası and Kışladamları *(4 hrs 10 mins)*

This is a day walk on the forested E side of the Hevek Deresi above Demirdöven. The route up to the mezra of Solerun is a steep and narrow path, but it's a pleasant and almost level walk along unsurfaced road from Solerun to Güzelce, a deserted mezra close to Karbasan. The walk down to the road near Kışladamları is a spectacular plunge into the valley down a little-used track. We also describe an alternative path up to Solerun.

Demirdöven is on the route from Yaylalar to Barhal and dolmuşes pass through morning and evening; get off here and walk N.

Crossing a narrow bridge just N of Demirdöven (A069), turn L and follow a narrow path to a stream valley (10 mins, A070). The path turns E up the valley to a junction with another path. Continue up scree on the L of the valley; from here, you can see over the valley to Taşbaşı, the upper mahalle of Demirdöven (15 mins). The route enters forest and climbs steeply with the stream valley to the R; as the trees thin and the path becomes less steep, it passes a çeşme (15 mins). The path rises gently over the rim of the valley, bearing L/NE towards the yayla, dipping slightly to pass a waterfall (40 mins).

The path, which has widened and become clearer, now rises towards the first substantial stone-and-timber houses of Solerun Mezrası, on the R and facing over the valley (5 mins, A077). Passing these, there are more, smaller, houses and barns on a bare and steep spur ahead. Turn R onto a path on the R of the spur, which keeps R to meet the dirt road running horizontally above the mezra; turn R and walk above the mezras (10 mins, A079).

Alternative route: Cross a substantial wire-and-plank bridge about 2.5 km N of Demirdoven. To the R of the bridge is a house and behind it a path climbs over loose scree E into the valley above. The first few hairpins of the path are in very poor condition and run over scree held in place by scrub oak. The path bears L of a headland over the valley and then R onto the headland; the going becomes easier. Here there are orchards and the narrow path heads up towards an isolated house with a mill and fields. Soon Solerun mezrası is in view ahead R/SE and the path continues to join the road just beyond the empty houses. Turn R on the road and follow it as it contours the valley, crossing a stream, to meet the main route above Solerun Mezrası (2 hrs). End.

> **Solerun and Duruklu Mezrası** have between them about 25 tall stone houses, mostly still in good condition, with wooden barns for the hay. They are both situated just below the dirt road, overlooking the Hevek Deresi, at about 2000 m. Only a few of the houses are inhabited, but the fields around are fertile and there is a good water supply; at one time there were water mills. In former times, during the summer the residents pastured their cows on Zitlop Sırtı, but there is more than enough grazing for the few remaining cattle.

From here, it's a walk of about 2.5 km SSW on the road to Güzelce Mezrası (45 mins). The descent from the road to the houses is steep and best done from the S end of the mezra (5 mins, A081).

> **Güzelce Mezrası** has about 25 deserted tall stone houses, all empty but mostly still in good condition, with wooden barns for the hay. They are mainly situated in a row just below the newish Karbasan road, but there are others at a lower level, on a SW facing slope overlooking a stream bed and meadows. Some of Karbasan's villagers still use the empty barns for storing hay and crops.

Descend from the road to the upper houses and find a narrow path running W, past some barns, aiming at a summit which juts out over the valley below, where there is a ruined barınak (15 mins). The path starts to descend in hairpins, then turns R/NW into forest, passing a pınar and continuing to descend to the mahalle of Vestel, with just 2 houses and a barn (25 mins). The path passes indistinctly down between the house and a barn and turns R to the edge of the forest on the N side of the yayla, where it plunges steeply into the lush forest (5 mins). At a deep, eroded valley it turns L and continues to hairpin down towards the valley floor. Close to the valley bottom it emerges onto terraces, close to the edge of the gully. Here the path is lost (40 mins). Descend the overgrown terraces diagonally L, and find a short, steep path, which takes you down to river level (10 mins, A093). Here the river is wide and shallow, so you can wade across to some newly built houses, adjacent to the road and about 1 km N of Demirdöven (10 mins).

WP	Lat (N)	Long (E)	Alt (m)
A069	40.91787	41.35223	1367
A070	40.91858	41.35261	1377
A072	40.91882	41.35570	1507
A073	40.91936	41.35911	1634
A075	40.92398	41.36625	1709
A077	40.92526	41.36885	1766
A079	40.92670	41.37084	1836
A081	40.89569	41.36857	2060
A082	40.89489	41.36004	1986
A085	40.89376	41.35561	1919
A086	40.89575	41.35531	1877
A089	40.89967	41.35096	1760
A091	40.90175	41.34802	1541
A093	40.90161	41.34561	1436

10.5 Kışladamları Mahallesi, Karbasan, Gravat Yaylası, Sura, Taşkıran and Sarıgöl (13 hrs 25 mins)

This route takes you from the central part of the Hevek Deresi E to Zıtlop Sırtı, and over the ridge to Taşkıran, in a valley descending to Sarıgöl. The ridge is about 2600 m high at the point where you join it, so the walk starts with a long climb, through villages and a yayla. The yaylas on the far side of the ridge have long been abandoned but their situations are beautiful, on E-facing slopes just above the tree line. From them, you descend to the northernmost valley, which leads down to Sarıgöl. You could link this route to route 10.6, or turn L on the ridge and walk N towards Barhal. Either way, as you approach the ridge, you should be careful to carry enough water, as there's none there.

Take a dolmuş on the main Yaylalar - Demirdöven road, to the concrete roadbridge at Kışladamları, which leads to Karbasan (it's about 5 km S of Demirdöven and 4 km N of the Mikelis bridge) (A094). Walk up the dirt road as it crosses the bridge over the Hevek Deresi, then a second bridge over the Alikolat Deresi, then for 150 m up a long diagonal climb to the NE (15 mins). An initially faint path climbs up R/SE through scrubby forest towards the sidestream valley. It turns parallel with the stream but above it and reaches the lower side of Alikolat Mahallesi. The path turns up on rough steps between the substantial houses then, at the top of the mahalle, turns R (25 mins). It continues to climb up the river valley, towards more forest, then contours below more houses to reach the stream near an old mill. This is a lovely spot, very secluded, shady and green (10 mins). Retrace your steps, turn up just before the village, leaving a house on your L, and climb the path out of the village into oak scrub. Hairpin L/N into a shallow gully then continue to climb on zigzags running NE up a ridge. The path meets the road on a bend and crosses it (30 mins, A106).

Just above the road, among pines, is a çeşme with an inscription and the date 1977. The path continues climbing steeply to an old road; turn R onto this and continue to the new road (20 mins). Cross the new road and climb onto an exposed and well-grazed hillside, just below the village of Karbasan. Soon you will see a rubbish tip on the R and beyond this the path narrows into a slot. Continue upwards/R into the village and climb between the houses to the top of the village and the new mosque (15 mins, A112).

> **Karbasan/Cabriket** is a flourishing village of maybe 200 people, with stone houses and wooden barns grouped around an old mosque. It is situated at 2100 m below woodland on a W-facing hillside and has meadows and grazing spread out below. A winding, steep dirt road links the village with the valley floor below. Several watermills line the road into the village and a new mosque is being built here, paid for by public subscription. It's likely that the old mills will be casualties of the new building programme.

To find the track to Gravat Yaylası, from the new mosque walk towards the old mosque, then turn uphill on a narrow alley between 2 barns (5 mins). You emerge on a level wide track leading E with a fence on lower side and the Alikolat Deresi well below that. A small yayla consisting only of a row of barns is visible above the stream on the R side of the valley ahead. Our yayla is high on the L bank of the valley, but not visible from here.

At a junction with a path leading downwards, keep straight ahead. At the next junction also continue straight. Gravat Yaylası becomes visible high above on the L bank of the valley, well above the stream and above a belt of trees (25 mins, A115).

Soon after, the path arrives at junction - the main path makes a sharp L bend but a narrow path leads straight ahead. Both routes lead to the yayla, but only the L path is passable by mules. Follow the L path until it turns back L again to enter trees. Here, again, you could continue straight ahead to join the other path. These minor paths enter the yayla from below, but the mulepath continues up more zigzags between and then above trees, then turns R to enter the upper part of the yayla. The zigzags are badly worn and very slippery, but edged throughout with a low barrier of branches (50 mins, A116).

> **Gravat/Kirayat Yaylası** is at 2300 m, on the N side of a wide grassy basin, about an hour above Karbasan and served by a good path. The 10-15 houses have a stone lower storey, with timber above, and face S. Families move frequently between the village and the yayla, which has good grazing pastures on the slopes above and opposite. A water channel, which is now not maintained, used to serve the village but there is still adequate water from pipes. A group of barns on the opposite side of the valley stores some of the hay used to feed a large herd of bulls.

Find the çeşme at the upper E corner of the yayla; it's fed by pipes along a water channel running through the trees above and R. From here you have a good view of the wide green valley above. It's divided by the Alibolat Deresi, with 3 main tributaries, and has several paths on the R/S bank, some leading up to the ridge above. To the R and L of the lower part of the stream, the walls are steeper, with rock outcrops and groups of pines. The aim is to reach the ridge R of the lowest point, just to the R of the widest eroded gully, which has reddish soil.

Turn downhill and descend a diagonal path from the çeşme to the streambed below R/SE, cross the stream on stepping stones and climb a worn R diagonal to the row of barns on the far bank; here there is a junction with a path going back towards Karbasan (20 mins, A120).

Just before the barns, turn L/E on a wide but ill-defined path running diagonally upwards across the slope and then passing over 2 rock outcrops above the stream. At the second outcrop, turn SE/upwards, aiming up zigzags towards a solitary pine tree (1 hr). Below the pine, turn L/NE and contour the hillside, following a definite path towards a side gully. It passes a water trough (a possible campsite) and continues across the lower part of a side-valley used for grazing bulls, then rises towards a second gully (35 mins, A121).

WP	Lat (N)	Long (E)	Alt (m)
A094	40.88381	41.34521	1460
A095	40.88511	41.34665	1477
A097	40.88429	41.34721	1553
A098	40.88334	41.34883	1581
A099	40.88358	41.34971	1652
A101	40.88199	41.35189	1686
A102	40.88164	41.35418	1705
A103	40.88251	41.35379	1761
A106	40.88415	41.35604	1888
A109	40.88489	41.35749	1946
A111	40.88436	41.36177	2070
A112	40.88499	41.36257	2104
A113	40.88563	41.36686	2110
A115	40.88749	41.37253	2194
A116	40.88904	41.37638	2326
A120	40.88691	41.37934	2300
A118	40.88735	41.38490	2671
A121	40.89012	41.39093	2679
A122	40.89222	41.38949	2698
A123	40.89394	41.39266	2805
A125	40.90027	41.39016	2733
A126	40.90927	41.38188	2630
A128	40.91742	41.38653	2588
A124	40.91654	41.39153	2350
A129	40.91597	41.39564	2264
A130	40.91686	41.39945	2135
A131	40.91796	41.40192	2014
A133	40.91892	41.40391	1913
A134	40.92153	41.41075	1728
A136	40.92356	41.40990	1673
A137	40.92559	41.41534	1613
A138	40.92331	41.41915	1567
A140	40.93824	41.44464	1245
A141	40.94523	41.47014	980
A142	40.95401	41.49741	840

10.5 Kışladamları Mahallesi, Karbasan, Gravat Yaylası, Sura, Taşkıran, Sarıgöl

THE KAÇKAR

Cross a stream in this gully - this is the last water before the ridgetop so you should fill up. Continue climbing gently L/N over a small outcrop, then contour until you reach the bank of the eroded wide gully with red soil. Turn uphill/NE and climb to the ridgetop of Zıtlop Sırtı, zigzagging up the open, grassy slope and keeping the gully to your L (1 hr 5 mins, A123).

From the pass, looking back, the peaks of the Altıparmak Dağları stand out sharp against the sky. Below them are the broad hillsides above Demirdöven, with steep, wooded slopes below them. Far below are the grey roofs of the village of Karbasan and the yayla of Gravat. This point on Zıtlop Sırtı is the junction of many paths. Looking E, you can see the tiny, deserted Satibe Yaylası, seemingly floating above the forest on a steep, grassy spur. There is a dry, badly eroded and ridged valley between the ridge and Satibe and the path is now unsafe. Another path on the R continues up the ridge, just to the R of the crest, and forms a link with route 10.6. On the L, a path runs downhill and L/W of the ridgetop. However, our route turns L/NNW along the ridge to the next high point, Velise Tepe (25 mins, A125).

Past Velise Tepe, below to the R/NE, are the 2 deserted yaylas of Kasmaleket and Patrikara, each with only a few houses, on spurs of the main ridge. On the third spur is our target, another deserted yayla called Sura. The first 2 can be reached by descending the grassy spurs (with care as they are steep) past some stone sheepfolds, but the forest paths below are overgrown, so we continue along the ridge. Ahead/NW is the conical summit of Sitele Tepesi; there is an unused path to the R of it but it's best to climb the hill and descend the far side to a dip in the ridge. Continue up a little rise, passing the remains of a yayla - the huts are now just hollows surrounded by stones. Cross the low rise of Avazan and descend the far side (1 hr 10 min, A128). This dip is the starting point for the decent to Sura Yaylası, far below on the grassy spur to the R/ESE.

Alternative routes: *The ridgetop path continues NNE, then NE towards Barhal, gradually descending until, beyond Satibe Tepesi, it drops below the tree line. The ridge is certainly passable to this point, and probably beyond. There are 2 possible points at which you could turn off: just before Satibe Tepesi, there is a steep wooded spur leading down to Aho Yaylası and somewhere between the hill and the yayla there is a newly erected mobile phone mast. This is linked by new dirt road to Doles, which is described in daywalk 10.2. The other alternative is to continue past Satibe Tepesi and branch off NNW onto Sapasımda Sırtı. This ridge divides and the R spur leads down to a forest road, which is connected to the network of roads which lead from Börekli to Barhal. However, both these ridges are mainly tree-clad and although the distance is short, route-finding will not be easy.* **End.**

The descent to Sura is steep and difficult, so you should take your time. Commence with a diagonal descent SE towards a pınar and trough, which is on a slope just to the L of the main gully leading down towards the R/S of the yayla. The pınar is marked by a bright green patch of grass which is not visible from the start of the descent but becomes clear as you approach the first trees. Fill up with water here, as the çeşme at Sura Yaylası has long since dried up (20 mins). Descend straight down/E from the pınar to the L of the trees below (the route becomes easier as you move onto thicker grass) and follow the crown of the ridge down in zigzags. Pass over a couple of low outcrops on the ridge where the former path is just visible and arrive at the yayla (45 mins, A129).

10.5 Kışladamları Mahallesi, Karbasan, Gravat Yaylası, Sura, Taşkıran, Sarıgö

Sura Yaylası has about 8 wooden huts, all in various states of collapse. However, at least one has a basement where you could sleep. There is plenty of firewood; if you need water, you will have to obtain it from the gully above and to the W of the yayla. Leave the yayla by the SE corner, where a trace of an old path leads into the woods and down the crown of the ridge. The path is an abandoned mule track and covered with pine-cones (but is otherwise good); at first it runs E, then ENE. At a clearing in the woods, keep diagonally L, still walking down the ridgetop. At a second clearing, ahead is a glimpse of an alpine meadow alongside a stream; a fallen log marks your turn to the L. In a third clearing, the path continues straight down, below large trees (50 mins, A133).

Just below a fourth clearing is a water channel and a junction with a path leading along it. Turn L/down on the path, which becomes clearer, but in places steeper, as it follows zigzags down, soon leaving the channel behind. It turns N from the ridge on more zigzags and emerges from the woods on the upper side of a sloping meadow with a couple of isolated stone buildings with timber roofs. On the opposite slope is a mezra and below that, in the valley bottom, more houses (1 hr). Keep R/down/NE alongside the woods, passing above a group of barns and some fruit trees and then a mill, which you could pass on either side.

The path emerges at a group of old stone houses (10 mins, A134).

Uban Mezrası is a group of 5 substantial 3-storey stone houses with tall timber barns, mostly in a good state of repair. The route passes through the middle of the group, where there is a (non-working) mill and a small courtyard stacked with timber for the winter. Only 2 families live here, arriving in June and returning to either Taşkıran or further afield in September. Around the houses are fertile hay-meadows, and above them orchards and woods. The area is reached by a dirt road from Taşkıran and Sarıgöl but Uban is the highest mezra in Büyük Dere and the last part of the road is undriveable.

Pass to the R of the lowest house, then turn L below it. Turn R down a field edge and follow a narrow path into a hedge and diagonally L/down towards the sound of water below. There are stepping-stones across the bubbling stream. On the far side, turn L on a rough, bulldozed dirt road and follow it downhill (15 mins, A137).

Soon, there is a bridge on the R to a yayla and a path L/upwards to Hacıoğlu Mezrası. Continue straight down; the track is now an attractive tree lined country lane with a stream on the R occasionally bubbling across the road (15 mins, A138).

It's a total of about 5 km from the highest driveable point to the village of Taşkıran in the valley below. Pass a turning to Kork, a mezra of just 2 houses high on the R bank. The road descends steeply through a narrow gorge, with the stream on the R. At Çarmenet, a large stream flows in from the L, with a footpath alongside it that leads up to more houses. These districts are all set above the road on the valley slopes. The first roadside village is Taşkıran (1 hr 15 mins, A140).

Taşkıran/Ziğrapor/Zapor is a spread-out village alongside the road along the valley from Uban to Sarıgöl, with a bakkal and teahouse and many well-maintained houses and gardens. A morning dolmuş runs to Sarıgöl and Yusufeli, returning after noon.

10.5 Kışladamları Mahallesi, Karbasan, Gravat Yaylası, Sura, Taşkıran, Sarıgöl

From here it is about 3 km along a concrete road, through orchards and fields with scattered houses, to Sarıgöl where you meet the main road just R/N of the bridge. Turn L to the main street (45 mins, A142).

10.6 Tekkale, Bölükbaşı Mezrası, Aşağı Gurp Yaylası, Bahar Yaylası and Dereiçi (15 hrs 10 mins)

This route takes you (by either of 2 alternatives) from Tekkale to Zıplot Sırtı, the ridge which divides the Yusufeli basin from the Hevek Deresi. This ridge was once a useful route between yaylas; an unused path, which once linked several yaylas, runs along it. From the ridge, the route descends to the long Dereiçi Deresi, which leads down to the Barhal Deresi, N of Yusufeli. The valley is green and lush at the head but becomes drier as it descends. You could also continue along the ridge to the N to join route 10.5 and descend further to the N. There is very little water on or near the ridge, so you should take sufficient with you.

WP	Lat (N)	Long (E)	Alt (m)
A029	40.83706	41.45789	1358
A032	40.84215	41.44973	1400
A033	40.84758	41.44336	1489
A035	40.85631	41.43492	1489
A036	40.85764	41.43453	1672
A037	40.86266	41.43280	1774
A038	40.86440	41.43266	1812
A039	40.86659	41.43064	1856
A040	40.86919	41.43015	1890
A041	40.86993	41.43139	1914
A044	40.87183	41.42906	2172
A045	40.87444	41.43176	2279
A046	40.87469	41.43358	2458
A048	40.87858	41.43397	2581
A050	40.88006	41.43463	2614
A052	40.88484	41.42565	2733
A053	40.88907	41.43299	2482
A055	40.89115	41.43694	2319
A056	40.89252	41.44020	2221
A058	40.89251	41.44350	2116
A059	40.89419	41.44751	2094
A062	40.89477	41.45082	1994
A065	40.89418	41.45757	1793
A066	40.89395	41.46637	1707
A067	40.89361	41.46737	1615
A168	40.88909	41.46269	1600
A169	40.89104	41.47153	1430
A170	40.89447	41.47070	1440
A171	40.88464	41.49421	1190
A172	40.87294	41.51248	870
A173	40.86250	41.53688	670

At the R junction in Tekkale (A180), turn uphill/WNW, walking past a teahouse and small bakkal on dirt road; the Güngörmez Deresi is on your R. Continue through the outskirts of Tekkale, past a concrete bridge to a district of wooden houses on the R bank (25 mins). Continue to a second group of houses; the road is now concrete. Pass a road, which rises L, cross a bridge and continue with the river on the L (25 mins). There are no more houses as the walls of the valley have closed in. There is no cultivation, just harsh stony slopes, until the road re-crosses the river on a concrete bridge (40 mins). Just after the bridge is the church of Dört Kilise; see route 10.1. 2 km after the church, as the valley broadens out again, there are houses on the outskirts of Bölükbaşı and open fields where the annual wrestling festival is held (35 mins). At a final river bridge above the festival ground, the road divides (10 mins, A029).

Turn R over the final bridge just before Bölükbaşı and continue NW past Alikolat Mezrası (on your L) to the 4 houses (2 inhabited) of Poysant Mezrası, on the R of the road just where a stream cascades down to join the Güngörmez Deresi (25 mins, A032).

Alternative route to ridge: Here, a path leaves the road for the houses of Poysant, crosses the stream and climbs SE to the forested ridge on the L of the stream, rising to cross the ridge S of Bavut Yaylası just above the treeline (1 hr 25 mins). This path can be seen from route 10.1 and is reported to be in reasonable condition. At the pass, turn L/NNW on the ridge to walk about 1 km to the yayla, then continue along the ridgetop path as it rises N. At a summit, where the ridge divides, descend NW to a slight dip. Pass a L turn to Sagüle Yaylası and continue either along the rising ridgetop or with the ridge to your L. At a second dip, pass a path coming in from Sagüle Yaylası and meet the main route (1 hr 35 mins). End.

The dirt road in the valley bottom climbs gently with the stream on the L. It rises in a hairpin away from the stream into beech and fir forest, running past a few houses on a bend. It bends back R along the R side of the valley and continues to rise towards Aşağı Gurp, which is visible ahead. As you approach the yayla, the road bends L and divides (40 mins). Keep on the higher/R road which passes above Aşağı Gurp and continues towards Yukarı Gurp (25 mins, A038).

Aşağı and Yukarı Gurp/Gupt are 2 lovely unspoiled yaylas at 1900 m, surrounded by fruit trees and forest, with 3-storey stone-and-sawn-timber houses and log barns, inhabited for 2-3 months per year. Several families return to spend holidays here. Both are on steep slopes facing SW and each has 5 houses and several barns; they are only 2 km apart. Hay is cut and taken down the rough, unsurfaced road to Tekkale to feed the cattle during the winter.

Just before the highest point on the road, about half-way between Aşağı and Yukarı Gurp, a stony path rises R/NNE of the road. It's difficult to find as the first part has been damaged by the road-building and blocked by a couple of fallen trees. After the blockages, a very faint path zigzags up the spine of a spur of the main ridge, becoming slightly clearer as it rises. At some rocks, keep initially to the R then, 50 m past them, turn L off the spur onto a straight, clear path which climbs parallel with the spine. It turns back/R in a hairpin, which rises steeply through the trees back to the top of the spur (1 hr 10 mins, A044).

10.6 Tekkale, Bölükbaşı Mezrası, Aşağı Gurp Yaylası, Bahar Yaylası, Dereiçi

Continue up, first on zigzags between trees, then onto an open, grassy area with a mound of stones on the spur crown. From above the trees, the deserted houses of Sagüle Yaylası are visible on the slope to the R, but there is a wide and steep valley between you and them. The faint path continues upwards and R, starting to contour around the first shallow valley to the R. It takes you to a gully where there is a small trickle of water, the last for some time, so you should fill up, even if you have to climb down the stream a little to do so (1 hr 5 mins, A045).

The aim is now to reach the top of the main ridge, Zıtlop Sırtı. Cross the gully and climb diagonally upwards to the top of a rock outcrop - the path is now just a few narrow traces in the grass. Continue to the top of the next rock outcrop, passing under an overhanging tree to gain a spur (20 mins). Turn L/up this wooded spur and climb it in zigzags, veering R towards a stack of rock (20 mins, A046).

Now turn up/NE towards the ridgetop, keeping a dry gully on the R. The ridge is scattered with small pines but, in general, you are above the tree line. Climb to the lowest point of Zıtlop Sırtı ahead (15 mins, A050). Looking down to the R/S, you are about 500 m above Sagüle, which has only 10 timber houses built above cowsheds, all in bad condition and unused for many years. Below the yayla is a zigzag path leading to a drinking trough, which is unlikely to have water.

The views back are over the wooded valleys to the Güngörmez Dağları in the SW. In front/NE are more wooded valleys descending to the Dereiçi Deresi; this side is noticeably drier, with lines of hills damaged by erosion in the E. To the L/N is a descending spur with Bahar Yaylası perched on it. Beyond is a second ridge dividing Dereiçi Deresi from Taşkıran Deresi, with several more abandoned yaylas situated in clearings on its crest.

Walk NW along the ridgetop for about 800 m, following one of several clear paths which run along the rising ridge. Ahead, choose a path which contours around the ridge on the R side of Kurugöl Tepesi; don't use the fainter, lower path as it has collapsed in places. After the hill, the path rejoins the ridge and continues wide and clear just L of the ridgetop. A stone cairn on top of a ruined animal shelter marks the start of the descent to the yayla (45 mins, A052).

On the L is a major gully with flowing water - in fact a waterfall - which is the only water source on the ridge. There are various side paths to this gully crossing a precipitous, grassy slope. Horses and mules left to run free in the summer months are said to drink here; you could also see wild goats. If the weather is good, you could camp on the ridgetop and look for wild animals at dawn.

Alternative route: This is a link with route 10.5, which crosses the ridge NW of here. Looking along the ridge to the L/NW, the ground rises and curves L to a steep sided summit called Bakat Tepesi, the highest part of the whole ridge. Instead of turning down the spur towards the yayla, bear L/W and continue up the slope of Bakat Tepesi in zigzags. Keeping L of the summit, turn R/NW and follow the highest section of the ridge for about 1 km around the head of the Güngörmez Deresi, either over the summits or with the crest of the ridge on your R. At the end of this section is Kondüsor Tepesi, where the ridge divides. Turn N and descend steeply towards a slight dip in the ridge. On the R, an unused and probably unsafe track runs over eroded ground to Satibe Yaylası, which has been unused for the last 10 or 20 years. Continue on the ridge to the next dip, just before Velise Tepesi - meet route 10.5 here. End.

Turn R and contour to reach the top of the spur which leads down to the yayla. The path starts as a faint track across stony ground but then becomes clearer as it turns down the spur on fairly easy going, mainly over grass. It keeps L of a pile of rocks then the gradient lessens. At a second rock pile, the track heads for a tree on the L of the spur and passes just above it, then down in zigzags - the ground below is stony and the going quite slippery underfoot (1 hr 10 mins, A053).

The final approach follows an old water channel on the L of the spur, which supplies the yayla with water from the waterfalls near the upper ridge (25 mins, A055).

> Bahar/Harmut/Daranev Yaylası has maybe 50 mainly wooden buildings, with cowsheds below and living accommodation above. It's on a steep E-facing slope at about 2100 m, just above the tree line, and has a forested ridge below. About 120 cows were pastured around this yayla on the steep slopes of Bakat Tepesi but now the water supply is in need of repair and only 2 families come for 2 months, moving up from Dereiçi, via Ketket Mezrası, where they also spend 2 months. There is plenty of grazing for the cattle and a bull and the old ladies make cream and cheese from the milk. Some of the hay and cream is sent down to market via the road which runs about half an hour's walk below the yayla. To the W is a second pınar which is piped down to a trough amongst the trees below the yayla. There is an occasional dolmuş from Ketket to Yusufeli.

The lower houses of the yayla overlook a slope leading down to the ridge below; a zigzag path descends the slope to a çeşme and trough made from a hollow log in a grassy clearing on the ridge (20 mins, A056).

You could continue to the R/SE to descend straight to the road below but a nicer descent is to continue ENE along the line of the ridge down to the junction of the Satalavat Deresi and Dereiçi Deresi below. The clear but narrow onward path starts just to the L of the ridgetop; follow it through forest to another clearing. Continue just L of the centre line of the ridge to a third clearing. To avoid a small, rocky hill, descend on clear path L of the ridgeline then hairpin back to meet the ridge crest at another clearing. A path descends L from this clearing direct to Ketket - it's well used and stony. However, our route carries on down the underused but more direct path following the ridgeline (1 hr 5 mins, A062).

It reaches a long open area with a shallow slope to the R and a tree clad summit ahead; the faint path leaves the ridge at the lowest point to run L of this summit. It rises slightly to an open area and then descends through rocks. Ahead is a hunting hide in a clearing at the ridge end (35 mins). The path descends steeply over a broad dirt slope just to the L of the hut, becoming more difficult and slippery. At the bottom, turn R, climb down some rocks and contour L to regain the ridge. Continue downwards on zigzags over a wide earth slope, until the path narrows and bends L (25 mins, A065).

At a large rock the path appears to stop and is very faint from this point on. Turn L and continue the descent on another slippery slope with a few rock steps. The path descends steeply on hairpins between rocks and seems to be approaching the end of the ridge. On the R, quite close below, are houses and the road but the slope to this side is sandy and steep and covered with dwarf oak scrub. Ahead there is a

10.6 Tekkale, Bölükbaşı Mezrası, Aşağı Gurp Yaylası, Bahar Yaylası, Dereiçi

seemingly impassable rocky outcrop (30 mins, A066). Approaching it, turn down diagonally to the R, keeping between firs and close to the rocks and find the continuation of the path about 10 m down, running horizontally along the R side of the ridge. It rounds a L corner on a built-up hairpin and continues downhill on zigzags to the next part of the ridge, then to the apex of a bend in the road where it has been cut by construction work (15 mins, A067).

The L turn goes to Ketket but we turn R on the dirt road, pass a waterfall and the well-built stone-and-timber houses of Aşağı Varnet, and meet the valley bottom road 500 m further on. Turn L onto this road, walk down to a bridge and cross it. Follow the road as it curves L under a rock face to reach Orta Varnet Mahallesi below. Turn R and cross another bridge over the Satalavat Deresi to meet the main valley-bottom road, where you turn R and continue to descend (35 mins). In this area are many wealthy-looking houses, lush hay-fields and orchards. In July, everyone is busy cutting hay and transporting it down to Dereiçi, where the animals are wintered. If you are offered a lift in one of the hay lorries, then accept it, as from the junction it is a walk of about 6 km over the dirt (later concrete) road down to Dereiçi.

After the initial groups of houses at Seku and Orta Varnet the road continues into a gorge, which has very little level ground for cultivation. As you emerge from the gorge, many more substantial houses, some renovated, line the slopes above the river, connected by bridges and winches to the road (1 hr 40 mins, A173).

> **Dereiçi** is squeezed into the gorge on both sides of the Satalavat Deresi, with houses stacked up the slopes almost on top of each other. It has a huge, modern mosque surrounded by old and new houses in good condition, most with hay and animal barns. Kahve and bakkal line the concrete roads and there are a few official buildings and a large school.

From Dereiçi to the main road is only 3 km - a bridge links the side valley with the Sarıgöl - Yusufeli road (45 mins). From here it should be easy to get a lift or dolmuş to your destination.

Chapter 11 **ROUTES AROUND BARHAL AND THE ALTIPARMAK DAĞLARI**

The Altıparmak district ranges in height from the valley of the Barhal Deresi at 1200 m, to the jagged Altıparmak summits at 3400 m. The upper parts of the valleys were eroded by glacier action which gouged out high-level lakes and U-shaped valleys but the lower parts are deep V-shaped, forested canyons, with rounded, grassy spurs in between. The valleys have winter and mid-season settlements but, until a few years ago, people and cattle moved to the upper slopes for the summer. Now only yaylas with road access are still active and even these are often populated by returnees from further W. Cattle farming, beekeeping, forestry and tourism provide seasonal income but many men leave their families at home and spend the winter working on building sites or bakeries in other parts of Turkey.

In winter, deep snow buries the mountains and even when the snow has melted on the ridges, ice and snow-bridges can remain all year in the valleys. Bears are numerous and when they are hungry, they raid beehives or orchards.

Barhal, officially Altıparmak, the central settlement on the Barhal Deresi, is active all year round, and in summer provides a lively hub for the area. Built at the junction of the Barhal Deresi and the Hevek Deresi, Barhal's huge wooden houses and barns are hidden in orchards and forest. Some new concrete buildings, including a fairly ugly mosque and various state buildings, have marred the lower part of the village. There are 3 pensions, all in old buildings. At the junction are several general shops, a bakery, kahves and cafés, as well as a primary school and health clinic.

Barhal is linked to Yusufeli by 30 km of narrow road, which is currently being widened and re-surfaced. Dolmuşes leave at about 7 am and return at between 3 and 5 pm. Dolmuşes to Yaylalar pass through about the same time.

Barhal is linked to Ayder and the Black Sea by the Kırmızı Geçit, the only mule-friendly track over the Altıparmak Dağları but, historically, this can never have been an important route.

11.1 Barhal, Amanesket Mezrası, Naznara Mezrası, Karagöl, (or Satibe Campsite) 8 hrs 5 mins

This is both a day-walk to Karagöl (a beautiful high-level cirque lake) and the route to Satibe Campsite, from which you could return to Barhal, reversing the first part of route 11.5. You could hitch a lift up the dirt road to the start of the footpath, which will save you about 2 hrs walking. Any of the pensions in Barhal can arrange this, although it would be cheaper to go with a group. If you choose to camp at Karagöl, you could explore the 2 villages in walk 11.2.

From Barhal (B001), walk up the unsurfaced road which rises WNW along the Bulut Deresi, at first mainly through forest. The road starts with the river on your L, then crosses to the opposite bank (here there are 2 roads off to houses on the L). Several km further on, the road re-crosses and, immediately before a rising bend, on the L of the river, is a picnic place with tables (1 hr 45 mins, B073).

There is a second rising bend, which takes the road into the upper part of the Barhal Deresi; another road leaves on the R on the bend. The road crosses the Barhal Deresi on a bridge and starts climbing in zigzags up the ridge (20 mins). Just after the river, turn L/SSW and climb to gain the old path running along the crest of the ridge. Turn up/R on a clear, well-used path climbing due W up the ridge. Immediately, you walk through Amanesket, (5 mins, B074), the first mezra, followed higher up the ridge by Naznara.

> Naznara and Amanesket/Amanezgit are 2 mezras of Barhal/Altıparmak situated on the ridge which leads up to Karagöl. Originally permanently inhabited, now the residents come from Barhal for 4-5 months to cut hay, pasture cattle, keep bees and grow a few vegetables. Both are linked by a dirt road, built in 2007, to Barhal, and electricity is installed. The houses (6-10 in each mezra) are substantial 2-storey buildings, mainly of stone, with separate log barns; there are also water mills, fed by the channel which descends down the ridge from Karagöl. The view down onto these mezras from above must be one of the most lush, pastoral scenes in all the Kaçkar.

Past the last mezra (40 mins), the path continues to rise, tending L/SW up the spine. It approaches an area of pine forest but does not enter it, instead bending further L and running on steep hairpins up to an almost level canal, which is fed from the outflow of Karagöl (the canal may be dry) (45 mins, B076). Ignore a path leading down/R but turn R/NW along the canal, and follow it below a crag and past several pines.

Beyond here, the canal almost disappears, but continue level towards the waterfalls, which cascade from the lake down the valley ahead. Below a small hill covered with rhododendron bushes there is a cairn, which marks the start of a narrow path (40 mins). Turn L/up and follow the path in zigzags up and over the hill, then turn R to a parallel ridge and continue upwards in more zigzags. Where the path divides,

WP	Lat (N)	Long (E)	Alt (m)
B001	40.96830	41.39257	1197
B002	40.96922	41.38188	1242
B071	40.97175	41.37087	1300
B072	40.98239	41.36500	1430
B103	40.98311	41.35708	1612
B102	40.98627	41.35504	1717
B080	40.98634	41.35054	1705
B073	40.98688	41.34564	1721
B074	40.98584	41.34240	1852
B088	40.98678	41.33038	2140
B075	40.98671	41.32461	2275
B076	40.98341	41.31831	2475
B096	40.98401	41.31315	2565
B097	40.98205	41.31235	2640
B077	40.98233	41.30822	2699
B097	40.98205	41.31235	2640
B078	40.97930	41.31623	2696
B098	40.97728	41.32442	2395
B079	40.97728	41.33541	2365

alternative route

11.1 Barhal, Naznara Mezrası, Amanesket Mezrası, Karagöl, (or Satibe Campsite)

turn R and continue climbing gently towards the outflow of the lake, then climb steeply over the rocky band retaining the lake. The deep, oval lake suddenly comes into view, surrounded until August by snow patches, set off by the cream rhododendron flowers (50 mins, B077). Cross the outflow stream to an area of flat rocks. It's possible to walk around the lake to a valley leading NW towards the pass between Altıparmak Dağı and the main ridge. 2 more lakes lie further up this valley, although there is no real path. This valley also gives access to Altıparmak Dağı, a non-technical climb with wide views over the whole range and down the far side.

Alternative route: To continue to Satibe, from Karagöl retrace your steps to the junction with the zigzag path. Instead of turning down the zigzags, continue level then climb up/R over a spur of Nebisatgur Tepesi.

Continue contouring across the grassy hillside on an almost level clear path; do not attempt to turn down amongst the rhododendrons below. As the path circles the hill, the view before you, as you look E, is of a long, wide, grassy spur called Satibe Sırtı, which just tops the treeline. The campsite is 3/4 of the way down the spur, on a continuation of the canal. As the slope on your L becomes less steep and grass replaces the rhododendrons, turn L/E/downhill. Follow one of many indistinct tracks onto the spur and descend towards the centre of the grassy area. There are a couple of steeper, rocky outcrops but a faint zigzag path runs down over both of them. As the slope becomes less steep, bear slightly L to the canal, and follow it to the campsite, which is marked by a çeşme gushing into hollow log (1 hr 30 mins, B079). **End.**

If you are just doing a day-walk, retrace your steps to the valley bottom and return to Barhal (3 hrs).

11.2 Bridge, Amanesket Mezrası, Sakser Mezrası, Bahgat Mezrası, Barhal road *(5 hrs 35 mins)*

This is another day-walk in the head of the Barhal Deresi, exploring the pine and fir forest and lively mezras on the N slope. If you have plenty of energy, you could climb up to the second Karagöl, a lake hidden in a cirque to the E of Marsis Tepesi.

From Barhal (B001), walk up the unsurfaced road which rises WNW along the Barhal Deresi, at first mainly through forest. The road starts with the river on your L, then crosses (here there are 2 roads off to houses on the L). Several km further on, the road re-crosses, and, immediately before a rising bend, on the L of the river is a picnic place with tables (1 hr 45 mins, B073).

There is a second rising bend, which takes the road into the upper part of the Barhal Deresi; another road leaves on the R on the bend. The road crosses the Barhal Deresi on a bridge and starts climbing in zigzags up the ridge. Stay on the road as it approaches Amanesket then turns away in a hairpin. On the far bank of the Barhal Deresi, a yayla, Yukarı Çatallar, is visible and below it a path rising through forest. Immediately before the next L bend, leave the road and climb down the muddy slope to reach a narrow footpath (this isn't visible from the road) (35 mins, B084).

Turn L/NE, continue a few metres across the upper edge of a field to a junction and keep L again. This path crosses a field, aiming at the yayla, to a stony track, with a wall on the L, which makes a short, steep descent towards the bubbling, rocky stream (10 mins). It leads to an unsteady log bridge; if you don't like the look of it, you could wade the stream a few metres further down. A lovely, well-used path rises

WP	Lat (N)	Long (E)	Alt (m)
B073	40.98688	41.34564	1721
B074	40.98584	41.34240	1852
B084	40.98757	41.33991	1888
B085	40.98875	41.33911	1898
B086	40.98981	41.33927	1883
B087	40.98869	41.34512	1903
B089	40.98922	41.34711	1878
B090	40.99060	41.34901	1887
B092	40.99192	41.35027	1883
B093	40.99103	41.35275	1905
B082	40.98732	41.35339	1790
B080	40.98634	41.35054	1705

to the R through the woods, crossing an irrigation ditch via a tiny stone bridge. It continues climbing gently, passing over occasional rock falls and above fields where cattle graze. Rounding a corner, you see in front and below the mezra of Sakser/Yeşilağaç. Cross a water channel and continue down stone steps leading straight down to the river valley, past a junction with a path on the R. As you approach the village, there is a beautifully paved section of path, with a water channel alongside (25 mins, B089).

> Sakser/Yeşilağaç/Demirkalem Mezrası and Bahgat/Balıyet Mezrası are on the far side of the valley from Naznara and Amanesket, and are both also administratively attached to Barhal. Sakser is the most substantial, with 35 houses of which 7 or 8 are now empty. Bahgat has about the same number but they are more scattered. Both have electricity and road access. In summer, families come and go from Istanbul, where they all live in the same district of Ümraniye. They grow crops, such as broad beans and alfalfa, to feed the cattle and themselves and cut hay on the surrounding slopes. The village houses were mainly constructed in the early part of the last century but have been well cared for and the original timber roofs replaced by corrugated iron. In former times the inhabitants also used higher yaylas for midsummer grazing, but now the number of cattle is fewer it isn't necessary. Sakser has a mosque, which was built several years ago by public subscription, and a communal picnic spot with benches set out on a viewpoint overlooking the valley.

Continue through the mezra, leaving by a track running NE/uphill in front of a row of houses and above the mosque. Continue to some picnic tables arranged on a rocky viewpoint overlooking the slopes beyond and the river below - it's known as Kayabaşı (10 mins). Continuing on level path from Kayabaşı, the path swings over 2 valleys then forks; take the branch which climbs away from an irrigation channel. It continues climbing through meadows, heading NE until it almost disappears at a junction with a path heading up the hill (30 mins, B093).

Alternative route: At this junction you could turn upwards then R at a mill and L again to climb up a ridge into the village of Kumru/Bogatget. Continue L then R, climbing out of the village to the edge of the forest beyond. Apparently there is a *path through the forest and on to the hillside beyond. This takes you N, parallel with and above the Başkaya Deresi on your L, towards Başkaya Tepesi ahead. Before you reach broken rock at the foot of the peak, turn L into the stream valley and follow it up to the cirque lake, which is surrounded by an almost complete circle of steep cliffs. The climb from Kumru is about 900 m and will take you upwards of 3 hrs, so you should be prepared to camp out at the lake if necessary.* **End.**

Turn down onto a faint grassy track, which runs along the edges of orchards towards a broad, grassy headland with a graveyard (15 mins). The path descends again past the houses of Bahgat to a road. Turn L on this and follow it down to the valley bottom (20 mins, B080). Turn L for Barhal (1 hr 45 mins).

11.3 Kurdat road, Pişenkaya Yaylası, Libler Gölü and return (4 hrs 10 mins)

If you have transport, you can drive to the start of this route from Barhal as there is a good dirt road going nearly as far as Pişenkaya. Otherwise, you could do it while based at Pişenkaya during the course of route 11.5 or you could visit Libler Gölü on the descent from the Kırmızı Geçit, route 13.5. The walk follows the Onbolat Deresi to the lake, first high on the S bank, to avoid a narrow valley, then on the N bank. It is an easy day-walk from Pişenkaya but you could camp at the lake and explore the area. Additionally, there is another lake hidden on the slopes of Lale Tepesi, which you could investigate. It's a delight in early season when the rhododendrons are in flower.

If you have transport from Barhal, then drive 3 km S down the Yaylayar road and turn R just before a bridge. Drive on reasonable dirt road up the Onbolat Deresi, crossing a concrete bridge and continuing along the N side of the river. Before a side-stream joins the main valley, the road makes a sharp bend R and climbs back towards Kurdat Mezra and up the hill towards Binektaşı. Leave your vehicle at the

WP	Lat (N)	Long (E)	Alt (m)
D168	40.95160	41.29715	1784
B134	40.95326	41.28869	1934
B136	40.95305	41.28396	2009
B008	40.95021	41.27358	2144
B057	40.94651	41.26476	2237
D159	40.94720	41.26078	2376
D158	40.94661	41.25801	2469
D157	40.94688	41.25665	2482
D156	40.94796	41.25600	2468
D155	40.94749	41.25183	2436
D153	40.94619	41.24574	2635
B065	40.94733	41.24328	2670
B069	40.94652	41.23965	2705
B070	40.94432	41.23789	2758
B069	40.94652	41.23965	2705
B065	40.94733	41.24328	2670
D153	40.94619	41.24574	2635
B171	40.93479	41.24356	2810
B172	40.94372	41.24941	2600

bend in the road (D168). Walk up the road and about 100 m uphill/NE from the bend. Turn L, climbing over a low stone wall onto a path which runs W across the top of a field and through scrub, then crosses the rocky sidestream on a bridge made from a single huge plank. The path climbs the far bank, passes below the few wooden houses of Norsel Yaylası and crosses a second sidestream. Climbing the bank, it undulates over open ground then enters woodland, passing between massive firs. After the fir forest, it rises on wide mule-track towards the fields below Pişenkaya. Approaching the village, turn R and walk, with a stone wall on your L, towards the houses (40 mins, B008).

> Pişenkaya Yaylası has about 40 houses and barns, built in tiers on a SE facing slope at an altitude of 1900 m, close to the valley wall. As there are plenty of massive trees in the area, the buildings are all of huge uncut timbers on stone bases. They are mainly roofed with corrugated iron; some of the remaining shingle roofs have partly collapsed, leaving the buildings in very poor condition. The yayla is used seasonally by only 2 families from Barhal, to pasture cattle and sheep for 2-3 months. They are joined by relatives from Istanbul. One house is unlocked and offers shelter if the weather is bad.

Leave Pişenkaya at the lower W corner of the yayla and follow a path which runs parallel to but above the river, passing above the first bridge then descending to the second bridge, which is by a large boulder. Cross the bridge and turn up to the R on a clear path, which climbs a slope close to the stream in zigzags (35 mins, D158). (In August 2007 over the river there was an ice-bridge which had completely buried the concrete bridge; the ice extended as far up the valley as we could see. If you have to cross ice, make sure you cross quickly, well beyond the point at which the stream exits.)

At the top of the slope is a level area and beyond that a rock wall which drops away on the R. Cross to the top R/W corner and find a continuation of the path descending towards the stream. It undulates a bit before reaching a crossing place (this too may be under ice) and passing over the stream to the broad meadows opposite (20 mins, D156).

Turn L and follow the path uphill past the remains of a few huts and up some zigzags. You reach an upper wide slope, cut by a couple of streams. The path is indistinct but there are occasional cairns showing the way, which is maybe 100 m above the Onbolat Deresi. Cross the first sidestream then continue to another stream crossing (15 mins, D153). Just beyond the stream is a junction of 2 paths. The mulepath climbs R/NW upwards towards the pass of Kırmızı Geçit, avoiding the lake, but the lake path runs L/WSW, climbing slightly, across a sloping belt of scree - mules are unable to cross this. At the far side of the scree, you approach the stream which exits from Libler Gölü. As there's no clear path from here on, you have 2 choices: either you can cross the stream and climb the rhododendron-clad slope beyond it, or you can stay on the N side of the stream and climb rocks and rhododendrons to the top of a low rise on the R. Either way, a short climb will get you over the rise and to the lake just beyond (20 mins, B070). Once over the moraine, the lakeside is level and sometimes marshy, with room for tents. The backdrop to the lake is spectacular, with scree slopes clad with snow until well into August. The R side slopes up to a couple of steep stony couloirs and by climbing these you can re-gain the mulepath to the pass. The climb is difficult with a full pack and groups should keep far apart to avoid kicking rocks onto those below.

Additional route: On the S side of the main stream, just above the crossing place, a sidestream enters from the S. Above this, there is a high bank clad with rhododendrons, and a long valley, which leads up to another lake, Davar Gölü. You can reach this by crossing the stream, climbing a path through the rhododendrons and continuing up the valley, mainly on the less-steep L side. The lake itself is on the R side so, above the crags, you will have to contour R to reach it. **End.**

Return to Pişenkaya then the road by the same route (2 hrs).

11.4 Pişenkaya Yaylası, Büyükaho T, Zekarat Yaylası, Sarnaven Deresi, Demirdöven (9 hrs 45 mins)

This long 1-day walk can be added to any of the routes passing through Pişenkaya. It takes you SE on difficult, unused paths up to Sarnaven Sırtı, the ridge to the S of Onbolat Deresi, reaching it at Büyükaho Tepesi. Sarnaven Deresi, on the S side of the ridge, is very different - completely treeless in the upper reaches, unvisited and with no occupied yaylas. There was once a system of water canals which supplied the upper yaylas but these have now broken down. Our downward route follows one of these canals E to the major mezra of ⊔rat/Sadat, from which you can descend SE on well-made mulepaths to the valley mouth and Demirdöven, on the bus route from Barhal to Yaylalar. We also describe an alternative, shorter descent which we have not used. Take plenty of water - you will not find any until you reach the larger mezras - and poles. A billhook or a saw would be helpful, especially if you are trekking in a group!

Cross the lower bridge at Pişenkaya (B008), and walk L/up the dirt road to a çeşme. Continue on the upper forest road into the trees and follow it until it ends at a stream where there is a confusion of scrub and fallen trees (10 mins, B010). Climb through the scrub just above the forest road and enter the trees on the far/E side of the stream. A clear footpath runs parallel with the forest road and about 5 m above it; follow it towards a river bed, which it crosses, heading ESE. The gently-rising path crosses a second open valley (maybe caused by an avalanche) and climbs diagonally up to an outcrop on the far side; the path is faint as new vegetation grows quickly in these areas. The path climbs up to a buttress in the forest; beyond this it continues steeply up and round a huge tree trunk and then less steeply in the same direction. Cross another wide avalanche trail on a gently rising trail, then cross some open areas. The path then turns R around some rocks; after the corner it's possible to see the top of the ridge ahead and R, with sheer towers of rock silhouetted against the sky. The path descends slightly through pines, then runs level across an open slope with many weeds and fallen logs to a headland overlooking the valley below. Norsel and Kurdat mezra and the valley road are visible far below (45 mins, B018).

The faint path makes a short diagonal descent to cross the steeply falling river below a waterfall and then climbs to the top of a rocky outcrop on the far side. Before re-entering the trees, climb a couple more hairpins; the path is totally overgrown. The next part of the path (maybe 200 m) is missing; many fallen trees lie jumbled in the area and partly covered in long vegetation. Scramble across the fallen trees then turn upwards and climb steeply into the standing trees, following the crest of a spur

SE and regain the path. Turn L towards another open area, passing over a headland overlooking a water-course (35 mins, B022). To cross the water-course, descend slightly through scrub and fallen trees, then climb to a headland on the far side. From here, there is a dramatic view of a fast-flowing mountain cascade on the opposite slope of the Onbolat Deresi.

In the forest again, the path hairpins up a couple of indistinct bends, then climbs a steep L diagonal through mixed woodland.

At the end of the diagonal, turn R onto more zigzags in the woods. It's now possible to see the rounded grassy top of a ridge more clearly (30 mins). Turn up/L/E into a flowery meadow of long grass with some scree patches. Zigzag steeply up to gain the lower side-spur where there are a few scattered trees. From the spur, above the edge of the main forest, is an amazing view across the Onbolat Deresi towards the Altıparmak Dağları. Around it is a sloping grazing area, no longer used; the ridgetop itself is only a short distance above. Cross the meadow to the SE to the start of a broad rising path, which climbs diagonally to a high point, where it rounds a rock. There are two more rocky corners to turn before the route arrives at the top of the main ridge (50 mins, B029). The top of the broad summit ridge gives views ahead/S down onto the deserted Sarnaven Deresi, where there are several unoccupied yaylas. Directly below, on the far side of the stream, are the substantial yaylas of Dibe and Dobet, apparently still in good condition. On our side of the stream is a smaller yayla. There are two ways down from this ridgetop.

Alternative route: It would be possible (but we didn't try it) to descend the slopes due S towards Dibe Yaylası. Just below the yayla is a river crossing and, from this, a path runs on the N bank of the river L down the valley to link up with our route far below. This route is shorter but initially steeper than our chosen route. **End.**

Our route turns L/ENE along the ridge, to a high point. Keep to the R of the hilltop and descend into a small bowl just R of the ridgetop. Below and in front are the 2 districts of Zekarat/Yukarı Yaylası, set amongst huge pines on the hillside only a short distance below the ridge. Take a trail over the edge of the bowl on a steep and slippery descent over shale to the water channel just W of the yayla. (The original trail ran further along the ridge and turned down from a dip immediately above the yayla but we were unable to find the route along the ridge) (55 mins, B032).

On the water channel, turn L and walk towards the yayla. The substantial but ruined houses are surrounded by a sea of nettles, which hides all manner of fallen roofing, tumbled walls and other rubble. It's best to stay some distance away from them. Walk across the top of the yayla to the edge of the woods then turn down to find an indistinct path, which leaves by a house in good condition at the lower E corner. Follow this path S then E/L around a corner to another yayla below. Again, avoid the houses and carry on above the yayla to 3 small barns where the path starts to rise. It climbs gently and diagonally across the valley slopes to reach a water channel which contours the hillside (50 mins). This long channel (it must be 6 km long) was a well-constructed and engineered solution to the shortage of water on the upper valley slopes. It took water from the upper reaches of the Sarnaven Deresi and delivered it to several yaylas along the northern ridge. It must have supported great herds of cattle as well as village life. Presumably the breakdown of the water supply caused the abandonment of the villages. It's difficult to see why the channel was neglected, as there seems to be no severe damage to it. The situation is

WP	Lat (N)	Long (E)	Alt (m)
B008	40.95021	41.27358	2144
B009	40.94832	41.27114	2136
B010	40.94846	41.27426	2176
B012	40.94809	41.27736	2218
B015	40.94834	41.27973	2238
B017	40.94818	41.28538	2269
B018	40.94727	41.28807	2249
B019	40.94597	41.28854	2227
B021	40.94542	41.29051	2253
B023	40.94550	41.29283	2311
B024	40.94400	41.29440	2344
B027	40.94226	41.29857	2481
B028	40.94235	41.30072	2524
B029	40.94164	41.30278	2544
B030	40.94231	41.30760	2535
B031	40.94273	41.31261	2476
B032	40.94122	41.31451	2361
B034	40.94044	41.31716	2263
B035	40.93874	41.31950	2277
B037	40.93983	41.32350	2309
B038	40.94223	41.32694	2295
B039	40.94072	41.32997	2268
B040	40.93724	41.33203	2254
B041	40.93705	41.33467	2176
B042	40.93505	41.33651	2159
B043	40.93489	41.33793	2140
B044	40.93231	41.33759	2059
B045	40.93025	41.33797	1978
B046	40.93203	41.33543	1976
B047	40.93230	41.33267	1923
B049	40.92989	41.33438	1788
B050	40.92664	41.33611	1750
B051	40.92315	41.33614	1765
B052	40.91899	41.33966	1616
B053	40.91876	41.34450	1536
B054	40.91644	41.35026	1420

reminiscent of the breakdown of Roman cities after their aqueducts were cut by earthquakes.

Continue walking along the water channel, which is built up on a stone wall for much of its length. You can see scattered yaylas far away on the lower slopes.

The channel winds L/NE into a huge gully then continues R/SE across grassy slopes into forest, where you have to dodge occasional branches. Beyond the forest, there is a stone wall above the channel; it has partly collapsed so you have to climb over fallen stone. Here the condition of the channel worsens and it begins to descend

11.4 Pişenkaya Yaylası, Zekarat Yaylası, Sarnaven Deresi, Demirdöven

more steeply. It rapidly becomes more overgrown with rose bushes and scrubby trees (50 mins, B040).

About 200 m beyond the wall, past a gully, turn diagonally down SE towards the highest yayla, Züdiye (30 mins). The small yayla is completely deserted, but the locked houses are in reasonable condition. Below a wooden house is a threshing machine and graffiti around the door proclaims that Cenk was here on 29th July 2007, 2 days before us. Again avoid the overgrown area between the houses and leave the yayla by the lower E corner (ignoring the second district immediately below) and contour around rocks towards a stream bed. Cross the stream bed and turn R/S onto a descending slippery path running through scattered pines. As the path bends L around the ridge, choose the lower/R path to descend through the woods towards a larger mezra, İrat/Sadat (35 min, B045).

> İrat/Sadat was a substantial mezra which must have once held 20 households - the houses are stone-built and some are huge but most are beginning to collapse. There are substantial barns between them. Electricity is connected and there seems no reason for the mezra to be deserted, except for problems with the water supply. The upper yaylas must have supplied plenty of grazing and hay for the winter and the forests above the necessary fuel. Overgrown orchards and walnut trees still surround the houses and the nearby hillside is terraced. It's sad and slightly spooky that a place with such advantages is now abandoned.

The fallen timber and roofing materials again make it difficult to walk between the houses; it is better to avoid passing through. However, there is water at the lower N corner so, if you need some, you should aim at the path below the huge house to the R. If you don't need water, look for a small fenced graveyard to the R/NW of the mezra and descend through the orchards and slopes below the forest to reach it. Below the graveyard is a wide mule trail contouring the slope (15 mins, B46).

The stone wall on the upper side of the trail has in places collapsed but, apart from that, the trail is wide and in good condition. It rounds a corner and descends NW. As it approaches a stream bed, it becomes very difficult to follow, as the wall has collapsed and willows overhang it; climb up above the willows, walk through the field and scramble across the stream before you re-join the path. Round another headland, our path descends again to a junction with a major path (30 mins, B047).

This is the junction with the variation described above. Turn L/SSE and continue to descend the valley past a dry water point and a seat to 3 old mills near the river bank. The path passes above the mills then descends to a flimsy bridge which leads to houses on the far side; ignore this turn. The mulepath now rises, running along a built-up wall around a steep face on the L of the river. It then descends to 2 more mills and a boggy area near the river, passing another bridge with a path rising to a house. The path climbs a little over green slopes and then descends rocky hairpins towards an area planted with great walnut trees under sombre rock walls. After the overhanging cliffs, the path continues to descend, walled on both sides and paved with stone steps. You are now approaching Taşbaşı and can see the village on its hill top ahead. Below is the minaret at Demirdöven. Before it reaches Taşbaşı, the path forks; turn R and descend on stone steps to the dirt road (45 mins, B053).

Turn R and walk down, over the river bridge, then swing L and continue to descend the dirt road, past barns and mills, to join the main road at Demirdöven. Dolmuşes stop at the village shop, which is just N of the lower river bridge (10 mins, B054).

11.5 Barhal, Sarıbulut Yaylası, Borasan Mezrası, Norsel Yaylası, Pişenkaya Yaylası, Okuz Gölü, Satelef Yaylası, Yaylalar *(14 hrs 20 min)*

This semicircular N-S route is a cross-country route from Barhal to Yaylalar, climbing Satibe Sırtı then descending to the Onbolat Deresi. From here, it follows the Bulbul Deresi to Okuz Gölü, a high-level lake close to the ridge which forms the SE boundary of the Onbolat basin. From here, a long and easy descent down the stark and beautiful Bulut Deresi takes you to Yaylalar. There are several tiny yaylas, plenty of campsites and water is abundant on the route.

We include an alternative route to Satibe Campsite, where you could spend a night, an alternative (shorter) route down the Onbolat Deresi, and an alternative (shorter) route bypassing Okuz Gölü.

From the centre of Barhal (B001), take the road towards Karagöl and, just opposite the turn to the Karahan pension, turn L over a bridge over the river. The path then bears R to a mill just below the valley slope. L of the mill a path rises diagonally L up the ridge. Follow it round the head of a small stream then past the ruins of a tiny chapel to a sloping grassy area on the ridgetop. Here is a small church (20 mins, B006); see page 48.

Follow the main path bearing R/WSW and up just before the church; it continues to rise WSW along the ridge to a hairpin over gravel (15 mins). It mainly overlooks several small settlements in the Onbolat Deresi to the L of the ridge. The path continues rising along the crest of the ridge aiming WSW, entering forest but passing through occasional open areas. For a short distance it is steep and eroded but improves again. At a large open area, where the path is indistinct, it changes direction, running WNW and climbing again into forest. Soon after this, it runs on the N side of a low hill, Çuvart Tepesi, with a drop to a tributary of the Barhal Deresi below R. Here the path is very distinct as the forest has been cleared on either side. Immediately after the hill, it crests an open pass, where it divides (2 hrs, B119).

The R branch climbs a ridge towards more forest, and probably goes to the end of Satibe Sırtı. Take the more distinct L/WNW branch, which descends on a gentle diagonal to the upper fields of Sarıbulut Yaylası. The path joins a stone wall and runs alongside it to the yayla, passing the first couple of old collapsing houses before reaching a crossroads in front of a fairly sound house (25 mins, B120).

Sarıbulut Yaylası has about 30 small wood-and-stone houses at 1900 m altitude, situated along an exposed, level grassy ridge pointing S over the Onbolat/Kışla Deresi. Although it has arable fields to the E, above and below these are extensive stands of tall pines. Sarıbulut is the last yayla on the climb from Pişenkaya, and the road doesn't extend as far as the yayla. It's almost uninhabited, although some of the houses are in fair condition and you could probably find somewhere to stay the night.

Alternative route to Satibe Campsite: On the N side of the yayla, on an open slope, are a couple of old mills which no longer have a water supply. Close to the mills is a path which runs upwards/N on the R side of a steep-sided gully. It climbs just on the edge of woodland then turns L around the head of the valley and rises on

THE KAÇKAR

WP	Lat (N)	Long (E)	Alt (m)
B001	40.96830	41.39257	1197
B002	40.96922	41.38188	1242
B004	40.96827	41.38011	1260
B006	40.96735	41.38601	1413
B003	40.96496	41.37603	1599
B114	40.96360	41.36869	1783
B116	40.96260	41.36477	1948
B118	40.96433	41.35640	2059
B119	40.96738	41.34858	2121
B120	40.96882	41.34274	2056
B127	40.97119	41.33785	1920
B132	40.96930	41.33279	1861
B121	40.96476	41.32518	1891
B124	40.96387	41.32137	1917
B126	40.95987	41.31940	1748
B129	40.95808	41.32329	1595
B130	40.95605	41.32203	1569
B133	40.95554	41.32157	1575
B131	40.95511	41.31005	1636
D168	40.95160	41.29715	1784
B134	40.95326	41.28869	1934
B136	40.95305	41.28396	2009
B008	40.95021	41.27358	2144
B141	40.94367	41.26459	2374
B140	40.93918	41.26335	2482
B142	40.93692	41.26086	2605
B143	40.93295	41.25793	2690
B144	40.93079	41.25716	2763
B160	40.92981	41.24856	3050
B161	40.92839	41.24796	3060
B146	40.92431	41.24937	2974
B147	40.92258	41.24779	3056
B149	40.92064	41.24504	2951
B150	40.91798	41.24436	2815
B151	40.91535	41.24238	2688
B153	40.90702	41.24725	2470
C120	40.90344	41.24802	2361
C119	40.90241	41.25395	2252
C117	40.89655	41.26449	2195
B155	40.89060	41.26911	2157
C031	40.88434	41.27240	2053
C116	40.87268	41.27567	1840
C028	40.86996	41.27256	1838

11.5 Barhal, Sarıbulut, Borasan Mezrası, Norsel, Pişenkaya, Okuz Gölü, Satelef, Yaylalar

zigzags to the grassy ridge. Turn L/W on the ridge and, just on the far side of the crest, you will find the çeşme which marks Satibe Campsite. It's only about an hour above Sarıbulut and makes a pleasant camp with wonderful views. End.

Below the mills and at the furthest N house, turn W and descend a good track which follows a line of telegraph posts into woodland. It descends into the valley NW of the yayla and passes over a landslip at the valley head (where the path is narrow and slippery) before turning L/SW and joining a stone, built-up path, which continues along the valley side, descending through more forest (25 mins). Below this path, on the far side of woodland, is a yayla, Uzunçalı. The path meets a bulldozed road in reasonable condition which climbs the hillside to a bend then descends past a few houses of Borasan/Kakrazor Yaylası to a junction. Ignore the R/upward road.

Just beyond the houses is a çeşme on the roadside (15 mins, B124).

Alternative (quicker) walk from çeşme: Continue for about 5 km down the village road, passing through the inhabited mezra of Binektaşı, then an area of extremely steep cliffs and bare rocks and above the mezra of Kurdat, until the road is almost at the valley bottom. End.

Turn L at the çeşme and walk SW across meadows, down a level, to the edge of the terracing above a wide stream valley, the Onbolat Dere. Pick up a path which descends into the valley with a stream bed below on the R. At the junction with an almost horizontal clear path (15 mins) turn L and descend slightly to Omergil Mezrası. In the middle of the houses, just after the highest point, turn R/down on a zigzag path which passes above the lowest house and descends on good hairpins over rock to the river. Here there is a flimsy bridge leading to meadows and the unsurfaced road (20 mins). Turn R and walk about 2 km along the road to the bridge. From the bridge it's almost 2 km to the R bend where the road starts to climb the hill. This is where the alternative route re-joins (1 hr, B134).

Walk up the road to a point about 100 m NE of the bend in the road and turn L over a low stone wall onto a path which runs W across the top of a field and through scrub then crosses the side-river on a bridge made from a single huge plank. The path climbs the far bank, passes below the few wooden houses of Norsel Yaylası, and crosses a second sidestream. Climbing the bank, it undulates over open ground then enters woodland, passing between massive firs. It becomes a wide mule-track which rises towards the fields below Pişenkaya and, approaching the yayla, turns R, with a stone wall on the L, towards the houses (35 mins, B008).

From Pişenkaya the track continues W, with the river about 100 m below on the L, passing above a concrete bridge and the junction of a side-stream with the river. It descends gradually to a second concrete bridge next to a huge boulder (15 mins). Across the bridge, climb the bank S then SE, with Bulbul Deresi on your L. Approaching a headland in the centre of the valley, the path swings R/SW, rising across a small stream and gaining a narrow stony path which rises in zigzags between overhanging rocks to the top of the headland (1 hr 5 mins, B140). At the top, bear L onto wide, grassy slopes, then upwards/SSW over faint zigzags to a gentle ridgetop. Past this, the path drops a little then continues SSE towards an area of scree. Here it turns R/upwards with a stone wall on the L and rises towards the scree slopes on the valley side. It then turns L and runs across the top of the scree, close against the valley wall. Continues on this gently rising path until it reaches Taş Yayla, a group of deserted huts with a stony patch below (45 mins, B142).

The path continues upwards across stones with the stream below L to a point where a headland divides the valley, with a branch of the stream on each side. The path approaches and crosses the R/W tributary. It rises to the top of the headland, where there are the remains of a small barınak. This is a good, level campsite (1 hr, B144) with views of the wide basin of the upper valley and the pass up to the SW. Okuz Gölü is out of sight behind grassy slopes R of the pass. There are good views from the headland down to the route that you have just climbed in the Bulbul Deresi but Pişenkaya is out of sight.

Alternative route direct to the pass: Walk SSW up the main valley to a barınak in the centre of what was an ox pasture. From the hut stay on the faint path which bears R around a rise and drops into a dip - the pass is clear ahead and marked by a cairn. *End.*

From the campsite, follow the L bank of the Bulbul Deresi WSW to Okuz Gölü (1 hr 5 mins, B160). At first the pathless route is not too steep but then it bends R and becomes steeper. Find a faint zigzag path which climbs up the steep slopes to the L of the stream and crests the bank retaining the lake. There is room for a couple of tents by the almost completely circular lake surrounded by steepish slopes. To rejoin the path to the pass, climb a faint path SW up the bank on the L of the out-flow stream and continue SW to the dip just before the pass (25 mins). The alternative route joins here.

The climb to the pass is a short diagonal running from R to L up the grassy slope to the dip in the skyline (10 mins, B147). From the pass, there are views back down the Bulbul Deresi; in front is Bulut Deresi, a wide glaciated valley leading up to the pyramid of Bulut Dağı and Çaymakçur Tepesi beyond that. The jagged curve of the main range is on your R. Below and L, Zarnevan Deresi descends towards Yaylalar.

The descent starts as a narrow and steep zigzagging path descending SW towards a gully. It turns L and continues with the gully on the R (15 mins). It tends L to descend below a rock buttress to a more level area with the ruins of barınaks. Here it bears L/down in indistinct zigzags, around the buttress towards the valley. It contours S then E across open hillside towards a gully; below/R is a grassy meadow above the level of the valley bottom. Before the gully and a rock stack beyond it, turn down towards the meadow and cross it towards a path starting in the SE corner (55 mins). The slippery, wide path runs in zigzags down the spur above a yayla to the valley bottom, with a side gulley on the L. At the base of the spur, you can either turn L and cross the gully for Satelef Yaylası (see page 103) or continue towards the main stream without crossing the gully. There is a level campsite between boulders close to the water (35 mins, C120).

Take a path which runs above the yayla and parallel with the river for about 100 m. It passes through a gap between boulders and joins a substantial path on a stone base, just above beds of raspberries. Cross a wide sidestream in a gully and continue on an old, wide path. Pass a second stream which is more like a waterfall splashing the route; the path here is slippery and narrow and continues almost level across a second gully and waterfall. After this, the path becomes a clear walled track, wide enough for a carriage, built up on a wall on the R and with a retaining wall on the L. Alongside are occasional ruined houses, water and drinking troughs and there are terraces in the valley below. It approaches the upper NW side of Körahmet, which stands on a spur looking over the valley (55 mins, B115).

Walk through the top of the village and turn down a stone staircase to gain the new road. Turn L and walk up the road for only about a km, until you reach Karamolla, where you climb L/up on a sloping track towards the centre of the village (15 mins, C031).

At a large çeşme flowing into a stone trough, turn down again on a footpath, which almost immediately crosses the road on a diagonal line. The path, heading down/S and initially steep and narrow, is an old mule trail which runs below the road around the sheer cliffs of the valley side to the old bridge over the Bulut Deresi, below Yaylalar. Ignore the 2 L turns on the path and, at the end, turn R, cross the old bridge and walk into Yaylalar on the road, crossing the new bridge over the Hevek Deresi just below the village (50 mins, C028).

11.5 Barhal, Sarıbulut, Borasan Mezrası, Norsel, Pişenkaya, Okuz Gölü, Satelef, Yaylalar

THE KAÇKAR

Chapter 12 **ROUTES AROUND YAYLALAR, OLGUNLAR AND THE KAÇKAR RANGE**

This area is the heart of the Kaçkar range and is the centre for trekking tourism. It includes the high hills between the Hevek Deresi and the main range, with the side valleys of the Bulut Deresi, Dobe Deresi and others to the S of the Hevek Deresi. It also includes several crossings of the main range via high passes and the climb of Kaçkar Dağı itself. This beautiful, stark area ranges in altitude between 1900 m and 4000 m and so is mainly above the treeline. The U-shaped valleys rise to the granite spires of the main range and the more rounded hills of its outliers.

Here, it takes a long time for the winter snowfall to melt and the trekking season is traditionally shorter: starting in mid-July and lasting until mid-September. But the lower-level day walks described below are possible earlier or later - certainly from the end of June to the end of September. In addition, heli-skiing has suddenly become popular. Skiers arrive by helicopter from Ayder, and are dropped S of the Hevek Deresi, in valleys which incline gently enough to make good ski slopes. The helicopter base is at the Çamyuva pension in Yaylalar - the pension has central heating and stays open for winter snow-shoers and cross-country skiers, as well as heli-skiers. The season lasts from January to March and, although there may be delays, the road from Yusufeli is kept open during this time.

There are only a few permanent settlements in this area: Demirdöven, Karbasan, Mikelis, Yaylalar and Olgunlar. Years ago, the land around was terraced for crops and supported a huge community who moved seasonally up to yaylas in the side valleys but, like most other yaylas, they have been abandoned. Now people who migrated from the area years ago are gradually returning to renovate old family properties in Karamolla and Körahmet and, if more roads are opened, no doubt more will return. That said, the current condition of the road is appalling - 30 km of riverside single track surfaced with tyre-tearing sharp rocks, which periodically slides into the river, leaving the villages cut off.

Yaylalar, at the junction of the Bulut with the Hevek Deresi, is now encircled by pine and fir forest, but this doesn't extend as far as Olgunlar. It is the hub of the area and until recently had a school and health centre as well as shops and bus services. Unfortunately, the Turkish State has had, since 1998, a policy of closing down smaller schools and the loss of this facility has caused many families with young children to leave the village. Currently, apart from bee-keeping and tourism, there is no real source of income. In the season, the 2 villages are humming with mules and their drivers, groups of climbers and walkers and the odd jeep group. Olgunlar is only 30 mins walk away, at the end of the road, and between them the 2 villages have 4 pensions and a few shops.

Yaylalar was linked to the S by passes over the Güngörmez Dağları to the Çoruh valley, which supplied the mountains with early fruit and vegetables as well as rice. From the N came roofing slats, salt and paraffin for lamps. Now most walkers use the Naletleme Geçiti to Yukarı Kavron but other mule-friendly passes include the Hevek Geçiti to Sırakonaklar and the Babur Geçiti to Ayder.

12.1 Olgunlar, Yaylalar (3 hrs 5 mins)

This is a short walk over the hill S of Olgunlar, into a secluded valley and along an old road back to Yaylalar. If you are staying in Yaylalar, you could just walk along

THE KAÇKAR

the road to Olgunlar to the start. Early in the season, the flowers on the banks and in the meadows are wonderful; a profusion of orchids grow in damp ditches. Olgunlar is famous for its butterflies, especially the blues, which congregate over the mud and puddles on the road and by the bridge.

Walk the road from Yaylalar to Olgunlar (35 mins, C063). From the W bridge in Olgunlar, cross the bridge and head straight up the bank to the S, straight towards the small hill Cudi Sırtı. The narrow and overgrown path runs straight up between low stone walls, then starts to zigzag, still between walls. It then runs diagonally on the open hillside to the L/SW, passes around a large rock and turns towards the summit, continuing to climb. It passes a junction with a narrow path; the main path runs straight on, then L and diagonally upwards past a walled enclosure on the L/E which has 2 stone pillars at the gate on the lower side. The path continues S between a bank and the wall of the enclosure (45 mins, C002).

At the end of the wall, our faint path continues into a broad bowl broken up by marshy areas. Across the hillside ahead there is a cattle track which runs into the valley leading to the pass; see route 12.8. Our route swings L across the broad bowl, still climbing gradually, then crosses the main stream to a path on the far side (15 mins, C251).

Turn L/downhill and descend as close to the stream as practical until the path becomes clear, running just above the gulley with the stream below on your L. It descends in a hairpin, then diagonally NW. The clear, well-used path crosses a gulley with a minor stream, then runs below a cliff. A second gully follows and the path continues downhill towards Yaylalar, passing an old house and barn on the L (50 mins). After this, the path is wide and clear and passes over a wider stream to run below woodland, still descending on a broad terrace. It turns round the head of a valley (where there is a çeşme and stream) and descends L/N towards the upper part of Yaylalar (25 mins, C006).

The path enters the village past a çeşme on the L. Descend to another çeşme, and a pink house set back on the R. Continue downhill past another çeşme to the road, which you reach opposite a pink house. Turn R on the road and walk 50 m towards the village, then turn downhill to another white stone çeşme. Our route continues downhill between houses; above a barn it turns R and continues across the slope to pass just below the lower mosque. Cross the wooden bridge over the stream and walk L to the bakkal and pension (15 mins, C028).

WP	Lat (N)	Long (E)	Alt (m)
C063	40.85956	41.23919	2076
C001	40.85479	41.24156	2279
C002	40.85495	41.24313	2315
C251	40.85222	41.24462	2382
C238	40.85633	41.24559	2241
C005	40.85986	41.24918	2180
C003	40.86304	41.25645	2000
C006	40.86642	41.26398	2034
C007	40.86796	41.26471	2001
C028	40.86996	41.27256	1838

12.1 Olgunlar, Yaylalar (3 hrs 5 mins)

12.2 Yaylalar, (Aksav Deresi) Modut Yaylası, Mikelis (6 hrs 45 mins)

This is a day-walk on wide and clear animal trails from Yaylalar to Modut Yaylası, a busy, friendly yayla above the tree line. From Modut, a winding, well-used mulepath descends to Mikelis on the main road, from where you can get a lift back to Yaylalar. Alternatively, part way along the path you could descend and join the old inter-village road (which winds along the cliff face) and goes directly back to Yaylalar.

Leave Yaylalar due S of the Çamyuva pension, at the bend in the concrete road, on the path to the R of the Mahlen Deresi stream-bed (C008). About 100 m along, cross the stream (there may be a log bridge) and soon after, re-cross. The path rises steeply to meet a path coming from the higher part of the village, starting above the old mosque. Re-cross the stream and continue on the L bank. The path is now less distinct. One branch of it rises up a side valley, but take the R branch and stay parallel with the stream (1 hr 10 mins, C011).

The path rises higher above the river, then, above the junction of 2 streams, it forks. Take the L turn on a path which continues rising above trees. A rising path from the yayla joins the footpath; keep L. Climb steadily SE up a sloping gully, then veer up the R bank. On the top of the bank is a well-made cairn about 2 m high (1 hr 40 mins, C012).

From here, you can see Aksav Sırtı, the ridge to the E. Crossing it at a low point is a clear path rising as a diagonal from the SE. You also have good views of the head of the valley, which is a broad bowl with a pass to the S. Aim for the start of this diagonal path, turn L onto the path and climb it to the ridge. On the ridgetop is a cairn and to its R, the path forks (15 mins, C014). Take the lower path - the upper/R one climbs to high pastures and a tarn. Descend the valley in front, passing a pınar and then contouring around the head of the valley in a boggy area (10 mins, C016).

Alternative route - return to Yaylalar by Aksav Deresi and the old road: Below, and on the far/E side of the valley is a small stone barınak with a corrugated iron roof, with animal pens nearby. Turn down the valley towards the barınak, keeping L/W of the scree slope. The route down the valley starts just in front of the barınak as a series of faint traces in the long grass. Continue N down the valley, zigzagging on a slight ridge between the stream and a scree band. After passing a boggy area with the remains of a yayla on the R, the valley broadens and the path becomes much clearer and less steep. Where the valley curves to the R/NE, cross the stream on a clear, wide path. This path runs down towards the main valley ahead then swings sharply L to run as good mulepath along the valley side. It descends past 2 water points, then passes around a headland. The final descent, on a wide path with houses along it, enters Yaylalar from the E and joins the concrete road about 150 m above the pension (2 hrs). **End.**

From the stream head, climb the hillside ahead to the low point, keeping clear of the scree on your L/N. The path runs on zigzags through rhododendrons and has lots of variations (25 mins, C017). There is a cairn on the hill-top and the view is of the rocky, dramatic Muratkaya Tepesi, with the Altıparmak Dağları in the distance and the Güngörmez Dağları as a backdrop for the hill. On the far side the path is clear and wide and sweeps across the valley to the next ridge. Descend the hill over 2 rock outcrops, to meet another path on your R coming in from above. Continue on the wide path and climb to the top of the ridge (30 mins, C022).

THE KAÇKAR

WP	Lat (N)	Long (E)	Alt (m)
C008	40.86811	41.27223	1875
C009	40.86148	41.27432	2010
C010	40.85567	41.27431	2232
C011	40.85364	41.27741	2386
C012	40.85119	41.27741	2456
C013	40.84942	41.28143	2590
C014	40.85184	41.28317	2663
C015	40.84973	41.28825	2754
C016	40.84831	41.29529	2679
C017	40.85248	41.29878	2625
C022	40.85380	41.30843	2720
C024	40.85144	41.31571	2557
C025	40.84911	41.31683	2494
C026	40.85091	41.31805	2451
C027	40.85203	41.32354	2332
C023	40.85903	41.33320	1956
C021	40.86172	41.33539	1760
C020	40.86665	41.33247	1605

Muratkayası is now on your L and in front is a low ridge that hides Modut, with conical Halime Tepesi on the L. The way down from this ridge has been badly cut up by the traffic of goats. Keep as far as possible to the R/SE (on grass) and descend to the valley path below. Aim at the R/upper path and use this to climb the next, lower ridge (45 mins, C024).

From this ridgetop you can see Modut but again the way down is not clear. There is a path visible in the valley below, above the junction of 2 streams, and you should aim for this. Head diagonally R/SSE and descend carefully. Cross the 2 streams and turn down/ENE to Modut with the stream on your L (35 mins, C027).

Modut Yaylası is on the steep NE-facing slopes of the Güngörmez Dağları, at a point where 2 small streams meet, with 2 more groups of houses further down the hill, known as Sakura Yaylası. In the yaylas, there are 30-35 houses, used for 2-3 months by people from Mikelis, plus many others who come home for the summer. The surrounding land is mainly cattle and goat pasture but an extensive terraced area on the hillside is used for growing hay. The path verges are cut as well; no foliage is wasted, so after the reaping, the paths are clear and unobstructed. The villagers use mules to move hay between the upper yaylas and Mikelis, where there are many barns. There is a half-built road to Modut, which has partly destroyed the old path and caused much damage to the forest. Up to 3 m of snow is reported in winter and some helicopter skiing takes place.

The people of Mikelis have a private festival on a local hill top, on the first Sunday in August: a family picnic for all the returnees, at which an animal is killed and roasted. The men put up tents on the Saturday while the women cook, then all bring up the food on Sunday.

12.2 Yaylalar, Modut Yaylası, Mikelis

Descend between the houses and find a stone-paved staircase dropping towards the stream where it meets a log bridge. Over the bridge, a clear path turns L/NE and down with a wall on one side. It descends between 2 streams and then crosses the L/W stream to Sakura Yaylası, on a bank below the forest. It continues, re-crossing a stream, to a couple of houses on a small hill top, then turns down/NW on a stone staircase to re-cross. Below this are many zigzags which take the path towards the edge of the fir forest but here it turns down again and meets the new road. Ignoring the continuation of the old path, descend a ramp L onto the new road (1 hr 10 mins, C023).

Walk about 300 m down the road, looking for a hidden R/NE turn onto the old path. Descend a steep, slippery path to a stream and çeşme. Across this, the path continues in zigzags, approaching the village of Mikelis. Just before the village, a path parallel with the beautiful Mikelis Deresi enters on the R. The path then turns L and passes between some gardens to a white house. Continue around the house and descend to a R turn between 2 barns; pass a çeşme and a house with a blue door; here you reach the concrete village road at its highest point. Walk L/down the concrete road through the village and, at the bottom, cross the concrete bridge onto the Yaylalar road (50 mins, C020).

12.3 Yaylalar, Karamolla, Sabahde Geçiti, Sulamenta Mezrası, Veknal Mezrası, Demirdöven *(8 hrs 45 mins)*

This semicircular day trek gives you the opportunity to trek from and return to Yaylalar using local transport. It also lets you admire the main ridges (Bulut and Kaçkar) from the pass over the rolling hills above Yaylalar. The first part of the walk is a long climb over grassy slopes on narrow paths; the second part runs through beautiful, well-kept villages where families from Istanbul or abroad return to spend the summer with their parents and siblings, looking after their cows and cutting hay for the winter. A long and well-used path descends to the road at Demirdöven, where buses to Yaylalar pass every evening.

We include an alternative route through the yayla of Tüspir; if you plan to do this alternative, bring overnight gear and camp out near the yayla.

Walk down the road going NE from Yaylalar (C028). The road immediately crosses a bridge, then a second one. Alongside the second bridge is a lovely antique Ottoman arched stone bridge. Just beyond this, an old track climbs the hillside going N (10 mins). This cobbled mule-track is the old route to Karamolla (see page 103) and stays well below the new road. 100 metres from the start, keep L through fields; later on, keep L again. The path climbs over a stream-bed then becomes a built-up track climbing around cliffs. It continues climbing to the dirt road, crosses this and continues to the village spring (45 mins, C031).

Continue through the village on a path which passes across a stream-bed. As this climbs up from the river, it passes a few poplars (10 mins). Opposite these is a gap in the upper stone wall where a narrow, overgrown and underused path runs upwards between 2 walls. The walls soon collapse but the path continues upwards then swings L/N, to a headland with a dramatic view over Körahmet and the Bulut Deresi and L to Karamolla and Yaylalar (25 mins). Just before the headland, the path turns R/S, re-crossing the stream and running about 100 m above 2 pine trees and the grove of poplars until it turns a corner towards the Tiğlap Deresi (15 mins, C034).

The path is now narrow and indistinct in places and it rises slightly as it runs towards the deep, narrow gully. On the far side, it disappears into the long grass and bog; head diagonally upwards for about 50 m and find a faint, narrow track continuing to a solitary pine tree on the ridge beyond. Here, the path turns upwards and zigzags on the crest, gaining more than 100 m altitude (1 hr 15 mins). As the gradient lessens, look out for a clear path running SE, which contours the next valley to reach a false pass on a spur. The path continues ENE to contour a second, larger valley, rising to Sabahde Geçiti, a pass over a ridge down from Saranlıya Tepesi, a 3000 m summit to the NW (1 hr 15 mins, C038).

From the ridge are views down the steep sided valley above Demirdöven and across the Hevek Deresi is the Gungörmez range, separating the Kaçkar from the Çoruh Nehri and the Erzurum plain. To the NE, the spikes and towers of the Bulut Dağları cut into the sky and below them are the slopes of the Bulut Deresi. On the ridge to the R is a barınak with a leaky corrugated roof; several paths meet here and you have to decide between the main and the alternative route.

Alternative route via Tüspir Yaylası: Our favourite path continues R/E below the barınak, along the crest of the ridge, descending over stones to a lower level. Ignore traces of side paths down into the bowl below on your L and others on the R. Continue SE with the spine to your R, down several levels onto a clear, stony track. There are spectacular views across the Hevek Deresi, far below, over to Modut and the Güngörmez Dağları in the S and to the grassy ridge above Karbasan. Now the descent becomes steeper, the path less clear and you move into forest. Stay with the spine, going NE, descending an open area at the edge of the trees. At the bottom, descend to the L of a pile of stones with the remains of some old graves. Pass 2 tree stumps cut off at waist height then bear L/W onto a footpath leading into forest. The footpath contours for 100 m then divides. Keep L/up and continue to contour. This path soon becomes a good mulepath; it rises over 2 headlands and passes 2 streambeds but generally descends gradually along the hillside, above dense woodland, to Tüspir Yaylası.

Tüspir/Tüzbir Yaylası is built on a sloping hillside, below forest and close to Sulamenta. There are about 10 substantial 2- or 3-storey stone houses with barns, all facing NE, with views as far as the Hevek Deresi. From July to the end of September, about 20 people from Demirdöven live there with their cattle. Below the yayla are sloping fields and past it is more grazing in the Veknal Deresi. A lovely path runs from the upper N corner, rising through the forest to Sorunpiyat.

Walk through the houses then branch slightly downhill/NE on a muddy narrow path which descends to the river, crosses it and climbs the far bank, above some beehives and 2 riverside huts. The route almost immediately meets a clear mulepath from Sulamenta Mezrası; this is the main route. **End.**

The shorter route leads to the burned-out mezra of Sulamenta and a distinctive white mosque, NE in the valley below. The initial direction is NE down the stream bed, keeping on the R of the stream and as low as possible. Descend through the rhododendrons, cross a side gully (where the path is very faint) then make a further descent to a second gulley where the rhododendrons stop. Descend through raspberries on a very slippery faint path until you are just above the stream bed, then turn parallel with the stream, passing below a scattering of large pines. Cross another stream bed and reach the yayla of Sorunpiyat (1 hr 10 mins, C043).

> **Sorunpiyat Yaylası** is a row of only about 10 wooden barns with living accommodation above, built in a row on the NW-facing slope of a hill just below forest. The former residents of Sulamenta, which burned down in 2006, use the yayla from early July to September. Below the yayla are streamside meadows with some vegetable gardens.

Continue below the barns to the çeşme at the end of the row and turn down on a path, which descends past pines then in zigzags towards the stream (15 mins). About half way down is a junction and a path leading R towards the forest and then to Tüspir Yaylası (see the alternative route). Continue downwards to cross the main stream, then the second stream and climb a steep zigzag path towards the mezra of Sulamenta. Approaching the mezra, past the first shells of the houses, the path branches and you turn R and walk on a mulepath below a row of the stone shells of burned houses (40 mins, C046).

> **Sulamenta Mezrası** now consists of a mosque and the shells of about 40 burned houses which were engulfed in an inferno in the early hours of the morning in August 2006. 1-2 houses, which are inhabited during the summer, remain and electricity is still connected. The land below the mezra is good for agriculture and the former residents, who have either been rehoused by the state or who live in Veknal below, come to cut the hay, grow vegetables and pasture their cattle.

Our path continues as good mulepath, running E past some barns, with the stream far below/R, to a fork where you turn R/down, passing under some crags, to meet the alternative route above the stream bed (15 mins). At the junction keep R and descend gently NE to Aşağı Veknal. The route passes a deserted white house with a çeşme opposite and a stone seat (40 mins, C049).

Just before the mezra, the path divides and a branch runs down to the houses; the main path continues above. Continue on the upper path, which is initially narrow, paved and runs along a watercourse, past a junction (where a path runs back to the yayla) then widens to a lovely mulepath. It crosses above a meadow, climbs around a small headland through woodland, descends around a SE-facing valley with a cleft in it and rises to another group of houses (15 mins, C050).

> **Aşağı and Yukarı Veknal/Varhal Mezras** cluster on a S-facing hillside above orchards and grazing land. The lovely tall stone-and-timber houses are well-built, divided by narrow paths and stairs and with barns clustered around them. They are inhabited by families who originally used Sulamenta; some are in residence year round, except when working on their lands higher up the valley.

The route climbs through forest towards a ridge then turns R/NE and descends the ridge on straight broad path. At an open area, it does a double hairpin and, from this point, the valley bottom below becomes visible (30 mins). From here the descent is ENE on steep hairpins down a ridge, passing the upper mezra of Demirdöven on the L and approaching the higher timber houses on the S side of the stream bed. At a junction, turn R and pass down a staircase, turning L to walk between the upper

WP	Lat (N)	Long (E)	Alt (m)
C028	40.86996	41.27256	1838
C116	40.87268	41.27567	1840
C031	40.88434	41.27240	2053
C033	40.88797	41.27048	2097
C034	40.88734	41.27262	2158
C035	40.89171	41.27240	2227
C036	40.88632	41.27875	2401
C037	40.88738	41.28377	2709
C038	40.88983	41.29653	2754
C040	40.89478	41.30232	2532
C041	40.89645	41.30390	2444
C042	40.89699	41.30655	2359
C043	40.89832	41.30938	2285
C045	40.90169	41.31024	2197
C046	40.90223	41.31239	2262
C047	40.90365	41.31672	2230
C048	40.90056	41.32042	2107
C049	40.90811	41.33118	1906
C050	40.91148	41.33370	1887
C051	40.91589	41.34178	1725
C053	40.91712	41.34832	1387
C044	40.91532	41.35022	1297

side of the houses and the forest. After about 100 m, you reach the end of a bulldozed village road (35 mins). Continue to a bend and turn R/downhill towards the main road and the village centre, passing a wooden mill with a huge millstone..On the main road to the L is the village shop and seating where you can wait for a return buses to Yaylalar. They run between 5 and 7 pm or even later (10 mins, B054).

12.4 Yaylalar to Olgunlar, Dilberdüzü Campsite, Deniz Gölü, Kaçkar summit and Dilberdüzü (14 hrs 30 mins).

This is the most popular trek in the Kaçkar. Most people take 2 or, more usually, 3 days to do it, spending either 1 or 2 nights at the large campsite at Dilberdüzü. Several tour companies have permanent base camps here with tents for cooking and stores so, in season, this is the busiest camp in the Kaçkar. A constant stream of mules takes their customers' rucksacks and kitbags to and from base camp. From the camp, the summit is a hard day's climb; you should not attempt the summit if visibility is low or the wind is strong. You could camp at Deniz Gölü, where there is room for 1-2 tents, but you should arrive early. Leave your large rucksacks at camp but use poles or, early in the season, an ice-axe and take a headtorch, food and warm, waterproof clothing.

From the pension in the centre of Yaylalar, walk up the road which turns R over the Mahlen Deresi stream and rises to the upper part of the village. Continue through the village and along the gently rising road with the Hevek Deresi far below on the R. Approaching Olgunlar, the road crosses a bridge to the N bank and runs above a boulder field. The road terminates in the centre of Olgunlar; there are 3 pensions here and a café on the way out of the village, between the 2 bridges (30 mins, C063).

Continue through Olgunlar to the café; cross the main bridge and walk the clear, gently rising track SW with the stream on your R. The path runs mainly along terraces, sometimes past animal enclosures, crossing several sidestreams to a yayla (1 hr 45 mins, D229).

> **Hastaf/Nastaf Yaylası** is a group of about 20 scattered small stone houses with corrugated iron roofs, on the S bank of the Hevek Deresi. It's seasonally inhabited from the end of July to early September by 5 families from Yaylalar and their cattle. The summit route runs right through the centre to a spring on the far side, so people are constantly coming and going.

The path passes through the centre of the yayla to a çeşme then continues rising uphill to a marshy area on the Karnovit Deresi. After crossing the stream on stepping-stones, there is a small hill on the L of the path, which is an alternative campsite. Be careful to position your tent fairly high as trails of cattle descend paths along the stream on their return to Hastaf Yaylası every night. The path continues WSW to rise towards the shoulder of Çağil Tepesi, where it turns SSE, on a short, steep climb to the campsite (2 hrs, C163).

> **Dilberdüzü campsite** is big enough for about 200 tents, and, since it's the base camp for climbs of Kackar, in summer it can be crowded. At the end of the season it can be distinctly unsanitary as there are no toilets and people use the lower slopes behind the camp. For this reason, you should take care either to boil or sterilise the stream water.

Start your summit attempt before sunrise. In August, first light is around 5 am and sunrise around 6 am, so you should start walking at 4 am. For the first hour you will need a headtorch but the route is relatively easy and a good warm up. If you wake up to mist, cloud, snow or rain, you have to assess whether it will clear or not; don't do the climb in poor conditions.

From the campsite follow the rising trail SW and cross the stream, ignoring the smaller path L to Hevek Geçiti. The path zigzags its way up the rocks to the top of the cliff overlooking the campsite, with the small stream on your L. Continue climbing the path, which bends R/NW; after a few minutes look carefully to your L to find a gushing pınar; fill your bottles here. Continue to a flat area with red scree straight ahead and many cairns around. L is a big rock which looks like a giant finger. Bear R and turn your back to the finger rock. The clear trail ahead will take you NW all the way to near circular Deniz Gölü (which usually has ice floating on it) (2 hrs, C262). The lake is so deep that an expedition failed to find the bottom; the surface is rarely completely ice-free so diving in it is a serious matter. To the S of the lake is a scree-covered slope leading steeply up to a pass; on the far side is Atsız Gölü (see route 12.7).

Find the outflow stream from Deniz Gölü; the trail continues R/NNW from here up a low hill. On top of the hill you will see your next target - a low pass NW. Keeping your altitude, traverse the slope towards the pass. The path disappears altogether and you have to walk between the rocks of a boulder field for a short time. Meet the path again directly under the pass and climb it to the top (1 hr 15 mins, C263).

WP	Lat (N)	Long (E)	Alt (m)
C028	40.86996	41.27256	1838
C007	40.86796	41.26471	2001
C063	40.85956	41.23919	2076
D230	40.84560	41.22813	2242
D229	40.83855	41.21225	2387
D226	40.82457	41.18771	2689
D225	40.82163	41.17745	2864
C163	40.81852	41.17247	2975
C261	40.81500	41.16959	3210
C262	40.81868	41.16317	3425
C263	40.82461	41.15774	3505
C264	40.83131	41.15981	3600
C265	40.83316	41.15692	3730
C266	40.83582	41.16171	3932

If the weather is clear, from the pass you will see in front of you the whole route to the summit. There is one key point, called "the balcony", due N - a flat ledge with a patch of green grass. It's accessed by a narrow path; note its location for later. First make a short, steep descent to a grey stone pile on the R of a small tarn (or ice), below the pass. Follow the ridge across the grey stones then turn L, keeping away from the pink-red rocks, and pass a short drop and another icy tarn on your R, followed by a snow-patch. Follow the snow in a curve to the R/NE. Where the trail starts to descend, follow the many cairns L onto rocks; there is no path or trail. There follows a gentle diagonal climb R/NNE; be careful not to climb too steeply into the boulders and keep looking for the path over scree to the balcony; it starts suddenly just 50 - 100 m before the balcony itself. There are many cairns but some of them lead to dead ends - be careful! Follow the path towards the balcony and, as you approach, there is 3-4 m of rock climbing for about 2-3 moves. No rope or security is needed but in July the climb can be difficult as snow-melt cascades down the rocks (1 hr 15 mins, C264).

Now, you are on the main mass of the mountain and there is only 2-300 m of ascent between you and the summit. The path continues straight then makes a 180° turn NW as it climbs onto the main mass of the mountain. The peak is in front of you but first go L/W, following the path and approach the summit in a long curve from the L/W side. Do not climb all the way up to the ridge as it is very rough and difficult to follow. Instead, climb on scree gently in a R curve, bearing further R just before coming to the ridge. The path becomes faint and narrow and sometimes disappears between the rocks but, as long as you gain height, you won't get lost. Don't gain altitude too fast; aim to reach the ridge at the dip just W of the main summit (1 hr 45 mins, C266).

At the summit is a cairn with a summit register in a box and a Turkish flag. Sign in and replace the register. Immediately around the peak are a jumble of granite spires, forming the main SW-NE wall of the Kaçkar range and leading to Verçenik Dağı in the SW and Altıparmak Dağı in the NE; Deniz Gölü nestles in a hollow. Beyond are the U-shaped glaciated valleys of (clockwise) Soğanlı, Davali, Kavron,

Çaymakçur and Hevek, divided by more rounded ridges. The horizon is formed by the Erzurum plain in the S, above the Güngörmez Dağları and, in the N the Black Sea, above rolling, wooded ridges.

Retrace your steps in the same gradual curve. A direct descent is a danger to members of your group and to other people who may be climbing as you will dislodge many stones. Then continue as before. After the lake, don't be tempted to follow the outlet stream as it enters steep rocks; it's dangerous to try to reach camp that way. Instead, after descending along the stream a little, turn L, following your upward route. If the weather is clear you will see your landmark, the finger-shaped rock, down below. If it's misty, follow the cairns and the path. Turn left again at the flat area under the finger rock and, after 10 min following the path, you will see the campsite below (3-4 hrs).

12.5 Olgunlar, Dibe Yaylası, Naletleme Geçiti, Yukarı Kavron (or Yukarı Çaymakçur) (9 hrs 30 mins)

This is the classic trans route from S to N of the range, linking the 2 major trailheads and used by most trekkers visiting the Kaçkar. It is a spectacular route, passing the beautiful head of the Dobe Deresi, climbing between the cliffs of the Naletleme Geçiti and descending past several lakes surrounded by rhododendrons. There are good camps at Düpedüzü and Deniz Gölü and the trail is easy to follow. Instead of descending via Yukarı Kavron, if you prefer a quieter, greener route, you could go down the Çaymakçur valley and we describe this alternative.

From the end of the road in Olgunlar (C156) continue through the houses until you see the bridges at the end of the village (15 mins) then turn R/N with the Dobe Deresi on your L, towards some tall poplars. The path to Dibe Yaylası is initially sometimes muddy and runs alongside the river, but soon it climbs to meet the original paved mule track below a stone wall (20 mins). Cross a sidestream and then another, wider one (25 mins). Cross two more sidestreams then pass the remains of a yayla. The path gradually deteriorates but continues to rise as you approach the L bend in the valley.

The path, now just a footpath, crosses a final stream bed where it breaks up into alternative paths, rejoining below Dibe Yaylası (40 mins, C067).

> **Dibe/Hayirli Yaylası** is a seasonally busy yayla, spread out on a SE-facing slope just above the river. The single-storey stone houses are topped by corrugated iron roofs and surrounded by walled enclosures for the cattle, some with roofs raised on pillars. To prevent wind or snow damage, when not in use, the corrugated iron roofs are stored inside the houses. 6 houses are inhabited by people from Yaylalar, who arrive in early August and stay until September. A spring on the upper side of the yayla is channeled through the paved alleys to carry off cow dung. Just beyond the village the river flows through a narrows with cascades.

The path above the yayla is confused. Start off above the spring and continue towards the riverbank then climb alongside the gushing cascade. Over a lip, the valley opens out and the path veers away from the stream (20 mins, C069).

Düpedüzü Campsite has plenty of room for tents on both sides of the stream, just after the junction with a sidestream, where there is a large boulder. On the SW side of the stream is a spring with a stone platform and trough. The hillsides and bogs

THE KAÇKAR

WP	Lat (N)	Long (E)	Alt (m)
C156	40.86054	41.24067	2097
C064	40.86920	41.23006	2333
C066	40.86909	41.22251	2396
C067	40.86824	41.21839	2458
C068	40.86788	41.21511	2515
C069	40.86343	41.20883	2604
C072	40.85988	41.20273	2699
C075	40.86042	41.19640	2842
C077	40.86040	41.19135	2906
C080	40.86175	41.18871	3007
C082	40.86303	41.18489	3047
C084	40.86477	41.18097	3126
C086	40.86574	41.17955	3185
C087	40.86790	41.17750	3159
C089	40.87077	41.17604	3047
C090	40.87174	41.17426	3000
C092	40.87391	41.17034	2926
C093	40.87486	41.16793	2870
C094	40.87518	41.16677	2812
C095	40.87462	41.16502	2961
C096	40.87298	41.16383	2911
C097	40.87646	41.16056	2832
C098	40.87705	41.15354	2610
C099	40.88113	41.14416	2463
C100	40.88239	41.13909	2360
C101	40.88384	41.13431	2266
D035	40.88415	41.13123	2225

around the camp are renowned for flowers - from orchids in the damp patches to poppies, campanulas and daisies higher up. The head of the valley is ringed with grey, snow-spattered saw-edged peaks which lead up to Kaçkar itself. They contrast with the lush green below them.

On the N side of the path, the ground is broken up by minor streams and bogs and path is unclear. The main path starts to climb W/up the hillside above the bogs, until you can see the stream which descends from the pass. Running SW, it crosses a shallow couloir which runs down towards the campsite (1 hr 10 mins). At a cairn on a boulder, it turns uphill towards the pass.

It levels a little, then turns R/NW around a rock and zigzags to the top of an outcrop on the edge of the stream with the sound of water beyond. At the top of the zigzags, the pass is in clear view, with a shallow cirque in front and steep cliffs just below the pass. The path passes a small pınar and runs close above the stream; on the R is a relatively level campsite or picnic place with room for a row of tents (40 mins, C080).

The path, running level, zigzags over smaller stones to a ridge and continues in a

2.5 Olgunlar, Dibe Yaylası, Naletleme Geçiti, Yukarı Kavron (or Yukarı Çaymakçur)

groove defined by larger stones. There is a permanent snowpatch in the cirque at the base of the pass, leading to zigzags climbing straight towards the cliffs and pass, just L of the biggest rocks. The path is extremely worn and gravelly; it becomes more difficult and steeper as you approach the pass (45 mins, C086).

There are plenty of rocky places on the wide summit of the pass to sit and admire the view. Naletleme Tepesi towers over the E of the pass and the sharper Kaçkar peaks are on the W. The view to the N is of a gently sloping rocky area and beyond that a narrow valley with steep walls, which slopes down to the Çaymakçur Deresi. In the bottom of the valley, but out of sight, are 2 lakes; 3 more lie over the wall to the L. On the S is the snow cirque with rock walls on both sides; behind is the grassy and rhododendron-clad wall of the Dupedüzü Deresi; beyond that, the Güngörmez Dağları is silhouetted against the sky.

The path runs NW down a shallow ridge over large stones, descending gently and keeping R of a buttress which divides the valley. It continues in hairpins down to the lower valley, with the steep buttress on the L. At the end of the hairpins, the path continues on the L of a straight ridge which divides the valley, passing R of a shallow hollow in the ridgetop (1 hr 5 mins, C090).

At the end of the ridge, the path continues R/down in zigzags then divides at a cairn. On the L is a small tarn and a stream linking that to Karadeniz Gölü below (15 mins, C093).

Alternative route to the Çaymakçur valley. For Çaymakçur, turn R at the cairn, bearing N. The narrow and faint path descends first straight, then in zigzags through some rhododendrons towards a campsite on the shore of beautiful Karadeniz Gölü, tucked into the hillside below the path. From the lake, there is an indistinct but gentle descent over grass into a shallow bowl - keep L of the centre line and walk to the rim. Bear R/NNE down a slope towards the R-hand stream (the outflow of Mesuk Gölü) where the path turns L and drifts above the stream on the side of a ridge.

You can now see Yukarı Çaymakçur far below in the U-shaped valley and Cennevit Deresi (the outflow of Karadeniz Gölü) is close on the L. Looking back to the R, you can see that all the 3 streams in the valley drop in torrents down moraine and rock faces below the rim of the upper valley. Behind the waterfalls are the peaks of the ridge. The path continues N as a clearer narrow slot then turns R as zigzags running down towards Yukarı Çaymakçur.

The path crosses the wide stream on stepping-stones and turns down more hairpins to a damp, stony patch. Cross to the far bottom corner then descends another small stream over slabs of rock which are the remains of the old path. Deep water sometimes flows over the rocks and leaves pockets of mud between the steep banks. At the bottom, cross the main stream via a wooden bridge, looking back to the view of the waterfalls up the valley. Walk on the narrow path up through nettles and weeds to the first house and join the dirt road just beyond.

> **Yukarı Çaymakçur Yaylası** has about 25 wooden houses at an altitude of 2250 m, situated in 2 districts 2.5 km above Aşağı Çaymakçur, at the end of a beautiful old stone footpath and a parallel road dirt. Only 8-10 houses in the yayla are occupied, giving a total of maybe 20 people in midsummer. The residents come from Çamlıhemşin; some pasture cows but others just come for a holiday.

Turn L and walk down the dirt road, then paddle across the concreted stream crossing. Now turn down and find the beautiful, paved path which runs parallel and below the modern bulldozed road. It continues for 1- 2 km to meet the new road on a bend just before Aşağı Çaymakçur (40 mins).

Aşağı Çaymakçur Yaylası has 2 districts with a total of about 40 houses. 3 are made entirely of stone, but most of panelled wood and stone. 1 district has been almost completely renovated; the other is neglected. Each year, from the first week in June until the end of September, 15 houses are occupied by about 40 people; formerly as many as 500 people lived on the yayla and kept cattle and bees. The Çağlayan Dağı Evi (mountain house) was constructed for trekkers but is now firmly locked up. A good dirt road leads from the yayla to Kaler Düzü and Ayder.

Turn L and continue down to the wide concrete bridge below the yayla. On the roadside are 2 springs; then another concrete bridge re-crosses the valley. Pass the junction on the L with the Palakçur dirt road and walk less than a km to the Ayder-Yukarı Kavron dirt road. If you turn R here, less than 100 m ahead is the campsite and roadside restaurant of Kaler Düzü (40 mins, C153).
From here you could take a minibus or walk down to Ayder (1 hr 30 mins). **End.**

Kaler/Galer Düzü is a level area above the Kavron Deresi where Yusuf keeps a campsite and small restaurant, open for 6 months per year. Without toilets and proper rubbish disposal, the site is often littered. It's mainly used by picknicking Turkish families.

At the cairn, continue L/SW on zigzags leading down to the stony stream crossing between the 2 lakes (10 mins, C095). Stepping-stones run diagonally L across the stream and the route on the far side is initially over a band of rocks. Climb long hairpins which rise up the grassy hillside to a dip on the horizon to the W, avoiding the rhododendrons (40 mins, C096).

On the far side is the Kavron Deresi, with its side valley, the Çinnaçur Deresi, descending steeply to the yayla below. Immediately ahead is a small tarn; Büyükdeniz Gölü is 250 m to the L/SSW in the head of the valley. The path descends SE from the smaller tarn down a slope in more hairpins to the Çinnaçur Deresi, and continues with the stream on the L. Approaching the valley and Yukarı Kavron, the path crosses to the S side, running around a small headland over the village (1 hr 10 mins). The final descent is over zigzags; at the first houses it turns R and runs between houses towards the bridge and crosses the river to Yukarı Kavron (see page 116) (15 mins, D035).

Between Yukarı Kavron and Ayder is 12 km of rough track; buses leave frequently in summer, the last at 5 pm.

12.6 Yaylalar, Karamolla Mahallesi, Körahmet Mahallesi, Satelef Yaylası, Babur Geçiti, Palakçur Yaylası, Kaler Düzü (9 hrs 10 mins)

This trek is a S-N crossing of the range, by the shortest route from Yaylalar to Ayder. From Yaylalar it climbs into the Bulut Deresi and, where valley curves L, it continues straight towards the impressive wall of the main ridge, slipping over by a well-hidden pass. The descent to Palakçur is long but easy and from there it's a walk of about 5.5 km on dirt roads to Ayder. If you're not in a hurry, take 2 days and camp in the upper Palakçur valley, perhaps at Derebaşı Gölü, surrounded by the pinnacles of the ridge and its spurs. Past the summit, you may run into mist or clouds and early in the season there will be snow patches on the descent from the pass - take poles for the snow and/or scree.

Walk down the road going NE from Yaylalar (C028). The road immediately crosses a bridge, then a second one. Alongside the second bridge is a lovely Ottoman arched stone bridge. Just beyond this, an old track climbs the hillside going N (10 mins). This cobbled muletrack is the old route to Karamolla and stays well below the new road. 100 m from the start, keep L through fields; later on, keep L again. The path climbs over a streambed then becomes a built-up track climbing around cliffs. It continues climbing to the dirt road, crosses this and continues to the village spring (35 mins, C031).

WP	Lat (N)	Long (E)	Alt (m)
C028	40.86996	41.27256	1838
C116	40.87268	41.27567	1840
C031	40.88434	41.27240	2053
C033	40.88797	41.27048	2097
C117	40.89655	41.26449	2195
B155	40.89060	41.26911	2157
C119	40.90241	41.25395	2252
C120	40.90344	41.24802	2361
C122	40.90586	41.24142	2375
C123	40.90533	41.23897	2380
C125	40.90645	41.23436	2521
C126	40.90849	41.23063	2606
C129	40.90769	41.22598	2758
C130	40.90899	41.22193	2817
C132	40.90891	41.21951	2944
C134	40.91037	41.21573	3071
C136	40.91179	41.21359	2940
C137	40.91147	41.21021	2842
C139	40.91203	41.20724	2729
C140	40.91161	41.20564	2700
C141	40.91332	41.20472	2666
C142	40.91806	41.20027	2564
C143	40.91967	41.19779	2511
C144	40.92196	41.19300	2442
C146	40.92469	41.18715	2416
C148	40.92538	41.18356	2353
C149	40.92834	41.17933	2232
C150	40.92730	41.17818	2172
C112	40.92980	41.16255	1914
C152	40.92575	41.15851	1826
C153	40.92777	41.14558	1691

12.6 Yaylalar, Karamolla, Körahmet, Satelef Yaylası, Babur Geçiti, Palakçur Yaylası, Kaler Düzü

Karamolla/Adatepe, which was originally at least partly Armenian, is now a prosperous village of huge, solid stone houses, often with a wooden top storey which was used to store hay. The village is quite tightly-packed and situated on a W-facing hillside, so the paths between the houses often take the form of stairs. There is a çeşme, with an inscription, flowing into a row of stone basins and above this a wooden pavilion where the women gather to drink tea, knit socks and gossip. It looks out onto terraced fields where hay is grown and to the slopes beyond where, in the evening, you may see bears. Recently, much repair and renovation work has been carried out and the village is bustling and lively in summer. In winter, a couple of families remain.

Continue through the village on a path which passes across a streambed, then to Körahmet, entering the village on the upper S side. Climb the concrete staircase, and continue NNE through the village to the wide track on the far side (30 mins, C117).

Körahmet (blind Ahmet), according to local legend, was named after a local robber chief; other sources say he was a woodman blinded in one eye by a flying woodchip. It's similar to but smaller than Karamolla and also busy in summer. In winter it's inhabited by just 1 or 2 families. The 2 are linked by well-made old road as well as the new dirt road, which has such an awkward bend that vehicles regularly reverse down it!

The track is wide and was once able to take a carriage; overgrown remains of houses show that it was once well used. After about 2 km, cross a gully with a waterfall running over it - the path narrows and is slippery (35 mins). Soon after is a second gully with a waterfall; here the path narrows again and remains narrow. As the path begins to bend W, it crosses a wide, gently sloping gully. From here on, it is less distinct, although the stone kerb is visible in places. It continues above an area of wild raspberries then, about 100 m before the houses, turns down slightly between rocks, aiming for Satelef Yaylası (30 mins, C120).

Satelef Yaylası contains about 10 single-storey stone houses and is set at an altitude of 2300 m around a valley mouth near the lower slopes of a spur of the range above, called Çaysıvak Sırtı. It's linked to Yaylalar by a well-made old road, which is still mostly in good condition. The yayla is only used seasonally, from mid-July to September by a few people from Yaylalar, who bring their cattle (including huge bulls) to graze on the damp turf. The best campsite is just after the village, amongst the huge boulders alongside the stream.

After the yayla, the path passes a çeşme, then a stream and runs past a large lichen-covered rock about 200 m after the village (10 mins). It continues rising gently - mainly indistinct but with occasional kerbstones - until it crosses a wide sidestream on stepping-stones; it's almost inevitable that you'll get your feet wet (40 mins, C123).

Soon after, cross another sidestream and climb over a moraine of stones and boulders to gain a low ridge close to the stream. Turn R/NW up the ridge, aiming for a zigzag path on the hillside ahead. The sidestream is close below on your R and the path stays close to it for much of the way to the top of the pass. At the top of the

12.6 Yaylalar, Karamolla, Körahmet, Satelef Yaylası, Babur Geçiti, Palakçur Yaylası, Kaler Düzü

first zigzags the path bears away from the stream and climb up to a rocky outcrop (50 mins, C125).

Continue NW/upwards parallel with the stream on a grassy slope. The path is indistinct but becomes clear again as the gradient steepens and it begins to zigzag towards the lip of a bowl with rhododendrons and a large rock on the upper side. It descends slightly into the bowl, passes under a small rock face and turns up/R around the rock. As it climbs above the bowl, the path zigzags between rocks; pass them and bear L, then R onto stones as you approach the stream again just as it descends over a lip. Cross the stream on large flat rocks into a boggy cirque with a pond or snow (25 mins, C129).

The character of the path changes here; it now is hemmed in by scree slopes and cliffs, and so is rocky, wet and often snow covered. The path climbs parallel with the stream up the cirque, keeping to the low rocks on the R side. The exit from the cirque is via zigzags climbing steeply over and between rocks. The path becomes easier as it climbs L/WNW above the rocky area towards a rock wall above (20 mins, C132). Above that is a towering, curved rock on the horizon and to the R/below you can see the wide valley leading towards the Lale Geçiti. Just below the wall, turn L on wet gravelly path then R on to more zigzags up scree and rocks. There is a cirque between the rocks on the R but keep heading WNW on hairpins towards the pass above (1 hr 10 mins, C134).

To the R of the narrow Babur Geçiti is a roofless barınak. The view ahead and L is of steep jagged spires of rock with snow patches in the crevices, hanging over the steep hairpins of the descent. They close off the view of Derebaşı Gölü but the wide, U-shaped valley of Palakçur Deresi is clear below. Behind, the Bulut Deresi stream sparkles far below as it runs straight down the valley.

A small headland divides the start of the descent over fine scree and the path switches R over a rock. The path is a clear descent in zigzags over scree and some grass, slippery in places but not too difficult. After a few bends, the path aims towards an outcrop on the R/NW. The path then starts a second zigzag descent over more grassy slopes, tending W (30 mins, C136).

Descend below the outcrop towards 2 large rocks on a low bank, then turn half R and continue with the Palakçur stream far below/L. The path leads downwards in hairpins, aiming at low moraine hills blocking the valley. Where it passes between the low bumps, it is very indistinct so follow the cairns, which mark the route L towards the stream (35 mins, C139).

About 200 m from the stream, the path reaches the bottom of the hairpins, and turns R/NNW, levelling off and passing several boulders. It crosses a sidestream above the junction with the main stream, then comes to a stone wall topped with wire which is a barrier to cattle. There's no gate so you have to climb the wall (25 mins, C142).

The clear but rough path continues, winding between boulders, gradually swinging NW and moving away from the stream. At a junction, a lower path heads towards the stream which, by now, is several hundred m below. Keep on the upper path, which climbs onto the grassy slope above the rocks and around the ridge, bearing R. Around the ridge, the scattered houses of Palakçur come into view; the path is now a clear slot in the turf, well used by cattle and muddy in places. It descends and passes over the top of a side gully, then crosses L onto the top of a low ridge (40 mins, C148).

This ridge runs between the main stream and the hillside, descending towards Palakçur Yaylası ahead (see page 118). At the end are the remains of houses buried in vegetation. Keep R and find a path descending the steep bank L towards the Palakçur Deresi below. Turn R along the stream bank and walk 80 m to the bridge (15 mins, C149).

It's 5.5 km walk down to Ayder, over pleasant dirt road, mainly through forest. Turn L over the concrete bridge and walk NW then W down the track, which soon enters woodland. It continues around the hillside to a major bend from which there is a view between the trees of the yayla of Yukarı and Aşağı Çaymakçur, but the forest is too steep for a path. The track then hairpins R/N and descends steeply towards the river, where it turns L again. At the bend there is a steel roadmakers' cabin. Continue down parallel with the stream to a place where the track has partly fallen away; here it joins the Çaymakçur road; turn R. Walk less than a km to the Ayder-Yukarı Kavron track. Turn R again; less than 100 m ahead is Kaler Düzü (50 mins, C153). From here you can take a minibus or walk down to Ayder (1 hr 30 mins).

12.7 Dilberdüzü Campsite, Hevek Geçiti, Davaliaşıtı, Apivanak Yaylası, Karmık Yaylası, Tirovit (18 hrs 10 mins).

This route is an E-W trans, running S of Kaçkar peak and over 4 substantial passes. It's a delightful way of accessing the upper Davali, Palovit and Karmık valleys, which are rarely seen by trekkers. The route stays high above the treeline and often above the yaylas, which means that there are superb views over various parts of the Kaçkar range and the mountains to the S as far as Erzurum. We include an alternative route into the upper Davali Deresi, over the pass to Atsız Gölü. Parts of the route are quite difficult and run over scree, so you should take walking poles.

This route starts at the campsite of Dilberdüzü (D223) (see page 96).

Alternative route via Atsız Gölü / Nameless Lake: from Dilberdüzü campsite, head SW as though you were aiming for the peak (see route 12.4). Here the Hevek Deresi stream runs in a steep valley and a path zigzags up, crossing from S to N and then back again. Past the head of the stream, the valley swings to the NW and continues climbing to the banks of Deniz Gölü. On the S side of the lake is a col (often snow-clad) with a steep and narrow path over scree to the summit, only about 80 m above the lake. Climb the path and you will immediately see Atsız Gölü on the S side. The descent is less steep than the climb, but longer, as Atsız Gölü is slightly lower than Deniz Gölü. Since it's S-facing, it's likely to have less snow around. You can camp on the margins of the lake. To join the route below, climb SW onto the top of a low ridge which descends into the valley below, running on the L/E side of the stream which forms the outlet of the lake and cascades in waterfalls down the valley. Follow a faint trail downhill over moraine and scree, to meet the other route at the junction of 2 streams. End.

Hevek Geçiti is due S of the campsite, in the R section of a semi-circular cirque. Climb the low moraine mass, which descends to the camp, aiming up a sidestream. Cross the stream and follow a ridge SSE and upwards - the faint path is marked by cairns. The path dips R then rises over another moraine ridge, aiming SSW at the R of 2 dips on the skyline, marked by a patch of red earth; we will actually cross E of this red patch (1 hr, D221).

Cross a shallow hollow, then pass over a series of small hillocks, still aiming at the red patch. Descend into the V-shaped valley which runs down from the pass and start to climb zigzags on scree to the R of the tiny stream. As the gradient lessens - and before an almost-permanent snow patch - cross to the L and start to zigzag upwards on a grassy ridge leading SSE (50 mins). As you approach a crag above, turn R then L and up some steep, loose hairpins over scree to a diagonal path leading R over some rocks to gain the pass (30 mins, D216).

From the top, you have impressive views N of Kaçkar and the N side of the Hevek Deresi and to the S lies the broad, green Soğanlı Deresi, bordered on the L by scree slopes and on the R by grassy slopes leading to Danma Gölü and Soğanlı Dağı. Far ahead is the large village of Sırakonaklar, in the valley below.

Cross diagonally R/SW across the bowl at the head of the Soğanlı Deresi to the L side of Soğanlı Dağı (25 mins). Skirt the L slope on a very faint trail running over the scree to reach a grassy valley with a stream which descends from the col you want to cross; it's clearly silhouetted above you. This could be a good campsite. Climb the S side of the valley onto a low ridge and cross diagonally onto the moraine bank which retains the lake - there's no path but it's easy going. Beyond the bank, the lake is far below in a steep-sided cirque (1 hr, C176).

Climb gently N to the top of the ridge on the R and head into the shallow bowl at the foot of the obvious col. On the L of the col is a low ridge leading NW - it's easy going to walk up the ridge, then bear R and over the top of some rocks, meeting the main ridge just below the col (1 hr 35 mins, C178).

A cairn marks the summit between 2 rock buttresss and, opposite, seemingly close enought to touch, is the craggy peak of Okuzyatağı Tepesi and beyond it the Kaçkar massif. The valley below slopes steeply down to the L and the head of the Davali Deresi and the peaks of the Verçenik Dağları beyond. At the head of the valley on the R is Atsız Gölü but it's hidden by moraine and scree. There may be cattle or goats and shepherds below. The descent at first looks impossibly steep but it isn't. The long, straight slope starts with muddy streaks alternating with small stone scree. On each side are rocky crags which may look easier but it's best to keep away from them as the rock is loose and crumbly. About 1/3 of the way down are several large rocks set in the scree - keep to the R side and descend on larger scree between the rocks and the crag. The descent then opens out a bit and you can continue R, where the slope is slightly less steep. The gradient gradually eases up and you finish on a grassy band which continues to the foot of the valley. To the L of the foot of the col is an enclosure with huge stone walls, once used for penning animals. The walls give some shelter for a camp, but the floor is stony; in good weather, a small mound at the entry to the enclosure is a better bet (45 mins, C180).

The route now countours Peşevit Sırtı, on the NW of the valley, to reach the highest part of the Davali Deresi. Start downhill SW and cross 2 streams at their junction, where there is a cairn. Continue downhill on cow-trails, aiming at the L side of the moraine mass below, passing L of a barınak and some marshy ground. Bear R/W towards the ridge, crossing several small streams and aiming at an open grassy patch surrounded by a circle of rocks (40 mins, C188). This is the start of a faint path leading NW around the ridge; it fades out as it turns the corner but then becomes clear again going NNW (30 mins, C191).

THE KAÇKAR

WP	Lat (N)	Long (E)	Alt (m)
D223	40.82063	41.17864	2882
D221	40.81444	41.18007	3023
D219	40.81020	41.18030	3102
D216	40.80698	41.18057	3271
C172	40.80470	41.17754	3255
C174	40.80268	41.17488	3270
C176	40.80068	41.16937	3256
C177	40.80305	41.16695	3325
C178	40.80310	41.16508	3368
C179	40.80415	41.16449	3405
C180	40.80567	41.16026	3191
C183	40.80364	41.15583	3112
C184	40.80238	41.15364	3082
C185	40.80050	41.15007	3015
C187	40.79904	41.14703	2919
C188	40.79853	41.14348	2846
C189	40.79776	41.14090	2807
C190	40.80030	41.13719	2825
C191	40.80603	41.13476	2874
C192	40.80530	41.13170	2870
C193	40.80683	41.12986	2924
C196	40.80770	41.12209	3024
C197	40.80908	41.11686	3080
C201	40.81081	41.11155	3080
C202	40.81194	41.11197	3128
C204	40.81368	41.11145	3061
C206	40.81555	41.11016	2971
C207	40.81679	41.10940	2874
C209	40.82271	41.10820	2745
C210	40.82482	41.10542	2795
C214	40.83574	41.09749	2616
C211	40.83949	41.09874	2533
C212	40.83696	41.09905	2548
C214	40.83574	41.09749	2616
C215	40.83626	41.09372	2709
C219	40.83431	41.08528	2849
C220	40.83548	41.08388	2808
C222	40.83386	41.08248	2752
E044	40.83526	41.07653	2667
E043	40.84115	41.07577	2598
C226	40.84863	41.07313	2518
C227	40.85308	41.07226	2513
E040	40.85696	41.07063	2490
C229	40.86125	41.06263	2450

12.7 Dilberdüzü, Hevek Geçiti, Davaliaşıtı, Apivanak Yaylası, Karmık Yaylası, Tirovit

THE KAÇKAR

On the far side of the ridge is a wide basin with plenty of water and grazing, ringed by the sharp-spired peaks of Kaçkar and its western extremities. To the R of a conical peak is the Kavron Geçiti and the Davaliaşıtı is WNW and out of sight. The basin forms a hanging valley above the Davali Deresi and below/L the path to the Hodacur Geçiti and Davaliaşıtı is visible in the bottom. Our pathless route continues across the basin to a ridge, Tepe Sırtı, crowned with rocks, between us and the pass. On its slope a path is just visible. Aim NNW and cross the first, wide stream at a pile of rocks where there's a cascade (10 mins). Continue cross-country to the base of a large rock buttress where there's a level, grassy area and plenty of streams. Continue over the streams and climb a bank to turn R on a narrow path which rise up the hillside - this is the path from Davali to the Kavron Geçit. Almost immediately, at some rocks, the path divides; turn L/up from the Kavron path onto the narrow but clear path which rises NW up Tepe Sırtı (25 mins, C193).

At the top of the hill, turn R to a large cairn (there is another below it) (10 mins). Cross a tiny stream on a straight, sometimes indistinct, path which runs W, straight for Davaliaşıtı, which is visible on the horizon and partly masked by the slopes of the hill to the R of it. The path, clearer now, rounds the ridge just before the pass, and the route rising straight from the Davali Deresi runs clearly on the hillside ahead (40 mins, C198).

There may have once been a path on our side of this ridge but rock-fall has made the slope dangerous. Descend to a cairn in the wide, boggy green bowl crossed by streams (15 mins). Cross the bowl to a second stream from which you can clearly see the pass and the cairns on its summit. Walk up the far side of the bowl to join the path from Davali. The path climbs straight NE and then over a series of gentle, wide zigzags to the pass (30 mins, C202).

From the pass, there's a good view down the huge, straight U-shaped Polavit Deresi below, to the 'dolls-houses' of Apivanak. Looking very carefully, you can see the path down the valley, crossing the stream from R to L and rising on the L bank, then running horizontally along the slope towards Apivanak. Behind, the Davali Deresi stretches out in a similar shape but to the SW is shallow Döner Gölü, in a basin on the far side of the valley. The pass you are standing on was once the divide between 2 huge glaciers.

The descending path runs in clear, built-up hairpins, straight down to the valley below but with an optional detour to the L to avoid snow (the pass faces due N). Its condition is excellent, mainly paved and with a retaining wall. There is a moraine and rock step jutting out over the valley part of the way down. Start the descent on zigzags leading to the bottom of the scree band. The diversion starts here but, unless the snow is deep and soft, there is no need to use it (25 mins, C204).

Continue down the main hairpins, towards the moraine step, where the diversion rejoins. The path runs close to a rock wall on the L and down to a headland below, then continues down the L of the headland. The path swings L/W; opposite and above is a tarn, Çukur Gölü, above a rocky bank. The outflow is a steep waterfall and the noise of water echoes in the valley. The last hairpin has very steep stone steps and the bottom of the pass is marked by a cairn (30 mins, C207).

The path continues for about 50 m across scree then seems to disappear. The original trail seems to be completely destroyed and you should not try to cross the jumble of large rocks, bogs and streams in front of you. Instead, turn R/ENE and

THE KAÇKAR

contour across the slope on a rocky path to a grass and boulder bank which slopes down towards the valley floor, on the E side of a secondary stream. Turn L and continue down towards the main stream bed; cross it at a line of stones and climb the opposite bank in a hairpin to find the old route below a large rock buttress (1 hr, C210). The faint, grassy path becomes a clear built-up path as it contours the hillside before descending a side valley towards the yayla (40 mins, C214).

Continue on the L bank towards Apivanak and cross the stream by a lovely old arched bridge (10 mins, C211). You could camp on the meadows by the stream.

> Apivanak/Hapivanak/Apivanag Yaylası, with 20 single-storey houses at an altitude of 2600 m, is set near the head of a wide, bare glaciated valley below the Davaliaşıtı S-bound pass which leads to Erzurum. The houses were originally built with an oak shingle roof, which was cut from the forest in the Palovit Deresi, on stone walls; nowadays most roofs are of corrugated iron. The majority of residents come from Pazar and Hemşin and stay 2 months with their cattle; they make cheese and cream. The access road is in very poor condition, and often not open until June-July.

Additional walk from Apivanak to Anadağ: Cross to the W bank of the stream via the charming hump-back bridge a short way S of the campsite. Head S up the valley, rising steadily, to a dry gully (35 mins). Turn R/W up the gully and climb for 10 minutes, before turning S again to contour the valley side on clear, built up path. Reach and cross a rocky sidestream beneath a massive rock buttress known as Dilbi Kaya (1 hr 40 mins). Continue S towards the broad, moraine filled head of the valley, crossing the main stream, then contour E around the head of the valley (boulder hopping across giant scree in places) to the foot of a prominent couloir (1 hr 45 mins). Scramble up the steep ridge to the R of the couloir (15 mins), emerging at the outlet of beautiful Anadağ Gölü (2970 m). A swim in the icy cold but crystal clear, snow-melt water of this exquisite cirque lake more than justifies the effort of getting here. Retrace your steps down the couloir, then drop straight down to the valley floor and follow the W bank of the stream back to Apivanak (2 hrs). *End.*

Cross the bridge upstream of Apivanak and climb the valley side to the R/SW to a level area near where the paths divide (30 mins, C214). Keep R and cross the shallow valley bottom; continue climbing a spur on your R towards a spiky ridge with an obvious col to the SW. Bear L/up towards a bank which closes off a small düzlük, zigzagging up alongside the stream to crest the bank next to the stream, which flows through a bowl of jumbled rocks. The faint path runs to the R of the stream and continues as a diagonal scar running from R to L just below the col. Climb the final zigzags to the crest of the col (1 hr 15 mins, C219).

Karmık Yaylası is now in view below, on the far side of the wide, empty U-shaped valley. From the col, descend a couple of zigzags before traversing R/N across the hillside on a long diagonal, passing over a small pınar. Turn L/down onto a mound, turn back L and recross the foot of the col. It's all easy going and if you are sure footed and have a light pack you could head straight down the grassy slope. Continue to the L/S, where the path becomes lost amongst stones and overgrown grass on a gentle slope, which you must negotiate to the bottom of the valley. Cross the Karmık Deresi to reach Karmık Yaylası (see page 137) (45 mins, C223).

12.7 Dilberdüzü, Hevek Geçiti, Davaliaşıtı, Apivanak Yaylası, Karmık Yaylası, Tirovit

The valley above the yayla is a long and wide glaciated basin, with no sign of habitation, and bordered by seemingly impassable scree except towards Yıldızlı Gölü; see route 14.4. Wander more or less N through the empty houses to the start of a faint track which runs down the valley. After some boggy, uncertain going the path becomes an old, paved road (50 mins, E042). The paved section, across marshy ground, soon ends. Stone-walled hayfields mark the approach to Tirovit and the path runs in narrow slots between these walls into the village (40 mins, C229).

From Tirovit it's 6 km down a badly maintained dirt road to Elevit (2 hrs). It is dull walking but, if you miss the bus, any passing vehicle will offer you a lift.

Alternative route: It is possible (and, if there's no mist, more fun) to walk down the N side of the Elevit Deresi, where there are a few scattered buildings but the path is so little used now it's almost impossible to follow. Persevere over bogs and rock outcrops until you approach Karunç Yayalası, on a slope above the rapidly steepening valley. Just before the yayla, you should turn down to the river and take the footbridge (B005) to a vehicle track rising R/W to the main dirt road. From here, walk between lush vegetation and patches of forest down into Elevit (D240) (see route 14.3) (4 hrs). *End.*

12.8 Olgunlar, Kanucar Geçiti, Dargit Yaylası, Yüncüler *(7 hrs 50 mins)*

This route, running SSE from Olgunlar, is also a little-used trans of the Güngörmez Dağları, leading up a steep-sided valley S of Olgunlar then crossing a pass into a wide valley headed by Dargit Yaylası. Below the yayla is a cluster of villages, famous for many years for their cloth and now known as Dokumacılar (the Weavers) and Yüncüler (Woolmakers). They are connected to Yaylalar by a daily dolmuş leaving around 7 am. No proper paths exist until you reach the yayla; you should take compass bearings and, if possible, use a GPS.

From the W bridge in Olgunlar (C063), cross the bridge and head straight up the bank to the S, straight towards the small hill Cudi Sırtı. The narrow and overgrown path runs straight up between low stone walls, then starts to zigzag, still between walls. It then runs diagonally on the open hillside to the L/SW, passes around a large

WP	Lat (N)	Long (E)	Alt (m)
C063	40.85956	41.23919	2076
C001	40.85479	41.24156	2279
C002	40.85495	41.24313	2315
C251	40.85222	41.24462	2382
C241	40.84978	41.24531	2449
C242	40.84796	41.24573	2533
C244	40.84306	41.24631	2695
C245	40.84071	41.24743	2746
C246	40.83745	41.25085	2850
C270	40.83340	41.25528	3070
C249	40.83102	41.25692	2975
C271	40.82625	41.26600	2800
C272	40.82079	41.27535	2570
C273	40.81131	41.27805	2340

THE KAÇKAR

rock and turns towards the summit, continuing to climb. It passes a junction with a narrow path; the main path runs straight on, then L and diagonally upwards past a walled enclosure on the L/E which has 2 stone pillars at the gate on the lower side. The path continues S between a bank and the wall of the enclosure (45 mins, C002). At the end of the wall, our faint path continues into a broad basin broken up by marshy areas. There is a cattle track across the hillside ahead which runs into the valley leading to the pass; join this path, then, as it approaches the stream, cross to the far side and continue upwards (15 mins, C241).

Cross a side valley - the path is clear but stranded and well used by cattle - then cross a mossy sidestream bed. The path runs alongside the stream, then turns L/up the hillside, then R again, climbing a rut in grass towards a bluff and zigzagging towards the top of a bluff. On top, the path becomes clearer and veers close to the stream gulley. It then climbs towards a bank across the valley and passes over a lip into a wide grassy basin which slopes gradually upwards and is bisected by a stream (1 hr 20 mins, C244).

Your overall direction is now SE. Cross the stream to the R and continue up a low ridge parallel with the stream then cross the stream to the L. Climb to the top of a low ridge, then to a small cirque below the pass, keeping the stream on your R. The faint path rises up a couloir then cuts L diagonally onto a scree bank and turns R over a boulder towards the pass (1 hr, C248).

Continue towards the pass on the R of the shallow couloir, on a faint path. From the pass, you can see - across a wide basin bisected by a stream bed - Dargit Yaylası. Rounded hills rise all around the basin, except behind the yayla, which commands the entrance to the valley of the Hüngemek Deresi. Descend SE down to the stream bed, which then swings S. At a junction of streams, cross the main stream bed and descend a ridge to the yayla (1 hr 20 mins, C273).

> **Dargit Yaylası** is at 2350 m, on a SE-facing slope above the junction of 2 streams. It's used for sheep grazing by people from Yüncüler and Dokumacılar, villages 7 or 8 km further down the valley. We don't have information about its current condition.

Turn L and cross the stream again to a second group of houses. Beyond the yayla, both banks of the stream are high and steep and the N bank is rocky. Turn down to the valley bottom and follow the track with the stream on your R for about 5 km downhill between juniper-clad slopes, past various groups of houses to Beşkavak, a mahalle of Yüncüler and the end of the dirt road (1 hr 40 mins).

12.8 Olgunlar, Kanucar Geçiti, Dargit Yaylası, Yüncüler

Chapter 13 **ROUTES NORTH OF THE RANGE – AYDER AND THE NATIONAL PARK**

This area is the most popular in the Kaçkar range. Ayder is the main gateway to the National Park and hosts thousands of mainly Turkish tourists each year. However, very few of these visitors are walkers so, although the dirt roads, picnic sites and Yukarı Kavron are extremely busy, noisy and sometimes dirty, you only have to walk a few minutes up one of our routes to find solitude and silence. The advantage of this tourist influx is that in Ayder there is a range of accommodation, a good choice of restaurants, plenty of public transport and the necessary shops. Ayder is also renowned for its vast, marble-lined, public thermal baths. The natural thermal pools (separate sections for men and women) are a good place to end a week's trekking - the steaming water soon soothes aches and overworked muscles and you can scrape off the layers of dirt and have a massage. Take a swimsuit and your own shampoo; towels are provided.

Ayder is a long ribbon of a village set between marvellous fir forests, often dripping with lichen, and with barrel beehives suspended in the treetops. Many buildings are still in traditional style and set amongst green meadows, but some concrete has intruded. Unfortunately, local day walks are strictly limited - most visitors don't walk and, due to lack of use, the old footpaths have closed up. Above Ayder, the trailhead yaylas of Yukarı Kavron, the Çaymakçurs and Palakçur are all set on the treeline in wide U-shaped valleys where trailfinding is not a problem and marvellous views open up as you ascend towards the granite ridges ahead.

Mist often rises up the northern valleys in the afternoon, so start walking early and try to cross to the S side before the mist rolls in.

13.1 Ayder, Huzur Yaylası, Ayder (6 hrs 45 mins)

A steep ascent through meadow and dense forest leads to Huzer Yaylası, situated on a grassy ridge above the forest. On a clear day there are lovely views E and SE to the main Kaçkar range. You could optionally explore the ridge before

WP	Lat (N)	Long (E)	Alt (m)
D006	40.95186	41.11951	1370
D008	40.95827	41.11975	1577
D009	40.96130	41.12074	1720
D010	40.96282	41.12278	1872
D014	40.96663	41.12136	2026
D011	40.96839	41.11824	2100
D012	40.97373	41.11704	2340
D011	40.96839	41.11824	2100
D014	40.96663	41.12136	2026
D015	40.96443	41.12423	2030
D016	40.96118	41.13838	1860
D017	40.95853	41.14241	1763
D123	40.95739	41.13392	1579
D121	40.95545	41.12974	1503
D006	40.95186	41.11951	1370

returning down to Periyatağı Yaylası. An easy descent on forest road, passing a couple of tumbling cascades, leads back to Ayder.

From central Ayder (C155), head ESE up the main Yukarı Kavron road to the sharp R bend approaching Avusor Deresi. The footpath begins just before the bridge at a çeşme near the Balcı Derviş café (40 mins, D006).

Ascend the zigzag path heading due N, passing through cultivated land to the highest of a scattering of wooden houses (45 mins). With the roar of the stream to your L ringing in your ears, continue zigzagging steeply upwards to the start of the forest (30 mins, D008). The clear path emerges briefly from the forest, with a wooden house visible at 150°, before plunging back into the trees (50 mins). It continues through forest onto a long, grassy ridge where it becomes less distinct (15 mins). Continue N, up steep meadowland, to a locked wooden house above the tree-line (5 mins). The path now runs E/up to another locked house, surrounded by nettles, just below a newly bulldozed forest road (15 mins, D014).

To explore the ridgetop, turn E on the dirt road and follow it E/SE as it rises up the hillside to Huzur Yaylası (50 mins, D012).

> **Huzur/Huzer Yaylası**, built in wood on stone foundations, is the highest of several on a grassy ridge which rises above trees just E of Ayder. It has wonderful views S to the Altıparmak Dağları. Currently almost abandoned, the new and ugly bulldozed road may well lead to reoccupation.

Alternative: From Huzur Yaylası, you could climb diagonally R/ENE towards the ridgetop. Here, turn R/SE and follow paths along the ridge towards Didiruba Deresi. After this valley, the paths decend to Periyatağı Yaylası where you join the bulldozed road. End.

To return directly to Ayder, turn R/W on the road and continue downhill. A small waterfall sprinkles water across the road (45 mins). The road joins the wider Ayder - Avusor Yaylası road at Taşlık Yaylası (10 mins, D017). Turn R/SW here and continue descending, passing a pretty waterfall to the L and a lone house above the road to the R (30 mins). The road crosses a stream, with a long, thin ribbon of waterfall away to the L, before meeting the Ayder - Kavron road (20 mins). Turn sharp R, cross the bridge, passing the Balcı Derviş café and return to Ayder (40 mins, D006).

13.2 Ayder, Hazındak, Pokut Yaylası, Sal Yaylası *(9 hrs 5 mins)*

A tough, clothes-tearing uphill walk through deep forest to Hazındak is followed by a lovely stroll on partly paved old road to Pokut. You can then either stay in Pokut Yaylası and complete the walk the following day, or arrange a lift down the dirt road to Şenyuva and Çamlıhemşin. We also describe the old ridgetop mulepath to Çamlıhemşin, now overgrown. If you attempt this route, go in a group, take sufficient water and be prepared to camp.

In central Ayder (D020), turn down the underpass close to the main bus stop. At the end of the paved road, continue towards the river towards a footbridge below the Yeşilvadı hotel. Turn up and R on footpath and pass above a deserted hamam building (15 mins, D021).

The path starts behind the hamam and climbs upward through dense deciduous forest with a messy understorey. It runs W, sometimes over streambeds, over roots and slippery rocks, to round a corner of a spur where it zigzags up to reach a water-

THE KAÇKAR

WP	Lat (N)	Long (E)	Alt (m)
C155	40.95463	41.09833	1182
D020	40.95257	41.09700	1182
D021	40.95111	41.09219	1376
D022	40.94864	41.09051	1451
D023	40.94472	41.08439	1850
D024	40.93806	41.07499	1770
D025	40.93436	41.07420	1820
D026	40.93224	41.07011	1970
D027	40.93664	41.07051	1960
D001	40.94335	41.06729	1960
D028	40.95257	41.05630	1885
D029	40.95752	41.04500	1990
D030	40.96090	41.03713	2018
D031	40.96323	41.03389	2067
D032	40.96203	41.02911	2059
D033	40.96277	41.02563	2051
D034	40.95938	41.01994	1969
D002	40.96535	41.01908	2060
D003	40.98150	41.02382	1870
D004	41.00121	41.02181	1600
D005	41.01183	41.02396	1470
D255	41.02453	41.01040	606
D254	41.02429	41.00927	620
D257	41.03000	41.00859	415
D258	41.02749	41.00409	370

alternative

fall and a small open area (45 min). Cross the sidestream below the waterfall and climb again into the undergrowth. The ridgetop is now intermittently visible. The path continues W/upwards, mainly on zigzags, diagonally across the slope to pass around a spur to a clearing where you have views back over the valley and on towards the yayla (1 hr 35 mins, D023).

Continue S, across a slope with rhododendron bushes alongside the slippery path, in dense but more scrubby forest, descending slightly and crossing a rocky gully. The path continues SW across the slope, descending towards a stream in the valley ahead. Across the steam, scarcely more than a trickle, the path turns up the valley through an open area, then again into trees, where it turns L/up a spur to zigzag across a slope and reach the S side of the yayla at a çeşme and graveyard (2 hrs, D025).

> **Hazındak Yaylası (Gazındağ, Hazındag, Hazındağ)** has around 25 houses situated at 1900 m on a ridge just above the forest. The houses are mostly timber and charmingly fitted with original hand-made locks and hinges. Inhabitants return from Bursa and Istanbul for the summer; the yayla is in use in July and August. Until very recently, access was on foot only, usually from Amlakit and Samistal, as the Ayder path is very steep and overgrown. A new road from Pokut is now complete but apparently it avoids the old paved path.

13.2 Ayder, Hazındak, Pokut Yaylası, Sal Yaylası

From the çeşme, walk due N along a ridge towards Pokut. The first section is with ridgetop on the L, through the upper levels of the forest, with views glimpsed between the trees, much bird life and occasional pig prints. The path bends L around a çeşme and stream head, then runs NW (45 mins). As the ridge drops, the path crosses to run over a paved section on the W side of the ridge where the forest drops away very steeply below the path. The path climbs to a second then third col where there is a well-constructed memorial fountain (35 mins, D029).

From here, the path contours for a while, then rises to open meadow with a few rhododendrons and many orchids on Oba Dağı. This is the high point of the walk and the views over the surrounding forest and valleys are magnificent, especially in the evenings when mist is rising in the valleys and the ridges look like islands in a sunlit sea. Beyond, the peaks on the horizon include Kemerli Kaçkar and the spikes of the Bulut Dağları. Pokut Yaylası is on a spur to the S and Sal Yaylası on the next spur beyond. A narrow path contours the hillside towards the yayla and descends to the upper houses (55 mins, D033).

> Pokut Yaylası has 55 mainly timber houses and lies on a ridge just above the tree-line, at about 2000 m. Up to 170 summer residents come from Konaklar Mahallesi at Çamlıhemşin, Ortan Köy and Boğaziçi Köy; a newly-improved jeep road leads to the yayla. There is a small pension (the muhtar's house at the extreme end of the ridge) but no regular transport or shop.

Alternative walk to Çamlıhemşin: There used to be a long (12 km) and well-used mule route from Pokut to Çamlıhemşin and you could investigate this. It was once partly paved but is now in an overgrown condition. Since it runs along a ridge, however, it has good views and should be fairly easy to find. From Pokut Yaylası, walk N, skirting the W side of Oba Dağı and follow the descending ridge which leads N between forested slopes. Keep L/W of a couple of summits on the ridge, above steep valleys on the L, then descend on hairpins to a col with a steep valley to the E/R. Here a path branches off L towards Şenyuva in the valley due W; it's unlikely to be usable. Climb up to the continuation of the ridge, which bends R/NE; the forest gives way to open meadow. The path branches around a summit; you could follow the ridge on either side. The route continues N in forest, descends steeply to a col, then passes W of a summit, E of another and continues to descend. By now, the route is in thick old forest with rhododendron understorey and probably quite indistinct.

It bends L/W and emerges on a tea plantation with 3 houses around it. Cross the plantation towards the W, walking along the eroded edge above a sheer drop, and descend a short slope onto the dirt track beyond. Turn R and descend to cross a stream then climb L on the far side. Here the condition of the track improves and, a little further on, the surface is concreted. At a fork, turn L and descend the slopes to a junction between an old house and a bridge, passing the water works buildings on the R. Turn R over the bridge to Konaklar Mahallesi, and R again on the road to walk 1-2 km to Çamlıhemşin. **End.**

A path from the lower part of Pokut Yaylası carries on to the ridge on the W and to Sal Yaylası (15 mins). A zigzag track descends Pilinçut Sırtı to Şenyuva, a walk of about 9 km, reaching the Fırtına Deresi road near the Muhtar's building just S of the Taşkemer bridge and the Doğa Hotel. In places you may be able to walk on the old path instead of the road, cutting the zigzags. Turn R and walk to the hotel where you could stay or ask them to call you a taxi (2 hrs).

13.3 Yukarı Kavron, Aşağı Kavron, Aşağı Çaymakçur, Palakçur, Avusor Yaylası (10 hrs 45 mins)

This route follows a series of paths, which connect the yaylas on the N side of the range. The first part (on an old road) and the last (past Büyük Göl) are very pleasant sections which you could do as day walks. Sections of this trek are also useful if you want to do 2 routes across the range in succession. Use the daily dolmuş from Ayder to Yukarı Kavron or to Avusor to access the route.

> **Yukarı Kavron Yaylası**, at 2260 m, has 100-120 mainly stone houses; temporary wooden buildings are used as cafés for day visitors. There is a kahve/bakery, a line of wooden buildings used as a pension and a kahve/shop by the bridge at the entrance to the village. The yayla is used as a starting point for trekking tours as it's only 8 km from Kaçkar peak itself. It is inhabited from the first week in June until the end of September or even later, but the peak tourism period is in August. At that time, it is overcrowded with day visitors (up to 1000 visitors per day); waste disposal is inadequate and waste water is discharged into the river. Some of the locals still keep cattle, but most are involved in tourism. A 12 km dirt road from Ayder terminates at Yukarı Kavron bridge.

The old road runs parallel to and below the new road to Aşağı Kavron Yaylası. Most of it is very wide and edged by huge kerbstones, often concealed under lush grass. Leave Yukarı Kavron (D035) by the new concrete bridge which is just above an ancient stone clapper bridge. Carry on down the road, until the old road below becomes clear, then descend and pass below a large rock just above the old path (10 mins, D036).

Cross a sidestream, then (55 mins) cross the main road at a bend onto grassy slopes. Almost immediately, re-cross the road and descend diagonally NNE over a headland high above the river; in this area the path is not clear. The upper mahalle of Aşağı Kavron Yaylası lies above our old road; the path passes through an area of weeds and mud, where it's unclear, then between the scattered houses of the lower mahalle, where it is paved with huge stones (45 mins, D043).

> **Aşağı Kavron/Kavran Yaylası**, at just below 2000 m, has 2 districts with some 6 wooden houses in each. The inhabitants come from Çamlıhemşin and keep cattle there for 3-4 months during the summer. The surrounding slopes are covered with rhododendron scrub, which restricts grazing.

Just past the second mahalle, the path meets a secondary bulldozed track leading down to the stream. Turn R and walk up the track to meet the main track (5 mins). Turn R on this and find a footpath which turns L off the road at the highest point above the yayla, on the L of some ruined buildings. This turns L/NE and climbs very gently across the hillside, crossing a tiny stream and reaching a ridge (15 mins). Here it turns R/SE to cross a larger sidestream, then NE again towards Meşe Tepesi, a small bare hill above the rhododendrons and scrub. Contour to the next slight ridge then bear R and climb up it to cross a couple of gullies, still amongst the rhododendrons (1 hr 25 mins, D054).

WP	Lat (N)	Long (E)	Alt (m)
D035	40.88415	41.13123	2225
D036	40.88720	41.12987	2217
D037	40.88992	41.13103	2089
C105	40.89385	41.13117	2074
D040	40.89890	41.13290	2077
D041	40.90136	41.13348	2045
D042	40.90545	41.13629	1991
D043	40.90808	41.13782	1969
D038	40.90918	41.14085	2000
D070	40.91060	41.14758	2120
D062	40.91880	41.15462	2180
D054	40.91373	41.16322	1920
D073	40.91114	41.16565	1980
D051	40.92112	41.16942	2100
D048	40.92609	41.16888	2170
D045	40.92686	41.17616	2100
C150	40.92730	41.17818	2172
C149	40.92834	41.17933	2232
D046	40.92938	41.18080	2238
D047	40.93057	41.18286	2319
D049	40.93241	41.18548	2461
D052	40.93414	41.19195	2717
D053	40.93693	41.18867	2772
D055	40.93798	41.18991	2734
D056	40.93699	41.19131	2719
D061	40.93908	41.19344	2629
D063	40.93928	41.19509	2613
D064	40.93921	41.19757	2644
D065	40.93743	41.19866	2650
D064	40.93921	41.19757	2644
D068	40.94214	41.19482	2522
D069	40.95145	41.19416	2428
D071	40.95145	41.19167	2370
D126	40.95255	41.19157	2307

Bear R around Meşe Tepesi about 100 m below the summit and bear L, descending the far side to meet the Aşağı Çaymakçur dirt road at a çeşme. Turn R and walk into Aşağı Çaymakçur (see page 101), branching L after the bridge towards the end of the road (25 mins, D073).

Walk through the upper district of Aşağı Çaymakçur on a rising path which runs NNE, climbing diagonally up the slopes through rhododendrons. After crossing some sidestreams, it climbs more steeply over a spur, crosses another gully and rounds a ridge to run ENE (1 hr 5 mins). From here, the route to Palakçur is a short and gentle descent to a couple of upper houses then more steeply to the road and bridge (20 mins, D045).

13.3 Yukarı Kavron, Aşağı Kavron, Aşağı Çaymakçur, Palakçur, Avusor Yaylası

> **Palakçur Yaylası** has 3 districts at 2100 m - either high on the steep slopes of the valley side or by the river. There are about 20 mainly wooden houses in good condition and others in a state of collapse. It's used by people from the Ardeşen area, arriving from the end of May onwards and departing in October; in July up to 85 people live in the yayla. A dirt road now links the yayla with Ayder, 5.5 km away, so families come and go by car. The road crosses the river by a concrete bridge and runs as far as the N mahalle. Electricity is connected and water comes from a çeşme at the top of the yayla.

There are 2 alternative routes from Palakçur to Avusor; only the first is suitable for mules.

Alternative (long) route: Follow the road to the end and climb up above the far district to find a well-used cattle path going NW and rising slightly across the hillside (ignore the lower path). Follow this N over a stream bed, then as it turns W and climbs towards a couple of houses on a ridge above rhododendrons and scrub. From here, Sele Geçiti is visible to the NW, immediately above the main stream gully. For 2 km, contour round the upper basin with the ridge on your L to reach the col. There's a faint path and the route is obvious; it's also easy for a mule. From the col, the direct (mule) route continues straight down towards the main stream and Avusor below. End.

The more direct route climbs steeply up the gully behind the yayla, almost directly to the col. Climb on zigzags to the highest house of Palakçur and pass L of it on narrow stony track which descends to the stream gully. Cross the stream, climb the far bank and turn R/uphill on the W side of the valley (15 mins, D046).

Climb steep zigzags between the river and the buttress ahead. Continue to a sidestream and cross it, then turn up/L on zigzags up a steep grassy slope. The gradient lessens and, looking back, you can see the village again, far below. Continue to zigzag up, crossing 2 small streams; there are a few scrubby rhododendrons in this area. Aim NE towards the skyline above the main gully, where there is a large, shallow cirque and a col (1 hr 45 mins, D052).

When the gradient lessens, with the cirque on your R, turn L/NW and climb a faint diagonal path to the ridge, aiming towards the second, western col on the skyline. Another path crosses the stream far below/R then climbs to meet our path, which becomes clearer as you approach the col diagonally (55 mins, D053). Avusor is on the far side of the valley below, with a confusion of deeply eroded stream-beds in front of it. Kemerli Kaçkar is on the R, but Büyük Göl is invisible in a cirque. The alternative (mule) path meets here.

The route to the lake (not suitable for mules) turns R on a clear path running E over a small headland, through rhodendrons and crosses a rocky bowl to the moraine bank retaining the lake. Start by descending gently along this clear path then, below a rock face, turn down onto a slight spur. Avoid the large broken rocks and scree and descend towards the stream bed below (25 mins, D061).

Turn R on a very faint, rough path which crosses the valley-bottom stream. On the far side, turn R on a better path leading up a ridge towards the lake (50 mins, D065). Büyük Göl is in a cirque, surrounded by scree and snow and fed by several small streams which cascade down the rocky walls surrounding it. The water is clear and mainly shallow but bitterly cold. The lake shore would be a good place to camp as there are pleasant level grassy areas on the N side. On the R is a peak decorated with a huge Turkish flag.

To continue to Avusor, return down the footpath over the moraine, then take the path running diagonally R/NW down a slope to the R of the stream (20 mins, D068). At the bottom, the path disappears so follow the L bank of a mill channel, which is ducted off the main stream near here, downhill towards Avusor (see page 124). As you approach a football field, cross to the R bank of the mill-stream and pass the mulepath coming in directly from the col (40 mins, D071). The final approach to the yayla is down a bank to the river, across a bridge and up hairpins to the houses on the opposite bank (15 mins, D126).

13.4 Ayder, Aşağı Çaymakçur, Yukarı Çaymakçur Yaylas, Körahmet Geçiti, Bulut Deresi, Satelef Yaylası, Körahmet Mahallesi, Karamolla Mahallesi, Yaylalar (15 hrs).

This tough route crosses the Bulut Dağları close to the Naletleme Geçiti. However, the ascent is from the upper Çaymakçur Deresi (rather than the Kavron Deresi) and the descent down the Bulut Deresi direct to Yaylalar (rather than to Olgunlar). Before corrugated iron was available, the pass was used for carrying wooden roofing shingles from the forests of the N to the yaylas in the S. It was used by walking groups in the 1980's but, with the rise of Yukarı Kavron Yaylası, was abandoned in favour of the Naletleme Geçiti. On the N side, the paths are in poor condition and the descent from the pass is now over scree, as access to the old path has been eroded. However, the descent down the Bulut Deresi to Yaylalar is an easy and pleasant one on good paths.

After crossing the pass, we include an alternative cross-country route over the head of the Bulut Deresi directly to Dilberdüzü campsite for climbing Kaçkar. The upper Bulut Deresi has a variety of terrain, including rhododendron bushes, is secluded and a good place for wild animal and bird watching.

You could camp on either side of the pass; take poles for use on the scree.

Take the dolmuş from Ayder to Kaler Düzü (C153) which is on the way to Yukarı Kavron. From here, walk to the junction just past the campsite and turn L onto the Aşağı Çaymakçur road.

Walk up the track, passing the L turning to Palakçur and continuing along the river. Cross the lower bridge at the remains of a small yayla; continue rising into the forest and round a hairpin bend then cross the upper bridge just below Aşağı Çaymakçur (1 hr 10 mins, D073). Walk up towards the village and turn R onto the old paved road, which runs SSE below the new road; the starting point is about 80 m above the bridge but it's not obvious.

Walk up the old paved road (a delightful reminder of a former way of life) parallel and above the river as far as a side stream, the Cennevit Deresi. Here, you will have to climb up to the modern road and cross by the ford (1 hr 10 mins). About 1 km further along the dirt road, it forks. Turn L/upwards to a building yard between a few cottages, with piles of sand and bricks (20 mins, D075).

Scramble up 5 m to the R and find a path rising across hillside, aiming at the valley from which the Cennevit stream issues. The path has an irrigation channel running alongside, and in places is flooded; in places stone walls edge the path. Climbing up zigzags, aiming NNE, the path gains a first ridge then crosses a dip to pass over a second ridge (1 hr, D076).

WP	Lat (N)	Long (E)	Alt (m)
C153	40.92777	41.14558	1691
C152	40.92575	41.15851	1826
D072	40.92108	41.16370	1852
D054	40.91373	41.16322	1920
D073	40.91114	41.16565	1980
D079	40.90301	41.17168	2040
D074	40.89659	41.17615	2268
D075	40.89799	41.17690	2335
D076	40.90138	41.17749	2385
D077	40.90131	41.17953	2394
D078	40.89977	41.18364	2490
D080	40.89852	41.18662	2560
D082	40.89666	41.19040	2712
D084	40.89737	41.19247	2801
D087	40.89827	41.19573	2937
D088	40.89571	41.20243	3014
D089	40.89323	41.20429	3135
D091	40.89349	41.20598	3169
D093	40.89210	41.20845	2994
D094	40.89154	41.21352	2931
D095	40.89138	41.21628	2874
D096	40.89130	41.21869	2788
D099	40.89055	41.22147	2729
D101	40.89185	41.22378	2665
D102	40.89419	41.22486	2636
D104	40.89587	41.22610	2593
D107	40.89774	41.22942	2513
D108	40.89950	41.23090	2485
D109	40.90214	41.23390	2406
C123	40.90533	41.23897	2380
C122	40.90586	41.24142	2375
C120	40.90344	41.24802	2361
C119	40.90241	41.25395	2252
C117	40.89655	41.26449	2195
B155	40.89060	41.26911	2157
C033	40.88797	41.27048	2097
C031	40.88434	41.27240	2053
C116	40.87268	41.27567	1840
C028	40.86996	41.27256	1838

You are now in a wide, straight and sloping valley, the Cennevit Deresi, with grassy slopes on the N and rhododendron-clad hills and hollows on the S. It runs SE up to a narrow, boulder-filled neck, with a headland on the R and rock slopes on the L. The path climbs parallel with the stream for 200 m and then turns down/L to cross it (10 mins). It rises up the N bank and turns uphill again, parallel with the stream. It is indistinct as it crosses a bed of boulders. At the junction of 2 streams, keep close to the L one. In places, the path is a well-defined mule trail but, in other places, almost invisble. It crosses a moraine mound and approaches a waterfall in the stream-bed. Keep on the L bank, rising towards the narrow neck and a wide bowl beyond it (1 hr 15 mins, D080).

The track swings L, away from the stream, to cross a band of boulders and then approaches the river on a diagonal. Cross the main stream to the R bank and turn upwards, then, soon after, re-cross and follow jumbled paths on the L bank over scree and boulders, through the neck, to a walled area which marks the start of the bowl. Past the enclosure there are flat camping areas, jumbles of rock and a headland on the R. On the L is a grass and scree slope, flanked by 2 large rocky buttresses, with faint tracks running up the grass. Ahead is a rock and scree cirque, with an obvious but inaccessible U-shaped col on the far side - this is just to the R of the one we will use and lower than our pass (1 hr 30 mins, D082).

If you walk up onto the rhododendron-covered headland on the R you have a spectacular view down the valley and to the Ayder area. During daylight you see the bulldozed tracks around Huzur Yaylası but, at night, you can see lights as far as the coast. There may be another path on the S side of the headland - there are some cairns here.

Access to our double pass is via the slope between the 2 buttresses, on a path running generally NE. Carry on up the main valley past the campsite until you are close to the R/SE buttress. Turn up a tiny stream running diagonally down the slope, until you find a path which runs diagonally L towards the L buttress. When you reach a rhododendron patch, turn R/upwards and zigzag up the slope between the rhododendrons (on your L) and a belt of scree. Where the gap between them narrows, cross the scree on faint path and continue diagonally R across the slope. Cross 2 more rock bands, then turn up/L and climb a low ridge, approaching the stream, which runs down the R side of the slope. Find a path and follow it up, crossing a final band of stones to gain the stream bank (50 mins, D084).

Follow the L bank of the stream, then cross to the R and to the L again, following the course of the stream. Turn R, following the stream into a grassy bowl below the pass. At the junction of 2 streams (15 mins), follow the R stream SE up a slope towards a narrow neck filled with boulders and a stone wall, to a second, upper bowl. Here is your first sight of the pass - the skyline has several cols but our pass is on the L/ESE, and appears to be the highest. On the R is a ridge, rocky at first then stony, which separates the bowl from the main valley below; this ridge is the best way to the pass (20 mins, D088).

Walk up zigzags on the ridge with a drop on the R towards the lower valley; the lower U-shaped pass is now close on the R and once could be accessed by a route across the top of a scree bank but this has fallen away. Continue up the ridge, bearing L/N towards the higher pass. It is divided by a small outcrop and has a steep and long scree bank below it stretching down into a scree- and snow-filled cirque beyond. On the R of the cirque is Bulut Dağı and to the S of the U-shaped pass is Çaymakçur Tepesi, recognisable by a distinctive sheer E wall (15 mins, D091).

The descent from the pass runs SE down the long scree slope to the cirque below - the start of the Bulut Deresi. From the top, the step between the scree slope and the

13.4 Ayder, Aşağı / Yukarı Çaymakçur, Körahmet Geçiti, Bulut Deresi, Satelef, Körahmet, Karamolla, Yaylalar

valley bottom is invisible so the slope looks dangerous; in fact, there is a faint horizontal path at the bottom of the scree. The highest part of the slope is over gritty consolidated earth with rock underneath. Below that, the L scree slope is white but the R is brown and with larger stones; between is an area with a few plants. Start by keeping close to the R side of the slope to avoid the outcrop and to get onto the scree as soon as possible. Then continue down the scree on the small white stones just to the L of the area with plants.

Follow the white scree to the bottom where there is a steep drop to the cirque below. You can either continue down a couloir to your R or turn across the bottom of the scree on a path running to a smaller couloir with a stream and descending steeply and awkwardly to the cirque below (50 mins, D093).

In the cirque is a long-lasting snow patch; turn L/E on this and descend to the main stream, which runs down towards a steep, narrow couloir (10 mins). Looking back up at the pass, you will see a hairpin on the grass on the W side of the scree - this is probably the best way to climb the pass but it's unclear how this route actually crosses the lip to the far side. Past a boulder on the L of the stream, find a faint path descending the L bank of the couloir; if there is snow, the descent is easy (30 mins, D096).

Cross the stream to the R and climb onto a rhododendron-covered ridge, which runs NE towards the main valley bottom. Descend the far side of this ridge and find a path running at the bottom of the slope (35 mins, D099).

Alternative cross-country route to Dilberdüzü: *Turn R on the path and contour the side of Bulut Dağı, aiming at the streams ahead/S. At the junction of 2 streams, turn up the valley on the R/W to climb to Şeytan Gölü, a small tarn between crags. Follow the stream above the tarn and climb the steep ridge, aiming SE. On the far side is a long, steep but grassy descent down the Pakin Deresi to Dibe Yaylası below.*

From Dibe Yaylası, walk up the Dupedüzü Deresi past the waterfalls to the upper basin of the valley. About 500 m out of the yayla, cross the stream to find a campsite with a çeşme with a paved surround on the far side. From here, a path runs SSW up a rhododendron-clad bank to a stream, then hairpins back and crests a lip to an upper bowl. Continue round the L side of the bowl to a grassy col to the SSE.

From the summit of the col, you can see down into the U-shaped Hevek Deresi and to Hastaf Yaylası, due S. From here, a faint path drops over grass, passes over a small headland and contours around a buttress. The hillside is very steep and in places scree-covered; the path not easy or clear. It descends the valley side in a long diagonal aiming SW, contouring around the side spurs and stream beds, until it reaches a scree-sided bowl where several streams originate. Cross 2 stream beds and just after the second stream turn down/S to follow a steep spur parallel with the stream to the valley floor. It reaches the valley bottom just before the path on the far side climbs up to Dilberdüzü campsite. Either cross the stream (which is deep) and follow the path up to the campsite, or stay on the R bank (which is boggy) and climb up to the camp.

You are now in position for an attempt at the peak. See route 12.4 for the climb of Kaçkar peak and the return to Yaylalar. **End.**

Turn L and follow the path back to the Bulut Deresi, cross it and continue NNE on clear path through the rhododendrons with the valley-bottom stream on the R. The path runs along a ridge then crosses onto a mound with a huge cairn at the centre (25 mins, D101). The path runs W of the cairn and above the main stream-bed, continuing NE on this line until the valley bends R. It is mainly a clear cow path through grass. At one point, it veers away from stream over a rocky headland and descends again on the far side. Soon after, it crosses a marshy area where it is confused and lost in puddles. It also crosses various streams en route. Looking back up the valley, the higher part is very beautiful, with a waterfall descending the slopes, and the pyramidal shape of Bulut Dağı on the R. As the path approaches the bend in the valley, it veers away from the main stream, and crosses a major sidestream (50 mins, D109).

After a second stream crossing (20 mins), the path runs even higher on the valley side and traces of old walls are visible along it (35 mins). It passes the junction with the path to Babur Geçiti and continues on a double-walled section to Satelef Yaylası (see page 103) (20 mins, C120). Below the yayla, between boulders and close to the main stream, there is a level campsite.

Take a path which runs above the yayla and parallel with the stream for about 100 m. It passes through a gap between boulders and joins a substantial path on a stone base, just above beds of raspberries. Cross a wide sidestream in a gully and continue climbing gently upwards on old path. Pass a second stream, more like a waterfall splashing the route. The path here is slippery and narrow, and continues almost level across a second gully and waterfall. After this, the path becomes a clear, walled track (wide enough for a carriage) built up on a wall on the R and with a retaining wall on the L. Alongside are occasional ruined houses, water and drinking troughs and there are terraces in the valley below. It approaches the upper NW side of Körahmet (see page 103), which stands on a spur looking out over the valley (55 min, B155).

Walk through the top of the village and turn down a stone staircase to reach the new road. Turn L and walk up the road for about a km until you reach Karamolla where you climb L/up on a sloping track leading towards the centre of the village (see page 103) (10 mins, C031).

At a large çeşme, which flows into a stone trough, turn down again on a footpath which almost immediately crosses the road. The path, initially steep and narrow, is an old mule trail which runs below the road, around the valley side, to meet an old arched bridge over the sidestream (Bulut Deresi), below Yaylalar. Ignore the 2 L turns on the path. Turn R, cross the old bridge and walk into Yaylalar on the new road, crossing the new bridge (1 hr 5 mins, C116) just below the village.

13.5 Ayder, Avusor Yaylası, Kırmızı Geçiti, Pişenkaya Yaylası, Barhal (11 hrs 30 mins)

This steep route takes you over the Kırmızı Geçit on a W-E trans across the range. Originally a trade route connecting Barhal to Ayder, this pass is now very popular as it's the most northerly that the mules can use. However, the route is not as easy as the Naletleme or Davali Geçits as the upper paths are very worn and need maintenance. The description is of the main mule route over the pass, but you could make a detour to Libler Gölü - see route 11.3, page 77.

There may well be an ice and snow bridge over the Onbolat Deresi, hiding the lower part of the descent and the river crossing; if so, cross diagonally and pick up the path on the far bank - don't go all the way down the ice as you may have difficulty getting off it as the valley narrows and steepens, or the ice may collapse under you. Take poles for use on ice and scree.

In season, there is a daily dolmuş from Ayder to Avusor, starting at 8.30 am from the main bus office. It is not always reliable, so try and check the previous evening if and when it will run.

If you want to walk up to Avusor, start up the main road towards Yukarı Kavron (C155). Continue past the stream crossing at Hoşdere and turn off on a dirt road running diagonally up/N and then NE with the lovely Avusor Deresi below R (30 mins, C114). Where the road crosses the river, you can cut the bend by walking R for about 50 m, then turning up a track which climbs the riverbank to the road. Later, as the road climbs away from the river, you could continue along the river on the old track and climb to meet the road at Taşlık Yaylası. From here, continue on the road through Dobet Yaylası to Avusor (3 hrs, D126).

> **Avusor Yaylası** is the last one on the approach to Kırmızı Geçit and the route to Barhal. At 2600 m, it has 25 single-storey stone houses, a small pension with 4 rooms, 2 bakkal and 2 kahves. Another, larger pension further up the valley is not currently in use. The older houses and barns, some with original turf roofs, are set into the ground to provide protection from the wind. Avusor generates its own electricity from a water-powered generator. One family is resident from April to October, but most of the mainly Laz residents use the yayla only from June or July until September, moving up from other houses lower down the valley. The road, which joins the Ayder-Kavron road about 1 km above Ayder, was constructed in 2002. In summer there is a daily dolmuş leaving Ayder at 8.30 am and returning at 3 pm.

From Avusor, start uphill/E on a wide track which leads towards a few houses in the valley above the yayla. Pass the last few buildings and continue upwards with the stream below on the R; there is no path but you should aim at the L side of the valley ahead. You could camp in this area, taking care to site the tent away from the routes of the cows up the hillside on the L. Continue along the river bank, near an irrigation canal but then veer upwards towards some boulders on the edge of a gully. There is a cairn on one of the boulders and this marks the start of a crossing place. A buttress divides the valley ahead and a path leads from the gully up to the L side of the buttress, following the L stream bed up a couloir. The definite path zigzags up to the rim of a high and wide basin, bordered by scree slopes descending from a semicircle of jagged peaks (1 hr 5 mins, D135).

This spectacular basin of mountains includes Kemerli Kaçkar on the W side and the obvious col of Lale Geçiti to the SE. Kırmızı Geçit is the dip in the rocky ridge on the E side of the basin; it's named for the red soil around it. At the entrance to the basin are scattered large boulders and the route continues SE past them across gently rising grass to the rocky bed of a sidestream on the L of the basin. Cross the stream and, on the far bank, take the R path. It bears L up the sidestream bank, weaving over scree and boulders (50 mins, D116).

The two paths meet again, cross a sidestream and turn up L/E towards the pass (30 mins). Our path climbs a low, stony ridge forming the R bank of a couloir, then zigzags up to a buttress on the R. Below the buttress, it turns L again; the path

THE KAÇKAR

WP	Lat (N)	Long (E)	Alt (m)
C155	40.95463	41.09833	1182
D006	40.95186	41.11951	1370
D121	40.95545	41.12974	1503
D123	40.95739	41.13392	1579
D017	40.95853	41.14241	1763
D125	40.96028	41.17414	2139
D126	40.95255	41.19157	2307
D127	40.95179	41.19533	2379
D113	40.95071	41.19959	2402
D128	40.95195	41.20378	2444
D129	40.95097	41.20750	2539
D130	40.95025	41.21177	2645
D135	40.94614	41.21617	2675
D115	40.94445	41.21907	2779
D116	40.94426	41.21988	2797
D137	40.94526	41.22204	2888
D119	40.94674	41.22495	3012
D141	40.94659	41.22712	3105
D143	40.94736	41.23140	3021
D144	40.94833	41.23370	3022
D145	40.94849	41.23627	2991
D146	40.94943	41.23917	2916
D147	40.94993	41.24061	2867
D148	40.94946	41.24276	2787
D149	40.94866	41.24275	2755
D150	40.94763	41.24156	2697
B065	40.94733	41.24328	2670
D153	40.94619	41.24574	2635
D155	40.94749	41.25183	2436
D157	40.94688	41.25665	2482
D158	40.94661	41.25801	2469
D159	40.94720	41.26078	2376
B057	40.94651	41.26476	2237
B008	40.95021	41.27358	2144
B136	40.95305	41.28396	2009
B134	40.95326	41.28869	1934
D168	40.95160	41.29715	1784
B131	40.95511	41.31005	1636
B133	40.95554	41.32157	1575
D173	40.95774	41.32936	1509
D174	40.95314	41.34560	1385
B137	40.94964	41.36861	1290
A185	40.96102	41.38351	1207
B001	40.96830	41.39257	1197

13.5 Ayder, Avusor Yaylası, Kırmızı Geçiti, Pişenkaya Yaylası, Barhal

surface is extremely slippery and well-worn and covered with small rocks and gravel. Cross the stream to the L bank and continue upwards on deeply grooved, steep zigzags. Below another buttress is a difficult, steep hairpin, where mule traffic has destroyed the thin grass. Turn R here onto the final approach to the pass (25 mins, D141).

At the top of Kırmızı Geçit, the basin and valley leading down to Avusor is spread out behind you but, in front, the view is a close-up of jagged peaks - Hızarkapı Tepesi on the L/N, Lale Tepesi and the Bulut Dağları to the R/S. A side ridge curls round SE over Libler Gölü and a buttress divides the valley into 2 parts.

The descent starts down the L/NE side of the valley, with a L hairpin on a well-worn path, leading to a grassy headland, where you catch your first glimpse of Libler Gölü (30 mins, D143).

Alternative route to lake: From here, you could descend to the lake, on a steep and dangerous path marked with cairns, which aims towards the head of the scree - walled cirque which contains the lake. It zigzags down avoiding the little streams and waterfalls which feed the lake. The final descent may be over snow. To rejoin the main route, leave the lake by the outflow stream and descend on your chosen side of the stream through a band of rhododendrons to rejoin the stream at a cairn, which marks the start of a traverse over a scree band. Do not attempt this route with full packs. See route 11.3. **End.**

Cross the stream on the L of the grassy headland and turn R onto a long ridge which descends gently down the valley. The narrow, stony path passes to the L side of the ridge (below and L of a roofless barınak) and continues almost level to the end. It then descend in zigzags over stony ground to a grassy slope (25 mins, D147). Just past a large flat-topped rock, pass through the rhododendrons on zigzags which lead towards the Büyükdere stream; turn R, parallel with the stream, to a crossing place. Cross on stepping-stones to the far bank where the clear, sandy path descends between rhododendrons, in wide zigzags, to re-cross the cascading stream just below a large boulder (25 mins, D149).

Turn L/E and continue down to the junction with the alternative path from the lake (10 mins). The path runs straight down over stones then re-crosses the stream on a wide, shallow crossing. It descends to the sloping düzlük above the main stream, (now known as the Onbolat Deresi) then, keeping close to the valley side, crosses another sidestream (15 mins). At the end of the upper valley is a small headland and below that a lower düzlük. Pass down an unclear zigzag path (with the remains of a few huts on the R) and cross the stream to a rising path on the S side (the stream may be bridged by a snow bank; in some years this melts very late) (20 mins, D156). Climb diagonally up the far bank on a path leading to the top of a buttress. At the top, the path passes under a higher buttress and, a few m further on, Pişenkaya comes into view on the far bank of the river below (15 mins). Descend on well-worn zigzags and cross the river, either on a snow bridge (avoiding the area around the mouth) or by the concrete bridge. Walk up the L bank and turn R to Pişenkaya, just a few hundred m further down (20 mins, B008).

From Pişenkaya, a path descends ENE, first down a field wall, then diagonally on a clear path toward forest. After the trees, cross the meadows below Norsel Yaylası and cross a bridge across a stream. Continue to descend gently, then cross a second bridge. Climb the bank and cross the upper side of a field to reach the dirt road (30 mins). Here, turn down to the valley bottom and walk about 5 km to the junction with the main Barhal - Yaylalar road. At the junction, which is by a bridge, turn L for Barhal, 3 km down the valley (2 hrs, B001).

For an alternative route to Barhal, you could use route 11.5 in reverse.

13.6 Yukarı Kavron, Derebaşı Gölü, Kavron Geçiti, Davali Yaylası, Taşbaşı Yaylası, Sırakonaklar, Soğanlı Yaylası, Hevek Geçiti, Dilberdüzü Campsite, Olgunlar (20 hrs)

This N-S trek loops around the W side of the Kaçkar massif and visits the wide glaciated valleys S of the peak, dipping to the beautiful scattered mahalles full of ancient stone houses which collectively form Sırakonaklar. It uses 2 high passes to cross the ranges and passes the base camp at Dilberdüzü. It's a long trek, but with no technical difficulties. However, the Soğanlı Deresi is a summer home for a herd of bulls; it's easy enough to keep clear of these huge, slow moving animals, as they cannot follow you onto rock or scree.

Take the dolmuş from Ayder to Yukarı Kavron (see page 116); if you are using a mule for this trek, the mule driver will meet you there, at the Şahin café near the bridge (D035).

The path to Derebaşı Gölü, due S, starts up a rough road from the W side of the village and stays on the W bank of the stream, rising onto slightly higher land away from the bank. It then curves towards the stream and, past a tributary from the E, crosses it on stepping-stones. The far side is quite marshy but the path stays close to the water. Before the moraine bank which retains the lake, the path re-crosses the stream; it climbs on zigzags amongst rhododendrons to reach the lakeside. On the W side of the valley, above the lake, is a small campsite which will take 3-4 tents, with large boulders above it (3 hrs 45 mins, D182).

The path continues above the boulders, climbing diagonally SW up the W valley wall then turning a corner into a shallow semicircle of cliffs. It zigzags up the cliffs to the lowest point on the ridge above where it is marked by cairns (1 hrs 45 mins, D185). From just S of this point is a sensational view of the Kaçkar N face and its spires and glaciers.

Turn L/SSE on a path which descends gently with the steep and craggy ridge on the L. To the R and below, a tiny tarn is visible; Anadağ Gölü is hidden in a cirque in the mountains. The path, paved with huge slabs as it runs over scree, rises to the Kavron pass on short, stiff, well-used and slippery zigzags (50 mins). From the top, there are views over the Palovit valley to the N; the jagged massif of Kaçkar rises on the E. To the S is a vast, semi-circular, SW-facing basin divided by a ridge; beyond this is the U-shaped valley leading down to Davali Yaylası and, beyond that, the lower mountains rolling towards Erzurum.

The descent is initially on a steep zigzag path over scree leading to a small hollow. From here, it becomes easier and leads to another tiny bowl with a pınar (25 mins). The path continues downhill and divides; keep to the L/E branch, which runs SSE below a patch of scree to a tarn; cairns mark the route. Continue over a low ridge to a small pınar in a bowl at the foot of the main dividing ridge; this is a good campsite (30 mins, D192).

Descend SSW towards a stream which runs down the S part of the basin and turn parallel with it. Walk down towards the basin lip, and find the start of a wide path which runs diagonally down the lip to a spring on the valley floor (1 hrs 45 mins).

THE KAÇKAR

WP	Lat (N)	Long (E)	Alt (m)
D035	40.88415	41.13123	2225
D179	40.87058	41.12747	2400
D184	40.85704	41.12765	2500
D180	40.84676	41.12822	2672
D181	40.84190	41.12709	2756
D182	40.83818	41.12732	2902
D183	40.83390	41.12017	3161
D185	40.82633	41.12664	3199
D186	40.82503	41.12695	3163
D187	40.81858	41.12983	3237
D188	40.81459	41.13202	3129
D189	40.81196	41.13250	3068
D190	40.81257	41.13677	3068
D192	40.80726	41.13954	2968
D195	40.80563	41.14134	2942
C190	40.80030	41.13719	2825
D196	40.79871	41.13649	2728
D199	40.79469	41.14054	2560
E105	40.79363	41.13950	2538
D200	40.79221	41.13937	2509
E107	40.78954	41.14238	2472
D201	40.78639	41.14444	2467
D202	40.78515	41.14528	2452
D204	40.77733	41.15290	2264
D203	40.76918	41.16271	2070
D205	40.76531	41.17424	1920
E111	40.76489	41.17878	1890
E112	40.76388	41.18202	1866
D197	40.76121	41.18661	1889
E115	40.76520	41.18926	1947
D215	40.76761	41.18802	1980
D217	40.77058	41.18455	2050
D208	40.77273	41.18429	2145
D209	40.77446	41.18195	2212
D210	40.78305	41.17717	2501
D212	40.78887	41.17716	2792
D213	40.79465	41.17838	2991
D214	40.80473	41.17958	3194
D216	40.80698	41.18057	3271
D219	40.81020	41.18030	3102
D220	40.81209	41.17958	3055
D221	40.81444	41.18007	3023
D223	40.82063	41.17864	2882
D225	40.82163	41.17745	2864

13.6 Yukarı Kavron, Derebaşı, Kavron G, Davali, Taşbaşı, Sırakonaklar, Soğanlı, Hevek G, Dilberdüzü, Olgunlar

There are huts around this area. At a junction, turn R/S from a çeşme and walk along a raised causeway towards the Davali Deresi, where you cross a stone bridge to Davali Yaylası (15 mins, D200).

> **Davali Yaylası**, at 2500 m, has about 40 stone houses on the W bank of the Davali Deresi, linked by an old stone bridge and a plank bridge with the far side. The houses are all single-storey with corrugated roofs and divided by narrow paved passages, with animal pens between the houses. The yayla is inhabited from July to early September, by people bringing cattle and goats from Sırakonaklar and relatives who come from Istanbul. The houses are often left unlocked, so you can easily find somewhere to stay. You may be offered tea or food; the cream, cheese and yoghurt are excellent and the shepherds friendly and kind.

The route passes over a wooden plank bridge reached by stepping-stones (the downstream stone bridge has collapsed) (10 mins). It continues SSE on a footpath running parallel with and E of the river, first over green meadows, then, as it approaches Taşbaşı, down rocky slopes where the path zigzags close to the river.

Above Taşbaşı is an open slope with the ruins of a couple of barınak below and a pınar hidden in the weeds about 20 m beyond them; this is the only possible camp site (50 mins, D201).

> **Taşbaşı Yaylası** is perched at 2350 m on a huge rock buttress on the W bank above the Davali Deresi. The 15 houses are of stone and are used for 2 months each year. The residents, who include returnees from Istanbul, keep cattle and catch the endemic red-spotted trout in the cascading river below. The route up the valley originally ran between the yayla and the river and, in places, is still in good condition. Unfortunately, the bridge which once crossed the river between Taşbaşı and Davali has collapsed, so the old route is no longer used.

Below Taşbaşı, the path descends steeply on tight zigzags - these are very difficult for the mules (20 mins). It then levels off a bit and runs over grass again, then between hazel plantations, still with the stream R/below. There are remains of old walls which once defined the path but these have collapsed in places and the route now largely avoids them (25 mins, E111).

The various mahalles of Sırakonaklar are now visible in the valley below and on the opposite slope are a few old houses. The path descends to a çeşme on an old track (15 mins, E112). About 50 m past it, the path branches R/down to the bridge in the valley bottom and the lower mahalles. *If you want to exit the route at Sırakonaklar, you should follow this path - see route 14.5, page 138.*

> **Sırakonaklar**, under its old name of Hodacur, was once a Christian village and had an extensive monastery complex on a ridge to the N as well as other churches. Now it consists of some 150 large stone farmhouses and many timber barns, where hay is stored and cattle are overwintered. It is spread out in several mahalles on slopes on both sides of the river, at many different levels, often close to forest. Hay is cropped on the surrounding slopes, hazelnuts and maize grow in the riverside fields and oxen are kept in the valley above.

To continue, keep on the old road which leads up to Akbaş, a mahalle of beautiful old houses (one with an Armenian inscription next to an arched window) (10 mins). Walk through the upper part of the mahalle and find a walled track rising along the hillside between fields. At a junction keep on the R/lower path. Just before Güneşli, the next mahalle, the path separates again and you should choose the L/upper path which climbs between walls towards old houses (20 mins, E115).

Pass under a walnut tree and meet the road running horizontally through the mahalle. Turn R and follow it down to a fork just before the river bridge, then choose the L branch which rises up zigzags through the remainder of the houses. The road climbs to the edge of the forest then hairpins R/N towards Dallıca Mahallesi. Just before the upper bridge over the Davali Deresi (40 mins), turn L and follow a footpath NW up the L side of the stream, first on a bank between fields then across the stream to a muddy area on the R side (25 mins). The narrow, well-used footpath rises on the stony bank, approaching cascades in the stream. It veers R/NNW onto hairpins which rise to a buttress (topped by sheep pens) then turns back towards the stream (40 mins). Crossing the stream above the cascades, the path climbs past the few roofless houses (all that remains of Soğanlı Yaylası) then up a ramp to the upper basin of the valley. It climbs steeply in zigzags on the L side of the stream, past a possible campsite by a sidestream (1 hr, D208).

As the valley flattens out, the path crosses the stream and continues N on the R/E side, aiming at the R of the pass above. Passing a tiny outcrop, climb gently to the pass on the rim of the valley (1 hr 10 mins, D214), where the serrated, snow-topped black peaks of the Kaçkar massif form a stunning contrast to the gentler Soğanlı Deresi. The headland of Çağıl Tepesi (just E of Dilberdüzü campsite) is below and to the L are the buttresses of Şeytan Kayaları.

Turn R/NE on a diagonal path down scree. This turns L on steep and slippery zigzags below a rock, leading to a small, snow-filled couloir just below the pass. Cross a tiny stream and zigzag down on scree (20 mins). At the bottom of the pass, follow a faint path NNE over jumbled moraine onto a low ridge, which leads down to Dilberdüzü campsite (see page 96) (1 hr 20 mins, D221).

From here, you could climb Kaçkar (see route 12.4, page 95) or return down the Hevek Deresi to Olgunlar and Yaylalar. The walk down the valley follows the descending path from the campsite, on the N side of the Hevek Deresi, passing Hastaf Yaylası then arriving at the bridge at Olgunlar (3 hrs, C063).

13.7 Ayder, Aşağı Kavron Yaylası, Samistal Yaylası, Amlakit Yaylası, Palovit Yaylası, Tirovit Yaylası, Elevit (12 hrs 20 mins)

This starts as a difficult route climbing the steep ridge between the Kavron-Ayder and Palovit valleys. The steep, indistinct path runs through large areas of rhododendrons or over wild hillsides where the path is often unclear. We also describe an alternative route from Yukarı Kavron to Palovit which is shorter and easier but misses the lovely yaylas of Samistal and Amlakit. From Palovit, the route crosses the next ridge to Tirovit and Elevit but you could continue to Apivanak and link with route 12.7 or 14.4.

Take the Ayder - Yukarı Kavron dolmuş, get off at the yellow sign marked 'Welcome to Aşağı Kavron' and walk R down a clear tractor track towards the village (D043). Ignore the first path L leading to the houses and take the second,

WP	Lat (N)	Long (E)	Alt (m)
D043	40.90808	41.13782	1969
D241	40.90693	41.13427	1940
D242	40.91167	41.13392	1945
D243	40.91304	41.12814	2100
D244	40.91227	41.11864	2450
D245	40.91300	41.10908	2830
D246	40.91136	41.09976	2450
D247	40.91036	41.09393	2510
D248	40.90338	41.08720	2480
D249	40.90648	41.07475	2130
D250	40.90255	41.07097	2030
D251	40.88281	41.08282	2250
D252	40.87122	41.08402	2350
D253	40.86958	41.07387	2630
D235	40.86684	41.06912	2770
D232	40.86159	41.06468	2470
C229	40.86125	41.06263	2450

heading S, through the sparsely inhabited stone-built houses (overgrown with nettles). Cross a small sidestream and head S then W to a simple wooden bridge over the Kavron Deresi (15 mins, D241). Turn R/N and follow a faint path across meadow and low shrubs to a distinct side valley plunging down from the W (15 mins). Head up the steep valley on the L bank, moving away from the main stream where it is joined by a smaller tributary. Keeping to a grassy spur L of the stream, climb in zigzags on a faint path, with increasing amounts of rhododendrons and rocky outcrops as you ascend. Higher up, the path is virtually non-existent as this route is now seldom, if ever, used by the locals. With the col clearly visible high above you (the lowest notch in the skyline, due W), just choose the best line. Sometimes you can follow the stream bed itself, sometimes you have to climb through rhododendron bushes. Finally, reach the top of the col (5 hrs, D245) where there is a small snow bank, even in midsummer.

The descent W to Samistal Yaylası, visible from just beyond the lip of the col, is on a steep, faint zigzagging path, with no rhododendron bushes to slow progress; it's a joy after the struggle up the other side (1 hr, D246).

> **Samistal Yaylası**, at 2450 m altitude, was once a huge yayla with 250 houses of good-quality traditional architecture. Currently, only 4 houses are occupied by cattle herders but the new access road from Hazındak may change the situation. The faint paths from Ayder or Yukarı Kavron are very steep; easier walks are from Amlakit or Palovit. You can camp on the soft, cushioned grassy meadow next to a çeşme, with excellent views down the valley.

The path leading to Amlakit Yaylası from Samistal is well used. Pass a tiny tarn, due W of and visible from Samistal, before contouring WSW then heading gently down, with a few cairns for guidance, to a steep gully (1 hr 15 mins). Descend the gully NW to reach a steeply sloping, flower-strewn meadow. Head diagonally WSW across the meadow until the corrugated-iron roofed houses of Amlakit Yaylası come into view on the far side of the valley below. Continue down the grassy area towards pine forest and follow an increasingly distinct path zigzagging down towards the river and yayla below. The path turns S into Amlakit, emerging next to the kahve (1 hr 15 mins, D250).

> **Amlakit/Hamlakit/Amlagit Yaylası,** at about 2050 m, has 40-50 mainly wooden houses, a mosque, bakkal, kahve and a newly-built, wooden pension. Property owners are usually here only in July and August and are working at restoring their houses. They come from the Pazar district, on the coast. Yukarı Amlakit, just half an hour away, is now abandoned.

From Amlakit, an obvious dirt road leads from the top of the village S/up to Palovit. Approaching Palovit, the road veers R/W up the valley side to the W district, where there is a kahve and shop. (1 hr 10 mins, D252).

Alternative route from Yukarı Kavron to Palovit: take the dolmuş from Ayder to Yukarı Kavron. From the upper kahve in Kavron, walk W straight up the valley side on tight zigzags which up a ridge partly clad with low rhododendrons. After a steep climb, you emerge at a düzlük with some pınar and grazing. From here the path continues bearing diagonally R/NW and up towards a spur which descends from the ridge. On reaching the top of the spur, keep the ridgetop on your L and continue WSW upwards towards the rocky col in the skyline ahead, not the smooth dip to the L. Approach the col with a scree belt on your L, zigzagging up towards the rocks on the skyline.

Beyond is a grassy bowl which slopes R/NW, a further col on the L/SW side and a headland due W on the far side of the bowl. Beyond that is the U-shaped valley which contains Palovit; wide, treeless, stony and edged with scree-banded hills.

Cross the col between rocks then descend slightly R/WNW to pick up a cairned path which descends R to a moraine mound in the bowl at the foot of the slope. Cross the valley floor and find a faint path which swings L/W and descends the valley. Continue, keeping the stream on the R (there is a barınak and spring on the far side of the stream). At the valley mouth, keep L towards some rocks and contour L around the hillside to your first view of Palovit. Descend diagonally L/SW towards the village, dropping sharply down the hillside before the boggy area above the village. End.

> **Palovit/Polovit Yaylası** has 150-200 houses spread at 2600 m on the bottom of a U-shaped valley. It has 2 kahve and a bakkal but no pension and is divided into 4 parts, used by people from Çilingir, Ortaköy, Çaneva and a separate area known as Meleskur. It is now the biggest yayla in the valley and the poor but usable road to Elevit, Çat and Çamlıhemşin passes just above/W of it. The road is opened in June and the yayla is inhabited until the end of September. Like other yaylas, there is no waste disposal and waste water pollutes the stream.

Alternative route to Apivanak: The valley becomes increasingly more alpine as you continue on the road towards Apivanak. Soon after leaving Palovit, the road forks and the main dirt road leads R/W. A lesser track continues straight ahead/S. Follow this across the Palovit Deresi via a ford (there is a small bridge just upstream if the water level is high). The road ends at Apivanak (see page 109) (1 hr 15 hrs, C211). **End.**

The road over the hill from Palovit to Tirovit Yaylası is steep, in poor condition and irregularly serviced by dolmuşes. To get the best views, walk over the hill via an old track which runs from the road on the W side of Palovit, starting S of the highest houses and running W, following telegraph posts. After climbing the hill in zigzags, the path follows a gully towards the col. Cross the col to the L of the dip and descend the steep hillside on more zigzags. Tirovit (see page 137) is right below you (2 hrs 10 mins, C229); you join the new road and turn R to the village.

For the descent from Tirovit to Elevit, see route 12.7, page 110.

Chapter 14 **ROUTES IN THE FIRTINA DERESİ AND TATOS DAĞLARI**

This area includes the second highest peak of Verçenik Dağı, its surrounding lakes and U-shaped valleys and the lower valleys to the N and E, the Fırtına Deresi and its tributaries. It's accessed via a newly rebuilt road from Çamlıhemşin, which runs alongside the river, passing Zil Kale (a 14th century fortress) and several slim, arched packhorse bridges. The steep-sided valley is surrounded by forest but, above the trees, rear grassy shoulders on which are perched elegant 19th century mansions, built by ambitious locals who returned from making their fortunes in Russia. The Fırtına is the most lively mountain torrent in Turkey, and attempts to dam it have so far brought forward determined resistance; a DSI (Turkish water authority) base remains on this road.

The 2 main branches of the valley once held major thoroughfares: the trade route past Başyayla or Kaleköy to Ispir, and the route over the Davaliaşıtı to the Çoruh and Erzurum; this once carried all official mail. Elevit and Hacıvanak have remains of churches or monasteries and there may have been others; it's likely that the monasteries once influenced trade.

There are 2 trekking bases - at Çat and Elevit, with a third possibility at Kaleköy. Çat is a busy village situated an hour or more N of Çamlıhemşin, where Hemşin Deresi and Elevit Deresi (2 branches of the lushly wooded Fırtına Deresi) merge. About 30 mainly new or reconstructed houses are situated along the river, with a district of 20 timber-and-stone houses on a shoulder of the hills above. Along the river are 2 pensions; the first doubling as bakkal and a kahve, the second has a riverside restaurant. A bathing pool has been scooped out in the rocky river bed near the latter. E of the river junction is an amazingly delicate arched footbridge, Çilanç Köprüsü.

On the E fork (6 km from Çat) is Elevit/Yezovit (officially Yaylaköy) and, facing it, the smaller mahalle of Tafteni/Taftenit. Both were yaylas but are now occupied mainly as holiday or retirement homes; everyone moves down the valley for the winter, locally to Çamlıhemşin, Pazar, Ardeşen or further afield. Elevit has about 50 wooden, stone/wooden or concrete houses spread on a slope, at about 1800 m, and surrounded by steep forested slopes; Tafteni has about 15 more. They have a new mosque, 3 bakkal/kahve, a simple restaurant and a pension (which also serves food and alcohol). Most returnees have rebuilt their homes, mainly in traditional style, but some are fairly tasteless and unattractive. The streams which merge here are fouled by rubbish and waste water. Above the village, both main and side valleys climb steeply and, as they rise above the tree-line, change to the classic U-shaped, bare valleys of the upper levels.

The third possible base is at Demireli Kesir Mahallesi, Kaleköy. There's an unsigned 4-bedroomed village pension on the dirt road; it would be a good base for exploring the castle, walking to the Tatos Gölleri or to Sarıncat/Balıklı Gölü before doing route 14.5.

Daily dolmuşes run from Çamlıhemşin to Çat at 9 am, continuing E to Elevit, Tirovit and Palovit (when the condition of the unpaved road permits) and returning after noon. The S branch of the road (also unpaved) is less well-used but, in summer, Saturday morning dolmuşes go from Hemşin to Kaleköy, Çiçekli Yayla and Başyayla; others, less predictably, go during the week.

14.1 Fırtına Deresi, Ortam Mahallesi, Fırtına Deresi (2 hrs 45 mins)

This is a short and easy walk which takes you along the E side of the Fırtına Deresi, through woods and past lovely old houses. It's is a good way to spend an afternoon while based at the Doğa Hotel.

Start at a concrete bridge over the Fırtına Deresi (D258) about 1-2 km S of Çamlıhemşin and 3 km N of the Doğa Hotel. Turn off the road onto the concrete bridge at Konaklar, just S of the Jandarma building. Turn R onto a concrete road and walk to the last house (15 mins, E015).

The route then bends L and continues up a concreted rising path. At a çeşme, turn L, then R and follow a narrow footpath up to an old road. Turn L/up and follow the road round a R bend; continue up zigzags until, at a L bend with a high stone wall, it opens out (35 mins, E008). Continue for about 300 m, then turn R and climb a bank on footpath. Continue S on an undulating path in forest and rhododendrons. This soon comes to a junction with a lower path and a pathside seat (50 mins, E010).

Continue S on this undulating path at the edge of woodland to a mahalle with several old houses just below the path on the R. One branch of the path continues upwards but follow the main path R/down a diagonal across fields to a village road. Turn R and follow this as it crosses 2 branches of a stream and descends towards the main road, a short distance N of the Doğa Hotel (1 hr 5 mins, E021).

WP	Lat (N)	Long (E)	Alt (m)
D258	41.02749	41.00409	370
E015	41.02413	41.00438	404
E014	41.02080	41.00202	528
E008	41.01958	41.00049	522
E009	41.01865	41.00090	548
E010	41.01820	40.99882	554
E021	41.00905	40.99207	408

14.2 Çat, Çat Yaylası (Vanski Yaylası), Çat (2 hrs 45 mins)

This is a short walk around Çat from the pension/bakkal in the village centre. It climbs to the upper mahalle from which there are great views, including a glimpse of Ziyırmat Yaylası, perched on a shoulder above the Hemşin Deresi. You could continue upwards to Vanski Yaylası. The walk returns past the old bridge.

Facing the pension/bakkal at Çat (E023), take the dirt track running NW in front of the L adjacent building and continue level between fields. Opposite the first house on the L, look R to find a small gate in the fence on the R with a level area between it and the track; ignore the bigger gate (10 mins). After the gate, turn L onto a level path through grass. Where it forks, turn R/up, crossing under some telephone wires and aiming at a few roofless houses on the hillside ahead (30 mins, E025).

Climb above the houses and then take 2 more hairpins up to reach the edge of the forest. Here a clear path climbs diagonally L into the trees, with occasional hairpins. Follow it towards a forested ridge leading NNE/upwards; the path reaches a small clearing, then turns R amongst giant firs, crosses a fallen tree and resumes. You are now on the ridge itself, and the path continues in steep zigzags to the top of the trees (40 min, E027).

Emerge into open meadow, facing the upper yayla of Çat. A broad field edged

WP	Lat (N)	Long (E)	Alt (m)
E023	40.86510	40.93742	1274
E024	40.86505	40.93432	1269
E025	40.86648	40.93273	1301
E027	40.86915	40.93315	1396
E028	40.87020	40.93578	1494
E030	40.87041	40.93841	1527
E031	40.86637	40.94326	1447
E032	40.86351	40.95553	1415
E033	40.86201	40.95788	1398
E034	40.86242	40.95035	1332
E023	40.86510	40.93742	1274

with a hedge slopes up to a line of trees and the lower houses. The road runs just above the lower houses and out of the far side of the yayla. Walk diagonally across the field, passing a post on the ruins of a house. Reach the village and turn R onto the unsurfaced road to the last house (30 mins, E030).

Alternative route: At a fork in the road you could turn up/L to the deserted Vanski Yaylası, 1-2 km above. End.

The lower road rounds a corner in forest to give views of the valley ahead. It continues as a pleasant stroll through forest, with views down the valley and to a yayla on the steep slopes opposite. At the junction with the valley road, turn R and walk back towards lower Çat (35 mins, E033). Your route passes an elegant and much-photographed arched bridge over the river, the Cilanç Köprüsü, then continues to the junction of the 2 rivers and the pension (20 mins, E023).

14.3 Elevit, Karunç Yaylası, church ruins (6 hrs 20 mins)

This is a day walk from Elevit to the remains of a church which once dominated the spur above the valley. It's now completely ruined but, on a clear day, the view up the valley towards Hacivanak should be compensation. In theory, you can descend from the church SW directly to Elevit, through the woods and crags above the village; we looked for this route but failed to find safe passage. Rather than return to Elevit, you could carry on to route 14.4.

Cross the bridge E of Elevit (D240) and walk up the road for about 3-4 km. The old road runs between walls (below the course of the present road) and you could try to follow this, but it seems overgrow and difficult for most of its length. When you have gained considerable height and before the road bends R to cross a sidestream, look L for a descending track which takes you to a footbridge across the main stream (1 hr 40 mins, E005). You can see Karunç Yaylası on the opposite side of the valley. On the far side of the bridge, climb R then swing L on a stony path which crosses a sidestream and continues towards the yayla (15mins, E006).

> **Karunç/Garunç Yaylası** has only 13 wooden houses (with about 4 in occupation) and is at 2100 m altitude. It's between Elevit and Tirovit on the S facing slope of the Elevit Deresi; Nafkar Yaylası is on the opposite slope and is occupied a farmer recently returned from Ankara.

WP	Lat (N)	Long (E)	Alt (m)
D240	40.85477	41.01318	1914
C236	40.85903	41.02580	2109
E005	40.86184	41.03502	2237
E006	40.86261	41.03469	2269
C232	40.86240	41.02302	2210
C233	40.85914	41.01509	2140

Behind the yayla, a clear path rises first steeply then gradually across grassy slopes below forest, aiming for the grass-topped spur above Elevit. Follow this easy trail which swings L onto the spur. Here there is a pınar as well as the church ruins, so the spur could make a wonderful campsite (1 hr 25 mins, C233).

It's better to return by road rather than risk a fall on the steep cliffs below (3 hrs).

14.4 Tirovit, Karmık Y, Yıldızlı Gölü (Hacıvanak and Elevit) (3 hrs 30 mins)

This is a 1/2 day walk from Tirovit to a lake perched in a cirque above Karmık Yaylası. Its fame derives from the fact that you should be able to see the rising moon, stars and rising sun reflected in the lake, so if the weather is clear and the moon full, you may want to camp. We suggest a continuation, which we haven't used, which turns this route into a circular 2-day walk.

Tirovit/Trevit/Trovit Yaylası has about 60 houses spread in the bottom of a bare valley at 2350 m, with windows facing in the Palovit direction. Most are recently restored or reconstructed for use as holiday homes; in spite of the lush grazing, there are few cows. There are 2 stone clapper bridges over the stream but cars use the adjacent fords. The stream is polluted by waste and waste water, so you should not drink downstream from here. In summer, locals spend evenings dancing a version of the horon but they are unfriendly to strangers. A visitors' house was built here but it's not currently operational; there is no bakkal or kahve but, in summer, a daily minibus service runs from Çamlıhemşin via Çat and Elevit at 8.30 am, returning at around 3 pm.

From Tirovit (C229), walk through the village to the upper bridge and take the track which starts above it (between stone walls) and with the stream on the L below the walls (15 mins). Continuing closer to the stream, mainly on difficult narrow paths, you come to a section of old, paved path which takes you across the worst of the boggy areas (20 mins) but doesn't continue for very long. You are now well into the U-shaped valley leading up to the main range and Karmık Yaylası is visible on the R slope, about half way up the valley; Yıldızlı Gölü is above the yayla but completely hidden. The path is mainly unclear but becomes visible as it crosses the stream descending from Yıldızlı Gölü, just before the yayla (1 hr 40 mins, E044).

Karmık/Garmık Yaylası has only 3 houses at 2600 m and may originally just have been a stopping place on route to Erzurum from Çamlıhemşin, as it is usually free of mist. The yayla is only used for a short time at the height of summer.

THE KAÇKAR

WP	Lat (N)	Long (E)	Alt (m)
C229	40.86125	41.06263	2450
E040	40.85696	41.07063	2490
C227	40.85308	41.07226	2513
C226	40.84863	41.07313	2518
E042	40.84400	41.07313	2578
E043	40.84115	41.07577	2598
E044	40.83526	41.07653	2667
C221	40.83055	41.06857	2895
E201	40.83118	41.06083	3180
E202	40.83118	41.05270	2930
E203	40.82724	41.04651	3130
E204	40.82645	41.03071	2850
E205	40.82111	41.02895	2740
E206	40.81368	41.03130	2630

The path to the lake starts at the yayla and climbs SW first gently, then steeply up the rocky W slope of the valley (1 hr 15 mins, C221). It crosses a stream running down from Zincirli Gölü and continues between the outflow stream and this stream. The lake, about 250 m above the yayla, is in an almost semi-circular cirque and there are campsites around the lakeshore. From the path you can see the col leading to Apivanak on the opposite side of the valley; this is described in route 12.7, and you could continue by walking this route in reverse.

Continuation to Hacıvanak Yaylası: The lake path once continued steeply W up the slopes past the N shore of the lake over an un-named col to a tarn called Karagöl. From there it continued WSW over a second col and swung S, descending gently to Hacıvanak Yaylası. We haven't walked this path and doubt if it is easy to find. The initial part is very stony and looks difficult but the Hacıvanak end is still clear. You could use the map to return to Elevit via this route, Hacıvanak Yaylası and the Hacıvanak Deresi. End.

14.5 Çat, Kaleköy, Başyayla, Kale Geçiti, Hacıvanak Yaylası, Hodacur Geçiti, Davali Yaylası, Taşbaşı Yaylası, Sırakonaklar *(20 hrs 10 mins)*

This is a multi-day NS trans of the range, which takes you from the steep-sided fir-clad valleys of the N to the broader, orchard-filled valleys of Sırakonaklar. The route runs via several high yaylas, and 2 major passes, over scarcely-used tracks with marvellous views, a huge variety of vegetation and some of the most friendly people in the Kaçkar area. Do consider walking from Çat to Kaleköy - we didn't but the valley is so beautiful that it warrants a close look. This trek is best done as a final expedition as the only bus from Sırakonaklar goes to İspir, from where there is a service to Trabzon but none to Yusufeli. In 2008, there may be accommodation in Sırakonklar; anyway there are plenty of places to camp. There are 2 alternatives described. If you don't want to do the whole route, you could return from Hacıvanak to Tafteni and Elevit along the Hacıvanak Deresi, but you would miss the magnificent Hodacur Geçiti. A second alternative is to join route 13.6 at Sırakonaklar and continue to Yaylalar.

From Çat (E120), walk down the R side of the S bound valley (Hemşin Deresi), on a unsurfaced road. The road stays on the W side of the valley, squeezed below steep wooded slopes and cliffs, past the remains of a couple of old bridges (2 hrs, E057). After a sidestream cascades down the valley side, the road crosses the river via a new bridge - the remains of Zocur Köprüsü are just upstream. Remains of old track are visible on the far valley side, but it is damaged.

After 1 km, the road re-crosses to the W bank and the valley starts to open out. After another km, you arrive at a junction with the Purnak Deresi where the main track continues SW along the Hemşin Deresi to Ortaköy and the yaylas on the W side of Verçenik Dağı (40 mins, E058).

Branch L over a concrete bridge with the old packhorse bridge alongside. The old road runs upwards between walls to the L of the new road (it's now so overgrow it is unusable) so follow the new road up zigzags to a group of houses on the shoulder. The new road now continues to Kaleköy proper and a branch swings L to the yayla of Yazlık on the L bank of the Purnak Deresi (20 mins, E060).

> **Kaleköy/Kale Yaylası/Hısarcık** is an extended village below the castle and along the old route across the range S to Erzurum. A road was built to the village in 1964 and since then a few people inhabit the yayla year round but most come for the summer months. The 40-50 houses are substantial stone buildings, surrounded by fertile meadows with plenty of grazing and barns for the hay. Electricity and telephones are connected and a dolmuş service runs from Hemşin. There is no bakkal but there is a small pension. Opposite Kaleköy is Yazlık Yaylası, which was burned down in the autumn of 2006; about 10 houses have been rebuilt in various materials.

At a çeşme, there is a second junction and a R branch goes up to the castle of Kale-i-Bala on the isolated summit on the R of the valley and Şehitler Mahallesi around it. Our road continues in the bottom the valley, with the old paved road still visible beneath the new surface and a new but unsigned pension on the L of the road. Amidst some houses, look L and see a bridge in the valley bottom; cross this onto a climbing path which aims towards a few houses on the valley side (1 hr 10 mins, E061).

Pass below the houses and continue L/up on a grassy diagonal path to Basyayla. This goes round a hillside into a valley with stream L/below, running through boggy areas with a myriad of autumn crocus in season. On the far side of the stream is a path which comes directly from Yazlık Yaylası. Our path continues closer to the stream, then turns slightly L, crosses a small sidestream and climbs a bank - the first house of Başyayla is visible on your R at the end of the road. As you crest the ridge

14.5 Çat, Kaleköy, Başyayla, Kale Geçiti, Hacıvanak, Hodacur Geçiti, Davali, Taşbaşı, Sırakonaklar

ahead, on your R is an old graveyard and behind that a düzlük where cattle graze. To the R and above are the scattered houses of Başyayla (1 hr 20 mins, E064).

> Başyayla/Hemşin Yaylası has 45-50 houses, at an altitude of 2470 m, on the old route from the coast dominated by Bala and Zil castles and leading S to Erzurum. Now it's used as a yayla by people from Hemşin and the surrounding areas and is inhabited for 3 months from 15th June to 15th September. There is dirt road access, electricity and phones but no supplies. A regular dolmuş service leaving Hemşin on Saturday mornings delivers supplies and returns either that evening or on Sunday morning. There are other, more irregular services during the week.

From the top of the yayla, the route to Hacıvanak is clear - it follows a ridge which runs ENE towards a dip in the skyline. Leave the yayla by a path which runs E to cross the stream on a small stone bridge (20 mins, E067), then rises L/up the ridge to a junction. The L path runs down to cross a stream on a causeway, then rises up the slopes of Vacakar Tepesi. This may be the end of an alternative route to Çat, which ran on the W slopes of the peak, passing Ziyırmat Yaylası - we didn't have time to investigate this.

Keep R and follow the ridgetop path to a junction marked by a cairn (15 mins). The path veers L, crosses a stream and climbs the far side past a large rock on the L. Ahead is a wide düzlük with a clear path continuing across it and the pass itself, Kale Geçiti, visible beyond. At the end of the düzlük, below a stony ridge which blocks the valley, the path divides (40 mins, E070).

Mules have to use the L alternative, which climbs the L valley side then contours R. Our path continues weaving through the jumbled rocks in the valley bottom. After about 100 m, turn R onto zigzags rising up the R of the valley towards the ridgetop (10 mins). Turning the top hairpin, continue ENE, climbing to the ridgetop on an intermittently clear path (15 mins). At the end of the ridge, the faint path descends slightly almost due E towards a stony gully which has a triangular rock with black stains on the far side. Before reaching the rock, turn L and walk down the far bank of the gully over difficult rocks downhill towards a small tarn, Çiçekli Gölü (20 mins). Just before the tarn, turn R and walk up towards the pass over gentle, grassy slopes. The faint mulepath joins again from the L (30 mins, E075).

On cresting the easy pass, if there is no mist, you can see Hacıvanak Yaylası straight in front on the opposite hillside. It looks very high because the valley bottom in front is so far below it. We now have to reach Hacıvanak without losing too much height but the slopes ahead are cut up by several stream beds and edged on the R by steep cliffs. A high-level path, starting on the R of the pass, contours the hillside and leads to 2 hidden tarns - if you have time and want to explore, you could take this alternative.

Descend over loose earth for 50 m to a nearly horizontal path, which marks the start of the descent. Turn L and continue down bends with a gully on the L. Descend between rocks to a lower level (15 mins). Turn half R/ESE and cross a slight dip, then continue on indistinct path which crosses a slope above rock fields and the stream beds on the R. Still continuing ESE, approach the streams just before the slope to the valley steepens. Cross the streams, then descend the steep hillside diagonally towards

The Kaçkar

WP	Lat (N)	Long (E)	Alt (m)
E120	40.86162	40.94151	1310
E121	40.85288	40.94656	1420
E057	40.83554	40.94525	1492
E058	40.82333	40.93883	1630
E059	40.81992	40.94060	1723
E123	40.81621	40.94504	1880
E060	40.80969	40.95053	1937
E124	40.79915	40.95857	2100
E065	40.79800	40.95966	2070
E062	40.80163	40.96465	2140
E063	40.80033	40.97175	2323
E064	40.80034	40.97495	2403
E067	40.79991	40.97993	2449
E068	40.80004	40.98466	2548
E070	40.80216	40.99239	2650
E071	40.80450	40.99744	2752
E073	40.80262	41.00043	2848
E075	40.80325	41.01145	2900
E076	40.80366	41.01711	2769
E077	40.80387	41.02333	2620
E078	40.80229	41.03323	2800
E079	40.80506	41.03593	2550
E081	40.80818	41.03948	2597
E082	40.80851	41.04365	2650
E083	40.80670	41.05040	2691
E085	40.80295	41.06112	2790
E086	40.80101	41.06818	2828
E087	40.79780	41.07408	2885
E089	40.79590	41.07719	2988
E091	40.79489	41.08230	3074
E092	40.79435	41.08634	3120
E094	40.79740	41.08783	3069
E096	40.80130	41.09915	2905
E099	40.80016	41.11574	2740
E101	40.79977	41.12058	2693
E102	40.79882	41.12784	2614
E103	40.79758	41.13237	2519
E105	40.79363	41.13950	2538
D200	40.79221	41.13937	2509
D201	40.78639	41.14444	2467
D204	40.77733	41.15290	2264
D203	40.76918	41.16271	2070
E111	40.76489	41.17878	1890
E116	40.75871	41.18640	1840

14.5 Çat, Kaleköy, Başyayla, Kale Geçiti, Hacıvanak, Hodacur Geçiti, Davali, Taşbaşı, Sırakonaklar

THE KAÇKAR

the valley of the Mihberçay Deresi ahead. Follow the grassy slopes R/up alongside the river and cross over a stone clapper bridge (40 mins, E078).

Bear L on a clear path which curves R around the hillside, rising on stone-paved hairpins towards the yayla. Below this path are the remains of the church of the Holy Cross, set between the 2 streams, with just its foundations visible in the gentle grass slope. After the stone-paved section, the path disappears on open grass; cross diagonally over until you reach a second stream where you turn R and walk up the bank (20 mins, E079).

Below/L is a second wooden bridge leading N to Hacıvanak Yaylası. Climb the bank and approach the yayla from below over boggy ground (15 mins, E081).

> Hacıvanak/Gaçivanag/Haçivanag/Gaçivonag Yaylası, the second highest yayla in the National Park, consists of about 80 1- or 2-storey houses spread over an altitude of 2200-2600 m, built in rows on a NE facing slope of one of the wettest valleys in the range. At its peak, it had 150 houses and was used by people from Çamlıhemşin, Yolkıyı, Şenköy and Zilkale. Many houses are built of good-quality squared stone, which probably came from the Monastery of the Holy Cross (Hac - cross, Vank - monastery) the foundations of which you can see on a grassy slope between 2 streams below the yayla. Now only about 3-4 houses are used so there are many empty houses where you could camp. A vigorous stream descends in waterfalls from Yedigözler Pınarı and flows down the NW side of the yayla, supplying fresh water. There is no access road and no facilities.

Alternative route to Elevit: If you want to return to Çat, you could walk on the path N from Hacıvanak to Elevit. Walk to the NW end of the village and cross the stream. Head NW/down past a small building aiming diagonally at the valley bottom. Just before the next stream bed, the path descends more steeply, but then continues approaching the Hacıvanak Deresi. The path veers NNW, running close to the stream and approaching cliffs on the R valley side. Beyond the cliffs, the path crosses the stream via a bridge and continues on the L/W bank. As you approach Teftani, you can cross the stream R to join the dirt road on the E side of the valley. This runs down to Elevit and joins the main valley-bottom dirt road just E of Elevit. Turn R and walk into the village (2 hrs 40 mins). End.

Küllük Deresi, the valley leading up to Hodacur Geçiti runs ESE from the yayla. It's a broad, glaciated valley with the spikes of Kocakurt Kayalığı on the R and an unnamed pyramidical peak behind them just to the R of the pass.

Walk out of the yayla via the E/upper corner on a faint diagonal path across the grassy hillside aiming upwards at the main path up the Küllük Deresi (10 mins). On the gently rising main path, cross 10 small gulleys; the path swings SE (25 mins). Head down slightly towards a major sidestream as it emerges from a gully and cross it about 100 m from the main stream. The path disappears but you should continue straight until you find it rising to cross another sidestream (30 mins, E085).

Climb up gradually, now heading ESE, crossing more sidestreams to a hillock with scattered rocks on it; this would be a good campsite. By now, Hodacur Geçiti (and a cairn on top of it) is clearly visible ahead (40 mins). The path leaves the düzlük beyond the hillock and climbs up a rocky bank in zigzags, then turns SE parallel with the stream and above it. It descends between rocks to the stream valley and crosses to the R bank (50 mins, E089).

14.5 Çat, Kaleköy, Başyayla, Kale Geçiti, Hacıvanak, Hodacur Geçiti, Davali, Taşbaşı, Sırakonaklar

The path zigzags over a small bank then descends and turns up a second rocky bank. It climbs on zigzags and, at the top, follows a rock and grass spur to its end. It descends and crosses a couloir across the stream, then climbs again between rocks on the R/N bank (30 mins). Three boulders block the path, so you have to climb over or around them. After this rocky area, bear L onto more zigzags which lead to a grassy area with lots of mountain goat prints in the soft soil. Continue up a few more zigzags to the pass and a large cairn on the summit (40 mins, E092).

Here are fabulous views over the wide basin of the Davali Deresi, with the peak of Kaçkar beyond. L of Kaçkar is the curving rock wall of the valley head; the dips in it are the passes to the Palovit and Kavron valleys. On the R is a col leading to Pinağros Yaylası. At the end of the season Döner Gölü, just below, is just a series of puddles. The path down/ESE then NNE towards the tarn is difficult to follow, as it has a snow patch and runs on soft earth between stones and rocks (25 mins). Cross to the R side of the stream descending from Döner Gölü. Continue down/E over well-used zigzags between rocks, approaching the stream again. Recross the stream and continue on the L bank towards a large rock (1 hr, E096).

The path now continues with the stream (now a river) on the R, crossing a small sidestream from Eylal Geçiti. The path drifts further from the Davali Deresi, then swings R and runs parallel to a sidestream, descending gently then more steeply around the top of 2 boggy areas. Cross another sidestream and descend steeply, a good distance away from the river. Below Davaliaşıtı, the path crosses a stream; you have now rounded the bend in the valley and can see a düzlük and Davali Yaylası ahead (50 mins, E100).

There are 2 more streams to cross before the path turns down and runs about 100 m from the main river bed (50 mins). The path is very rough as it descends towards the yayla, passing a white rock face where the path to Davaliaşıtı goes up the valley side (30 mins). The final stream before the yayla descends from Atsız Gölü. At the junction with the path from Kavron Geçiti, turn R/S from the çeşme, walk along a raised causeway towards the Davali Deresi and cross a stone bridge to Davali Yaylası (see page 129) (15 mins, D200).

From the S side of the yayla, the route passes over a wooden plank bridge reached by stepping-stones (the original stone bridge has collapsed) (10 mins, E107). It continues SSE on a footpath running parallel with and E of the river, first over green meadows then, as it approaches Taşbaşı, down rocky slopes where the path hairpins close to the river. Just opposite Taşbaşı is an open area with the ruins of a couple of houses below. There is a pınar at the S end of the houses and you could camp here (50 mins, D204).

Below Taşbaşı Yaylası (see page 129), the path runs on tight zigzags descending steeply - these are very difficult for mules (20 mins). It then levels off a bit and runs over grass again, then between hazel plantations, still with the stream R/below. There are remains of old walls, which once defined the path, but the route now mainly avoids them (25 mins). The various mahalles of Sırakonaklar are now visible in the valley below and there are a few old houses on the opposite bank. The path descends to an old track and turns L to a çeşme(15 mins, E112).

50 m after the çeşme, turn off the track onto a path which descends to Çavuşlar Mahalle in the valley bottom and, close to a mosque, crosses a bridge to the far side of the valley. Turn R onto the dirt road which runs with the river R/below down the

valley (E116). A dolmuş runs down the valley from Sırakonaklar to İspir at about 6 am every morning.

If you have time to explore, the valley is beautiful, lush and green, with mature walnuts and fruit trees. Several of the ridges descending to the valley once had churches on them - the first is NE of Dallıca, another E of the bridge at Çavuşlar, another opposite on the W ridge and another on a slope S of the first side valley. The valley bends L then R to Yonca Mahallesi and continues to a junction of 3 valleys at Cücebağ/Cicibağ Mahallesi, 5-6 km below the bridge. Here, the mosque is a converted church (1 hr 15 mins). Just below Cücebağ the road crosses the river to the W and continues into a narrower and steeper, uninhabited section of the valley. It runs for 8-10 km down to the main Çoruh valley, which it joins about 45 km W of Yusufeli.

14.6 Kaleköy, Tatos Gölları, Tatos Geçiti, Yedigöl Yaylaları (8 hrs 45 mins)

This is a straightforward N-S trans route, from Kaleköy to Yedigöller, following the main trade route to the E of Verçenik massif. The route follows 2 major U-shaped valleys: the Purnak Deresi leads up to the Tatos Gölleri and the Tatos Geçidi, and the Aktakan Deresi leads down the far side to Yedigöl, the Çoruh valley and İspir. We haven't done this route and so are not quite sure how much of it is now vehicle track or of the accuracy of the times but on the N side the driveable track continues for several km past Çiçekli Yaylası.

From the pension at Kaleköy (E124), walk S along the village road and turn up to Çiçekli Yaylası, either via a path which climbs in zigzags on the edge of woodland, or via the longer road. In the yayla, turn SSE and walk level along the valley side, gradually approaching the main valley-floor road (1 hr 15 mins, E126).

Turn R onto this and walk S towards the Tatos Göllerı and the Tatos Geçiti. The road continues to climb past seasonal yaylas for about 4 km then crosses the stream (1 hr 10 mins). After re-crossing, it swings R/SW as it approaches the lakes, drifting away from the stream. The path crosses a sidestream to Sulak Gölü. Turn L in front of the larger lake and climb SE towards the steep and narrow pass (1 hr, E129); there is a col to the W which links the E and W sides of Verçenik Dağı.

There are good views of the huge massif of Çatalkaya Tepesi due S; Verçenik

WP	Lat (N)	Long (E)	Alt (m)
E124	40.79915	40.95857	2100
E125	40.79634	40.95273	2370
E126	40.78251	40.96009	2180
E127	40.75453	40.95219	2600
E128	40.73976	40.94563	2880
E129	40.73396	40.95397	3170
E130	40.71891	40.96627	2780
E231	40.69794	40.97641	2350

itself is beyond and SW. Below the pass to the L/NE are 2 tarns. Descend due SE, on a path that runs down between 2 streams then switches to the R side. The path continues with the Aktakan Deresi on the L, crossing a sidestream. After passing the bulk of Çatalkaya Tepesi, the path crosses the stream and runs on the L/E bank (1 hr 30 mins, E231). The path continues down the valley until it eventually runs alongside an irrigation ditch and then enters the lower part of Dağancık Mahalle, on the hillside above the junction of the Aktakan Deresi with the Aksu Deresi. Below here, it meets the main route from Yedigöl, running E and parallel with the Aksu (2 hrs 30 mins). You may be able to find an early morning bus from Yedigöl; otherwise walk downstream to the junction of the Aksu with the Çatak Deresi (1 hr 20 mins) and find a dolmuş or lift from Çatakkaya to İspir.

Appendix A SETTING UP AND USING YOUR GPS

All the points on the lists in the route section and on the website were taken on a Garmin Trek GPS unit. Before you use your own GPS, you should change your settings to match the ones we used.

System setup:
  Mode: Normal
  Offset: +2.00 (difference in hrs between Turkish time and GMT)

Navigation setup:
  Position format: hddd.dddd (degrees in decimal format)
  Map datum: WGS 84
  Units: Distance - Metric, Height - meters, Pressure - millibars, Angle - degrees
  North ref: Mag 004° E

Waypoints, routes and maps

There are 32 routes, and a total of about 700 points. The 4-character waypoint identification has no special significance. Nearly all points were taken in situ and are accurate to a few metres. A few are estimated from a map source; these are less accurate but are still good enough to be useful. If you find any inaccurate waypoints, please take a new one and let us know.

Some GPS's have a maximum of 20 routes; some have a maximum number of points for each route. Check what your model will allow before you start loading points. You can load maps to some GPS's, but we have not done this and so can't recommend any specific maps. You can load waypoints manually or via a computer and communication cable, controlled by the manufacturer's or third party software.

Loading via a computer

You need software supplied by the manufacturer, or third party software (for Mac users, we can recommend Mac GPS Pro, www.MacGPSPro.com) and a special cable to connect the GPS to a USB port on your computer.

Log onto the website www.trekkinginturkey.com, go to Online books and maps, then choose GPS and maps. Read the notes to find your login; look at your copy of the book to find the password and follow the instructions to download a file onto your computer, in .txt format. Use a text editor programme to edit this file: delete the routes you don't want and/or combine shorter routes and so reduce the number of routes to your maximum. Then convert the file to your required format (.kmz, .gdb, or other). The manufacturer's instructions or the instructions in your software package should tell you how to do this; it could be as easy as re-naming the file.

Upload the modified file to your GPS, copy your software and the file to a cd and bring it and the cable with you. Then you can re-load routes to your GPS as required.

Loading part of the route

If you are only walking a short section, you can manually enter waypoints. On a Garmin Trek GPS, first take a number of waypoints, corresponding to the number you want to enter. Then go to the menu, choose 'waypoints', and find the first point that you entered; enter takes you to the 'review waypoint' screen.

Click down the fields to the elevation; press enter to go to a new screen to edit the elevation. After editing, press ok. Repeat for the N and E fields.

Using the 'new route' option, you can then assemble the points you have entered into a route or series of routes. The disadvantage with this method is that the number of the waypoint on the GPS does not correspond with the identification we used, so you have to make a manual note in the margin of the book.

Other makes of GPS let you enter new points more easily.

Appendix B USEFUL INFORMATION

Useful websites

www.trekkinginturkey.com is our site with everything you need to know to supplement this book. The update page contains any amendments to the book; check it before you trek.

www.turkeytravelplanner.com is a mine of information about planning your travels around Turkey

www.akut.org.tr The Rize search and rescue team is not yet functioning but, before you trek, check this site - click on Rize - and if details are available take them with you. The central (Istanbul) phone number is 90 212 217 0410.

www.choruh.com is the English/Turkish site of the UNDP project encouraging nature tourism in the Çoruh valley. Includes accommodaton information and trekking routes (with GPS points) and extensive information on the Georgian churches. Also bird, butterfly and plant check lists and birdwatching locations.

www.kackarlar.org Produced by the Doğa Derneği (Turkish nature society) in both English and Turkish, it has moderately useful information on everything from local foods and possible walking routes to history and wildlife.

www.kuzeymavi.com Of interest if you can read German or Turkish, this professionally-produced site has detailed information on the Black Sea side of the range, with emphasis on Hemşinli culture and the summer pastures (yayla).

www.wunderground.com has weather information for Artvin and Rize.

www.milliparklar.gov.tr is the official site of the Turkish National Parks.

www.tourismturkey.org, www.gototurkey.co.uk are both official sites of the Turkish Culture and Tourism Ministry.

www.alternatifraft.com, www.adrift.co.uk, www.waterbynature.com are sites of three companies offering rafting on the Çoruh river.

Guide books

Title: Trekking in Turkey
Authors: Marc Dubin and Enver Lucas
Publisher: Lonely Planet O/P 1989
ISBN: 0-86442-037-4

Although some of the information is now a little dated, it was a well-researched guide and definitely worth trying to get hold of second-hand - particularly if you intend trekking or walking elsewhere in Turkey. 16 of the guide's 148 pages are devoted specifically to the Kaçkar.

Title: The Mountains of Turkey
Author: Karl Smith
Publisher: Cicerone Press
ISBN: 9781852841614

Smith's book filled the gap left by the discontinuation of Lonely Planet's 'Trekking in Turkey'. It is slightly more comprehensive than LP's 'Trekking in Turkey', but lacks the colour photographs and maps which enliven its predecessor. A Turkish translation of Smith's book (from Homer books at a fraction of the cost) is the 'bible/koran' of Turkish trekkers.

Title: Kaçkar Dagları
Author: Tunç Fındık
Publisher: Homer Kıtapevi (www.homerbooks.com)
ISBN: 9758293184

A 140-page mountaineering guide to the range, with diagrams and instructions for 36 routes, sketch maps and background information. It also includes a short trekking section describing the main routes. In Turkish, but expected to be translated.

Title: Bulbous plants of Turkey and Iran
Author: Peter Sheasby
Publisher: Alpine Garden Society (www.alpinegardensociety.net)
ISBN: 978-0-9000048-77-7

A comprehensive guide to the bulbs of Turkey and Iran, illustrated by colour photographs. It has a short section on habitat and a main body arranged by family. No keys are included but distribution and habitat are well described.

Title: The most beautiful wild flowers of Turkey
Author: Erdoğan Tekin
Publisher: Türkiye İş Bankası Kültür Yayınları (www.iskulturyayinlari.com)
ISBN: 975-458-628-4

A completely pictorial guide, with high-quality detailed photos, to 1000 flowers, arranged by colour and number of petals. Additional information (given by diagram) is height, distribution, altitude range, flowering season, and habitat.

Title: Flowers of Turkey
Author: Gerhard Pils
Publisher: privately published in 2006

This is Turkey's first flora with colour illustrations, although without keys. In 464 densely packed pages, it covers 4153 species of ferns and flowering plants in Turkey. One or two colour photos illustrate each species, with brief notes on altitude, habitat and distribution within the country.

Title: A Field Guide to the Butterflies of Turkey
Author: Ahmet Baytaş
Publisher: NTV Books (www.pembooks.demon.co.uk)

A newly-published photographic field guide to the butterflies of Turkey. It includes over 750 photographs of butterflies taken in their natural habitats and the species accounts of 344 species.

Background reading

Title: East of Trebizond
Author: Michael Perriera
Publisher: Geoffrey Bles 1971

An engaging account of exploring the Pontic Alps on foot and by local transport, though the author and his companion do not 'trek' in the true sense of the word, nor do they visit the alpine zones. Contains some very accessible and interesting local history.

Title: The Towers of Trebizond
Author: Rose Macaulay
Publisher: NYRB Classics
ISBN: 159017058

An ill-assorted group of travellers make their way from Istanbul to Trabzon, encountering evangelical Americans, obstructive policemen and other difficulties en route. An eccentric take on 1950's Turkey.

Title: My Travels in Turkey
Author: Dennis Cecil Hills
Publisher: George Allen and Unwin Ltd 1964 O/P

A fascinating account of mountain wayfaring in Turkey in the 1960's, when much of eastern Turkey was still 'off-limits' to most outsiders. Hills lived and taught in the country for many years, and his love of the people and their homeland shines through. Unfortunately only one short chapter deals with his adventures in the Kaçkar but essential reading nonetheless.

Title: Journeys in Persia and Kurdistan
Author: Isabella Bird
Publisher: Virago Travellers
ISBN: 9781853 810558

Although much of this fascinating travelogue deals with the redoubtable Bird's travels in Iran and the south-east of modern-day Turkey, her account of her party's passage over the Pontic Alps via the Zigana pass to Trabzon is charming:
'Villages of chalets with irregular balconies and steep roofs ... with a blue background of pines, above which tower spires and peak of unsullied snow.'

Title: The Persian Expedition (Anabasis)
Author: Xenophon (Translated by Rex Warner)
Publisher: Penguin

This account of the retreat of the Athenian leader Xenophon and his band of 10,000 (actually closer to 14,000) mercenaries from Mesopotamia to the Black Sea at the very end of the 5th century BC is a classic in every sense of the word. The account of their encounter with azalea honey will put you off ever eating any.

Title: People of the Hills
Author: Charles Burney and David Marshall Lang
Publisher: Weidenfileld and Nicholson O/P

A very readable account of the archaeology and history of the eastern and northern Anatolian highlands, with particularly informative sections on the civilisations of Urartu, Georgia and Armenia. The text is admirably supported by well-chosen black and white photographs.

Title: Armenia
Author: H.F.B. Lynch
Publisher: Khayats (Beirut) O/P

The last great Victorian traveller/scholar, who recorded his prodigious travels through this region of the decaying Ottoman Empire in some style. In addition to crossing the Pontic chain, he made a well-planned ascent of biblical Mount Ararat.

Title: Armenia: A Year at Erzeroom
Author: Robert Curzon
Publisher: Cambridge Scholars Press
ISBN: 1904303080

Despatched to Erzurum in 1843 to help fix the boundary between the Ottoman and Persian empires, Curzon spent a year in this harsh city, whose weather he describes thus:
"The atmospheric peculiarities of this climate are such that the weather, as a general rule, may be considered as on the way from bad to worse". *Curzon twice crossed the Pontic range from Trebizond (Trabzon) to Erzurum.*

Appendix B: Useful information

Title: Eastern Turkey: An Archictectural and Archaeological Survey Volume 2
Author: T.A. Sinclair
Publisher: The Pindar Press
ISBN: 0907132332
This volume (the second of four extremely comprehensive books covering virtually every monument in Eastern Turkey) has detailed information on the historical sites of the Black Sea region (including the Kaçkar themselves), the Georgian valleys and Erzurum. It also contains useful maps and plans and describes how to reach each site. Compiled in the 1980's, it was prohibitively expensive and is now difficult to obtain; try a specialist archaeological library.

Title: Rural Architecture in the Eastern Black Sea Region
Editor/Author: Prof. Dr. Afife Batur and others.
Publisher: Milli Reasürance TA.
ISBN: 975-7235-68-7
This huge book is a compilation of photographs of historic buildings of the region, with texts on the history, architecture and building traditions. Detailed illustrations show carving, decoration, layout and materials of both private houses and public buildings. Compiled from exhibition material, it presented in English and Turkish. The photos are superb; just a glance evokes the atmosphere of the lush and mysterious northern slopes.

Title: Black Sea Coast of Turkey.
Author: John Freely
Publisher: Redhouse Press
ISBN: 975-413-070-1
Covering the whole Black Sea coast, from Istanbul to the Georgian border, this is an engaging guide to both the major and minor historical sites. Freely is an old Turkey hand and very knowledgeable about the country. He uses quotations from source material liberally (everybody from the Greek mercenary Xenphon in the 5th century BC, through the Georgian monk Mercule in the 10th century to the British explorer Hamilton in the 19th century).

Title: Turkish Region
Authors: Ildiko Beller-Hann & Chris Hann
Publisher: James Currey/School of American Research Press 2001
ISBN: 0-85255-279-3
A readable and informative anthropological study of the region of which the Kaçkar are a part, dealing with everything from the economy through to marriage customs, the roles of Islam and the state through to the ethnic minorities (Laz, Hemşin and Georgian). It shows how, compared to other Turkish regions, the women have had to become independent and self-sufficient.

Title: Black Sea
Author: Neal Ascherson
Publisher: Vintage
ISBN: 009952046X
Only one chapter of this eloquently written book deals with the Pontic region, but it is essential reading. It is an unbeatable introduction the ecology, culture and history of the Black Sea in general.

Title: The Black Sea - A History
Author: Charles King
Publisher: Oxford University Press
ISBN: 0-19924-161-9
King takes as his starting point the idea of the Black Sea region as a place where cultures, ethnicities, religions and states have interacted rather than clashed. Well researched and readable, it covers everything from the early days of Greek colonisation to the setting up of the Black Sea Economic Co-operation Region following the collapse of the Soviet Union.

General Guides for Independent Travellers
Title: The Rough Guide to Turkey
Publisher: Penguin
ISBN: 1-84353-606-4
The most comprehensive of comparable guides, it includes relatively detailed historical and cultural information about the country, as well as how to get around, where to stay, where to eat, etc. Two of its authors, Marc Dubin and Terry Richardson, are also keen trekkers and have written about the Kaçkar and other mountain areas in Turkey.

Title: The Lonely Planet: Turkey
Publisher: Lonely Planet
ISBN: 1-74104-556-8
The Lonely Planet has a greater number of city and town plans and sells more copies than the Rough Guide. It is also updated slightly more frequently. Although it lacks the depth of the Rough Guide, it does have a newly-introduced section on trekking in Turkey by Kate Clow.

Title: Undiscovered Heaven - Yusufeli
Publisher: Yusufeli Governor's office
A local Turkish-English guidebook which lists all the attractions of the area including historical sites not covered in this guide, festivals, white water rafting and the mountains. Includes a list of driving routes and another of local hotels and pensions. Nicely produced, with illustrations showing the mountains in all seasons and many other aspects of the area. Available at a tourism office 50 m N of the otogar in Yusufeli.

A film
Title: Lignes de pente - Kaçkar Sugar
Producer: Dominique Perret
This exciting DVD is full of the thrills and spills of heli-skiing in the Kaçkar. It's done wonders for promoting winter sports in the region; in French but action speaks louder than words. The Swiss-Turkish company which offers heli-skiing packages in the Kaçkar can be found at www.turkeyheliski.com.

Appendix C TURKISH FOR TREKKERS

Turkish is unrelated to most European languages, but uses a European character set augmented by six specials - Ç,ç, (ch), Ş,ş, (sh), Ü, ü (eu) and Ö, ö (ew) as in German, I, ı, (hard i as in milk) and ğ, which lengthens the preceding vowel. Other characters are sounded as in English, except C,c, which is sounded as j in jam. There are no compound consonants, each is sounded separately.

Make words by adding suffixes (endings) to a basic stem. For verbs, endings give the negative, the voice (active or passive), the tense (present, future, past) and the case (I, you, he, etc). For nouns, endings give the case (subject, object, from, at, to) and the possessive, and also make related words. There is no gender, and no word for 'the'. Endings are regular, and, in village Turkish, frequently omitted.

Vowels are divided into two groups; the hard (a, ı, o, u) and soft (e, i, ö, ü); endings always use a vowel from the same group as the last vowel in the stem.

The Black Sea accent is very soft - there is a well-known t-shirt which reads 'celdim, cördüm, cezdim' - this is the way locals pronounce 'geldim, gördüm, gezdim' - (I came, I saw, I toured around). The last vowel is also often lengthened - as in 'hoş celdiiiin' (welcome).

Greetings:
merhaba - *hi, hello, greetings*
günaydın - *good morning*
iyi akşamlar - *good evening*
iyi günler - *good day,* iyi geceler - *good night*
Selaamın aleykum - *go with God;*
answered by - Aleykum selaam
hoş geldin, hoş geldiniz - *welcome;*
answered by - hoş büldük
nasılsınız? - *how are you?*
iyiyim, teşekkürler - *fine, thanks*
fena değil - *not bad*
ne var, ne yok? - *what's the news?*

Politeness:
Bey - *Mr,* Hanım - *Mrs (used after first name, eg.* Mehmet Bey, Fatma Hanım)
amca - *uncle;* teyze - *aunt,* dede - *grandfather*
abi - *brother,* abla - *sister,* kardeş - *sibling (these are used as honorary names for non-relatives)*
lütfen - *please,* teşekkür ederim - *thank you*
teşekkürler - *thanks*
özer dilerim, pardon - *excuse me*

Saying goodbye:
görüşürüz - *see you*
Allahısmarladık - *go with God*
hoşçakal - *stay well (when you leave)*
güle güle - *go with a smile (when you stay)*
gitmek zorundayım - *I must be going*
yine bekleriz - *we wait for you again*

Time:
sabah - *morning,* öğle - *noon,* akşam - *evening*
gece - *night,* gün - *day,* geç - *late,* erken - *early*
ilk bahar - *spring,* yaz - *summer*
son bahar - *autumn,* kış - *winter.*

Weather:
hava - *weather,* açık - *fine*
kar - *snow,* buz - *ice*
bulut - *cloud,* sis - *mist*
fırtına - *storm,* sel - *flood*
şimşek - *lightning,* yıldırım - *thunder*
rüzgar - *wind,* güneş - *sun*
serin - *cool,* sıcak - *hot,*
soğuk - *cold,* ıslak - *wet*
yağmur - *rain,* çağmur - *mud*

Trailfinding:
aşağı - *lower,* yukarı - *upper*
küçük - *small,* büyük - *big*
dağ - *mountain,* dağlar - *mountains*
bel / geçit - *pass,* boğaz - *narrow neck or gorge*
tepe - *hill,* tepeler - *hills,* zirve-*peak,* yamaç - *face, slope*
kaya - *rock,* çarşak - *scree,* taş - *stone*
yüz - *face,* sırt - *ridge*
uçurum - *cliff,* vadi - *valley*
dere / çay - *stream*
sazlık, bataklık - *marsh, swamp*
taşlık - *stony area*
şelale - *waterfall,* buzul - *glacier*
cağlayan - *small falls/cascade,* su - *water*
sarnıç - *cistern,* kuyu - *well*
oluk, kanalet - *ditch, irrigation channel*
yalak - *animal feeding trough*
köprü - *bridge*
deniz - *sea,* lake, göl - *lake*
tarla - *field,* arazı - *enclosed land*

düzlük / ova - *plain*, çukur - *hollow*
çanak - *bowl, cirque*
yol - *road, way*, yürüyüş yolu/patika - *path*
aşıt - *paved path over a pass*
kaldıran - *paved path between villages*
karayol - *asphalt road*, toprak yolu - *earth road*
stabilize yolu - *stabilised road*
yayla - *highest summer pasture*
mezra - *houses used in spring/autumn*
mahalle / semt - *district*
köy - *village*, kasaba - *town*
ev - *house*, barınak - *shepherd's hut*
yurt - *summerhouse*, çadır - *tent*, ahır - *stable*
cami - *mosque*, kilise - *church*
harabe, kalıntı - *ruins*
hisar - *fortress*, kale - *castle*
meydan - *village square*
işaret - *sign*, iz - *trail, track*
dörtyol / makas - *crossroads*
köşe - *corner*, viraj - *bend*
bakkal / dukkan - *shop*, lokanta - *restaurant*

Animals, birds and insects
boğa - *bull*, okuz - *bullock*, inek - *cow*
eşek - *donkey*, katır - *mule*, köpek - *dog*
koyun - *sheep*, keçi - *goat*, yılan - *snake*
kertenkele - *lizard*, kurbağa - *frog*
domuz - *wild boar*, ayı - *bear*
geyik/ceylan - *deer*, kurt - *wolf*, tilki - *fox*
kuş - *bird*, kartal - *eagle*, atmaca - *buzzard*,
şahin - *falcon*, kargı - *crow*
böcek - *insect*, kelebek - *butterfly*, sinek - *fly*,
arı - *bee*, eşekarısı - *wasp/hornet*
balık - *fish*, alabalık - *trout*

Trees and flowers
orman -*forest*, ağaç - *tree*, çam - *pine*
ladin - *spruce*, meşe - *oak*, kestane - *chestnut*
kavak - *poplar*, ardıç - *juniper*, köknar - *fir*
çiçek - *flower*, ot/bitki - *plant*
soğanlı bitki - *bulbous plant*

Equipment:
sırt çantası - *rucksack*, çadır - *tent*
uykutulumu - *sleeping bag*, mat - *mat*
el-feneri - *handtorch*, kibrit - *matches*
çakmak - *lighter*, ışık - *light*
bot - *boot*, ayakkabı - *shoes*,
terlik - *indoor shoes*, çorap - *sock*
çeket - *jacket*, yağmurluk - *waterproof coat*
pantalon - *trousers*, şor - *shorts*
buz kazması - *ice axe*, tozluk - *gaiters*
gömlek - *shirt*, t-şor - *t-shirt*
eldiven - *gloves*, şapka - *hat*
ocak - *cooker*, tencere - *pan*
şise - *bottle*, su şişesi, matara - *water bottle*

tabak - *plate*, bardak - *glass*, fıncan - *cup*
çatal - *fork*, kaşık - *spoon*, buçak - *knife*

General chat:
anlamadım - *I didn't understand*
daha yavaş konuş - *talk more slowly*
yok - *no, none*, (eg. şeker yok - *there's no sugar*)
var - *yes, there is* (e.g. su var - *there is water*)
hayır, yo *(or a quick lift of the head)* - *no*
evet - *yes*, tamam / olur - *ok*,
bir dakka - *just a minute*, sakın ol - *take it easy*
geçmiş olsun - *may it soon pass*
afiyet olsun - *enjoy your meal*
elinize sağlık - *health to your hands (to the cook)*
iyi yolculuklar - *have a good trip*
bu - *this*, şu - *that*, biraz - *a bit*
biraz fazla - *a bit more*, değil - *is not*
bu temiz - *this is clean*
şu temiz değil - *that isn't clean*
şu en büyük dağı değil - *that isn't the biggest mountain*, bu daha büyük - *this is bigger*

The following endings denote position:
Add -e/a - *to*, -de/da - *at*, -den/dan - *from*
eg: sola git - *go to the left*, burada dur - *stop here*, evden gel - *come from the house*.

Add them to any other word:
bana, bende, benden - *to me, with me, from me*
(su bende - *The water is with me, I have water*)
sağ - *right*, sol - *left*
ilere, ilerde, ilerden - *to / in / from the front*
arkaya, arkada, arkadan - *to / at / from the back*
üst - *above*, alt - *below*
bura - *here*, ora - *there*, şu - *over there*
karşı - *opposite*, yanı - *next to*, arası - *between*
kenarı - *the side of*, oteki - *the other one*

Pronouns and possessives:
ben - *I, me*, biz - *we*, sen, siz - *you* (sing/plural)
o - *he/her/it*, onlar - *their*
-im, -imiz - *mine, ours*, -in, -iniz - *yours*
benim - *mine*, bizim - *ours*
senin, sizin - *yours*, onun - *his, hers, its*
şekerim var - *(lit. there is my sugar) I have sugar*
yumurtan yok - *you have no egg(s)*

People nouns:
eş - *wife or husband*, eşim - *my wife/husband*
arkadaş - *friend*, arkadaşınız - *your friend(s)*
misafir - *guest*, misafirimiz - *our visitor(s)*
yabancı - *stranger, foreigner*
gavur, kafir - *non-muslim (a mild insult)*
erkek - *man*, kadın - *woman*, çocuk - *child*,
kız - *girl*, oğlan - *boy*, bebek - *baby*
anne - *mother*, ana - *mummy*, baba - *daddy*
avcı - *hunter*, çoban - *shepherd*, çiftçi - *farmer*
bekçi - *watchman*, jandarma - *rural police*

İngiliz - *English*, Amerika - *USA*
İngilizim - *I'm English*
Amerikalıyız - *we are American,*
Londralıyım - *I'm a Londoner*
Romalıyız - *we're from Rome*
Questions:
ne zaman? - *when?*, nerede? - *where?*
nasıl? - *how?*, kaç tane? - *how many?*
ne kadar? - *how much?*
neden, niçin? - *why?*
kim? - *who?*, kimin? - *whose?*
ne istiyorsunuz? - *what do you want?*
adınız nedir? - *what's your name?*
nerelisiniz / memleket? - *where are you from?*
bu nedir? - *what's this?*
saat kaç? - *what's the time?*
Add mi/mı? to make a question:
kızın mı? - *is this your girl (daughter)?*
göstermiyim? - *shall I show you?*
iyi misiniz? - *are you ok?*
Basic Verbs:
ol(mak) - *(to) be, exist,* al - *take,* ver - *give*
git(mek) - *(to) go;* gel - *come;* kal - *stay*
dur - *stop,* yürü - *walk;* sap / dön - *turn*
kalk - *get up,* otur - *sit,* yat - *lie down,*
konuş - *talk,* de - *say,* sor - *ask*
anla - *understand,* anlat - *tell*
pişir - *cook,* temizle - *clean*
gör - *see,* göster - *show*

ye - *eat,* iç - *drink,* sigara iç - *smoke*
iste - *want,* tarif et - *direct*
kat - *add, put on,* çık - *go out*
Add the possessive endings:
gelin, geliniz - *you come,*
sorım, sorımız - *I ask, we ask*
Add me/ma to the root to give the negative:
alma - *don't take,* almayın - *don't you take,*
görmem - *I don't see*
Emergency:
imdat - *help,* tehlike - *danger,*
ilk yardım - *first aid,* yangın - *fire*
yaralı - *injured,* hasta - *sick,* kan - *blood*
kaza - *accident,* doktor - *doctor*
Adjectives:
çok - *very,* daha - *more,* en - *most*
az - *less, a little,* hiç - *none*
iyi - *good, fine,* fena, kötü - *bad*
temiz - *clean,* pis - *dirty*
büyük - *big,* küçük - *little,* güzel - *nice,*
güneşli - *sunny,* yağmurlu - *rainy*
zor - *difficult,* kolay - *easy*
hızlı, çabuk - *quick,* yavaş - *slow*
geniş - *wide,* dar - *narrow*
düz - *level,* dik - *steep*
yakın - *near,* uzak - *far*
bir, iki, üç, dört, beş - *1,2,3,4,5*
altı, yedi, sekiz, dokuz, on - *6,7,8,9,10*
yüz, bin - *a hundred, a thousand*

Appendix D **GLOSSARY OF MOUNTAINEERING TERMS**

Basin: the area of land drained by a river and its branches.
Bowl: a relatively small depression or hollow in a mountain landscape.
Buttress: a part of the mountain or rock that stands out from the main face.
Col: a low point between two mountains or along a ridge or spine.
Contour: a line joining points of equal altitude; also used here to mean keeping to the same height/level when walking across a hill or mountainside
Couloir: a stony, steep gully which may have snow or ice.
Cairn: a pile of stones used to mark a route or route junction.
Cirque: a deep and steep-walled basin on a mountain formed beneath the start of a glacier at the top of a valley.
Fork: a place where a route splits (forks) into two routes.
Glacier: a slowly moving permanent mass of ice.
Gully: a wide, shallow ravine on a mountainside.
Hairpin: a tight bend or turn in a path.
Hanging Valley: a side valley that joins a larger valley at a higher level than the main valley floor.
Headland: part of a hillside jutting out over a valley.
Moraine: an accumulation of unconsolidated debris which is left behind by the melting of a glacier.
Outcrop: rock standing up from a hillside.
Pass: a route between two mountains or two highpoints on a ridge.
Precipice: a very steep, sheer cliff.
Ridge: a long crest or row of summits between valleys or lower ground.
Scree: loose rocks and stones that cover the slope below a cliff. Scree slides under your feet with every step.
Spine: a narrow ridgetop, usually with summits along it.
Spur: a side-ridge sloping down from a main ridge or spine.
Summit: highest point of a mountain or ridge.
Tarn: a small mountain lake.
Zigzag: a path with very sharp turns running up/down a slope.

Appendix E **PHOTOGRAPHS**

The photographs in this book were taken by Kate Clow and Terry Richardson using digital photography or Fuji Sensia slide film. Photographs are listed clockwise from the top left of each page

Page 161 -

Büyük Deniz Gölü under ice, Village shop in Elevit, Kate's boots, Playing football in Naznara Yaylası

Page 162 -

Looking down from the summit of Altıparmak, Woman and child at Davali Yaylası, Old stone bridge at Başyayla, Misty river in Elevit, Yayla houses at Salent

Page 163 -

Cairn on Hodacur Geçiti, Overlooking Aşağı Çaymakçur Yaylası, Gentian, Drinking trough at Bahar Yaylası, Relief carving on the Georgian church at Barhal

Page 164 -

Suleyman and his horse at Davali, Old village road in Saksera Mezrası, Elderberries in the Onbolat Deresi, Summer returnees at Davali

Page 165 -

Şimşek (Lightning) grazing on the Okuz Gölü Geçiti, Girl in Yaylalar, Curious cow in Tirovit, The bridge at Sebekdüzü

Page 166 -

Zil Kale, Copper pot at Avusor Yaylası, Door hinge from Samistal Yaylası, Chapel above Barhal, Georgian church of Dört Kilise, Tekkale

Page 167 -

The Çılanç Köprüsü at Çat, Packhorse bridge at Apivanak, Hinge from an old house in Ayder, Spring at Hazındak Yayalası, Cairn on the Tepe Sırtı

Page 168 -

Polygonums above Palovit, Butterfly on a centaurea, Dung drying at Apivanak, The Georgian church in Barhal

Page 169 -

Crocus scharonjani at Okuz Gölü, Rosehips in the Onbolat Deresi, Bayır Kilise near Tekkale, Yayla house at Pokut, Yayla house at Hazındak

Page 170 -

Winter berries above Olgunlar, View from the Hevek Geçiti , Snow bridge in the Mahlen Deresi

THE KAÇKAR

Page 171 -

    Olgunlar under November snow, Trekkers crossing the Naletleme Geçiti, Muscari, Karagöl from the slopes of Altıparmak

Page 172 -

    Tim above Modut Yaylası, Trekkers crossing a stream en route to Kaçkar summit, Crossing the Davali bridge

Page 173 -

    Campsite at Dilberdüzü, beneath the Şeytan Kayaları, En route from Adyder to Huzur Yaylası, Aqualegia near Olgunlar, Feeding a kid in Başyayla

Page 174 -

    Looking over Elevit village towards Hacivanak Dersesi, Karamolla Yayalası, Kaçkar from above Derebaşı Gölü, Pokut Yaylası

Page 175 -

    Kate, Lem and Jane above Apivanak, Hacıvanak Yaylası in autumn, with crocus vallicosa in flower, Village house in Ortam Mahallesi, near Çamlıhemşin, Aşağı Gurp Yaylası

Front cover -

    Kaçkar range glimpsed from Hastaf Yaylası, in July

Back cover and map front cover -

    Cairn on the Hodacur Geciti, with Kaçkar in the background

Map back cover -

    Village girl from Veknal carrying Kate's pack

Inside front cover

    Bull fighting at the Kafkasör Festival near Artvin, Kaçkar summit in bad weather, Grandmother from Taşbaşı Yaylası, Wrestlers compete at the Tekkale Festival, Soul and Blues near Okuz Gölü, Breakfast tray with a local cheese speciality, muhlama.

Appendix E Photographs

When you are travelling, there are small moments...

Like the first time you observe a wild Brown Bear or the peace and quiet after a long day, when you are watching the glorious sunset and sipping coffee made with snow-melt water. Or the moment you see the first snowdrops bursting through the snow. Or suddenly, when you are exploring an ancient site, the words of the guide bring the ancient days vividly to life.

These are the moments which turn an ordinary touristic visit into a unique travelling experience. Our job is to make sure that you will be in the right place at the right time to capture these moments.

Our task is to create unique travelling experiences

Middle Earth Travel Gaferli Mah. Cevizler Sok. No:20 Göreme / Nevşehir
Tel: +90384 271 25 59 Fax: +90384 271 25 62
www.middleearthtravel.com e-mail: info@middleearthtravel.com

161

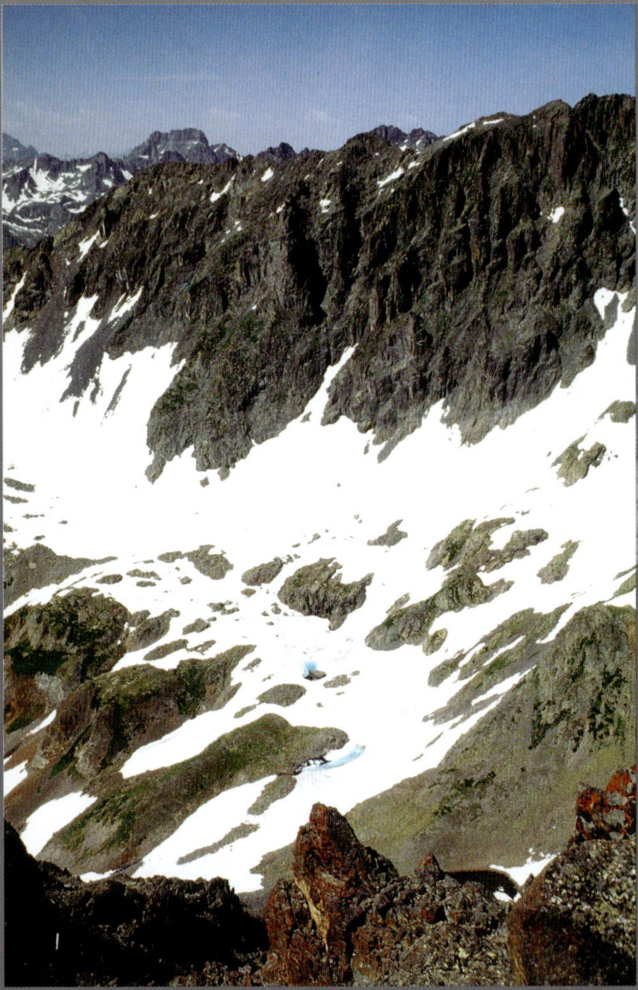
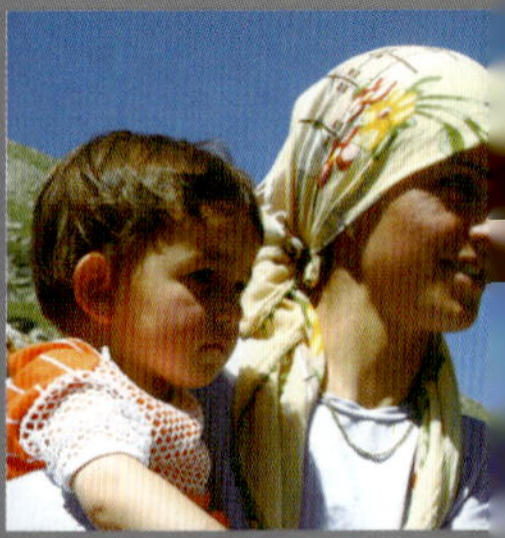
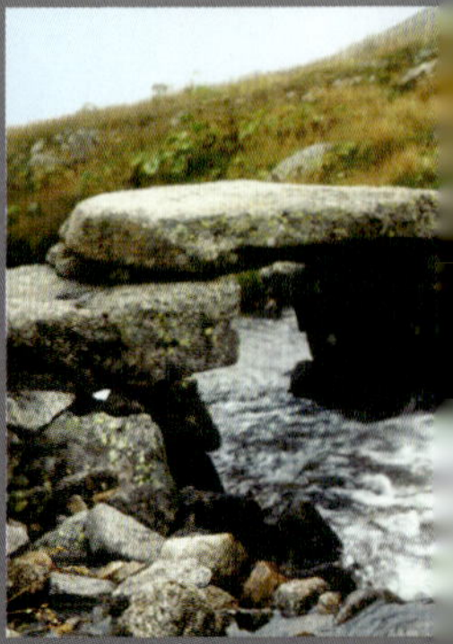
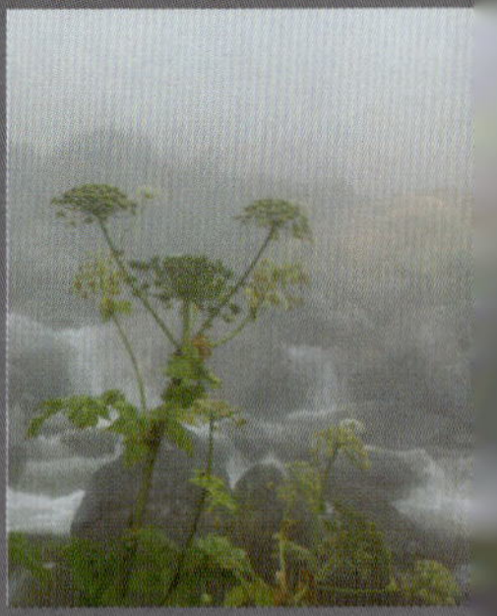
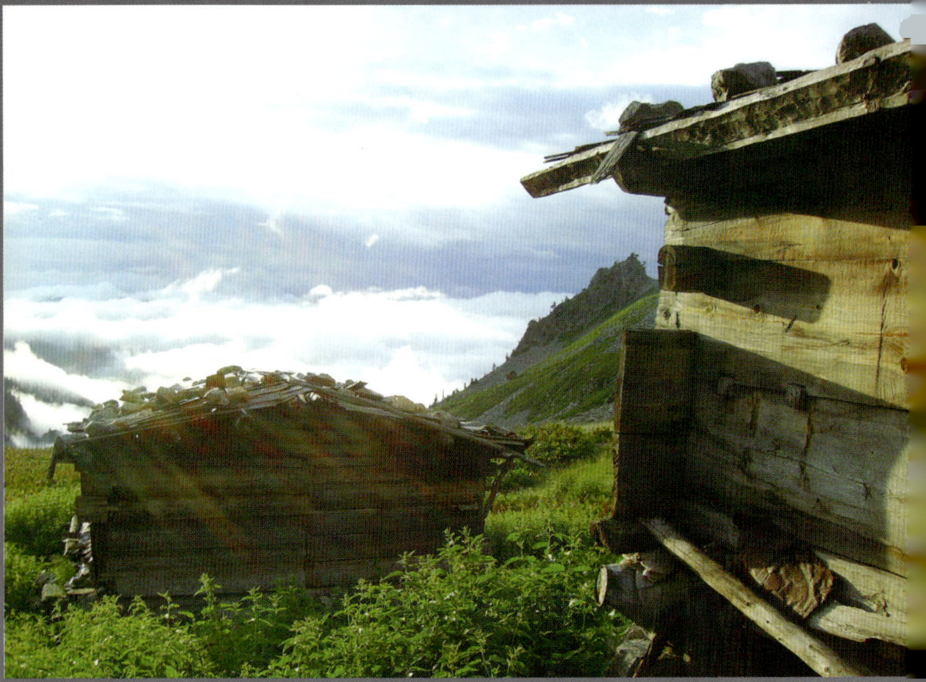

163

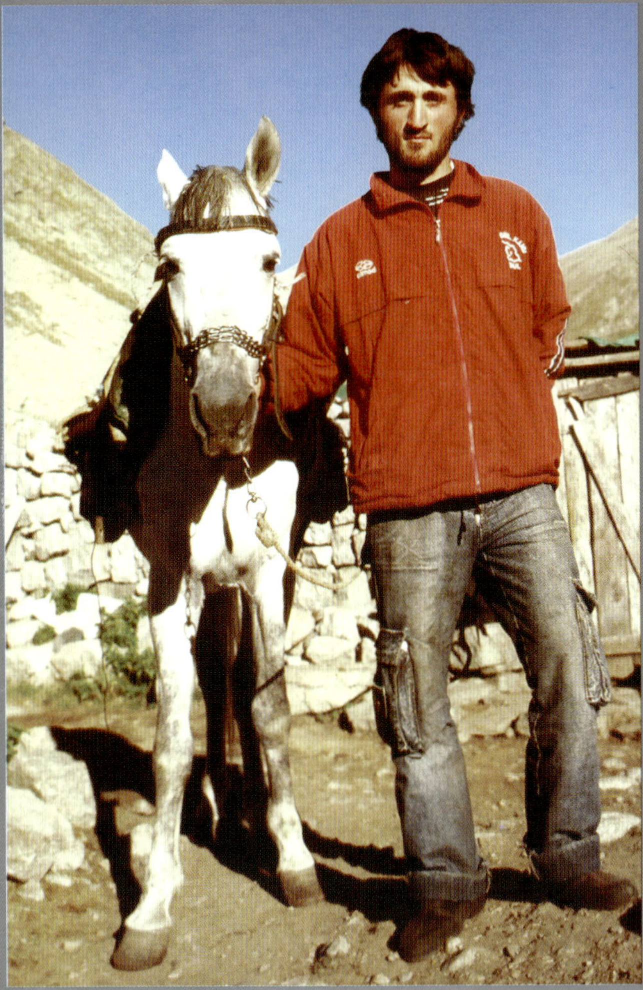

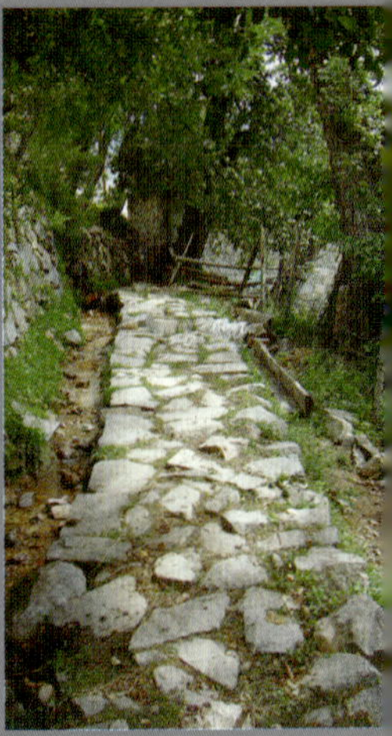

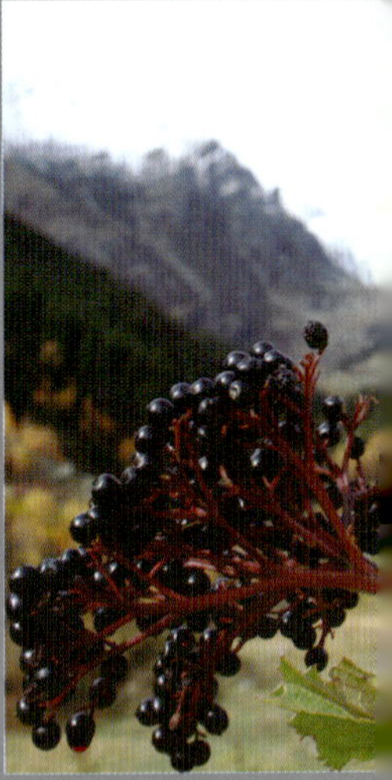

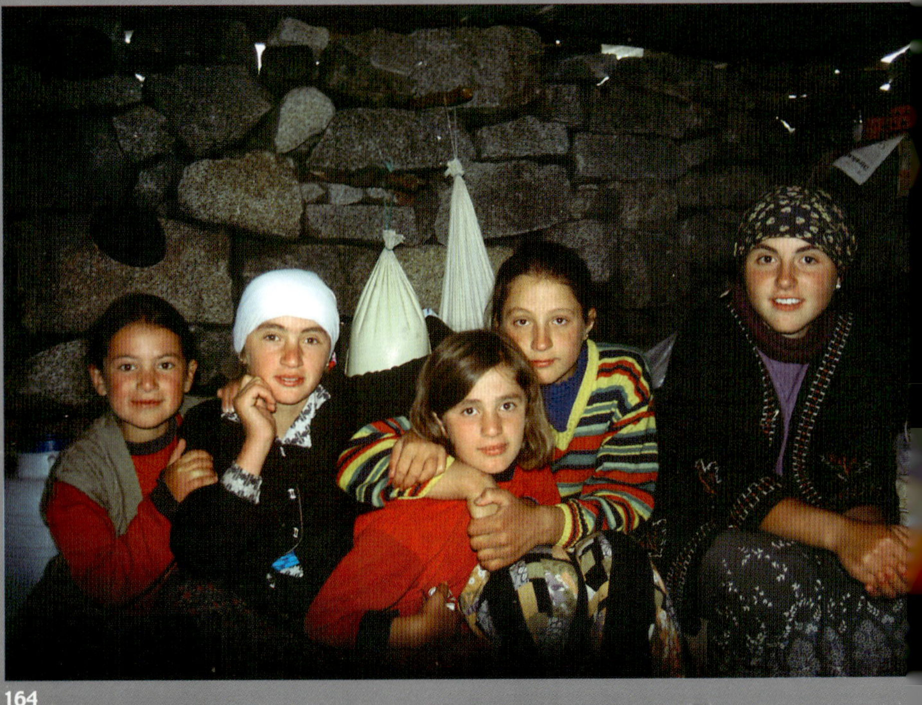

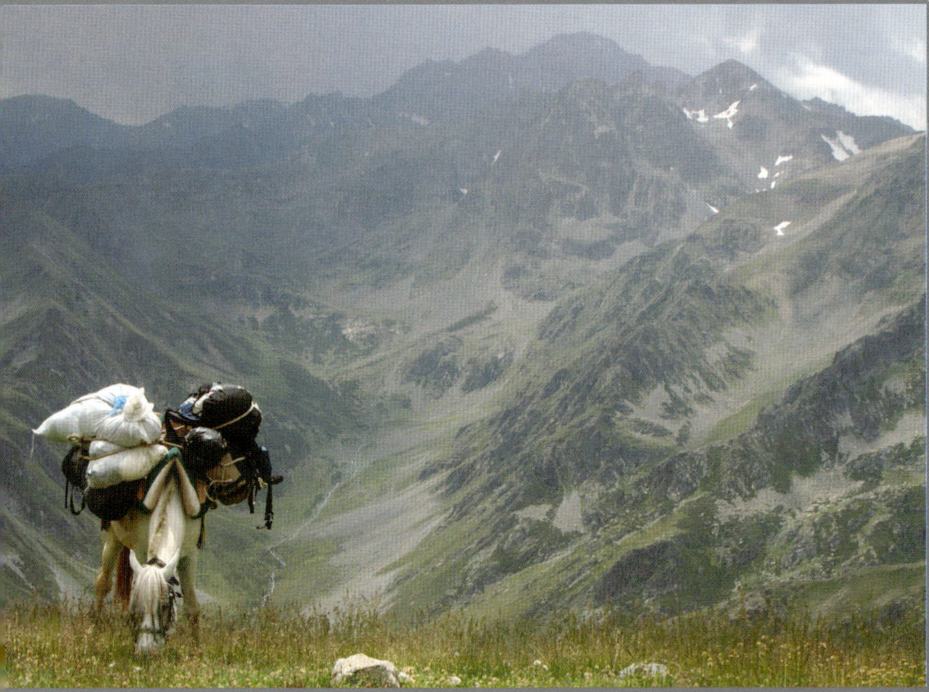

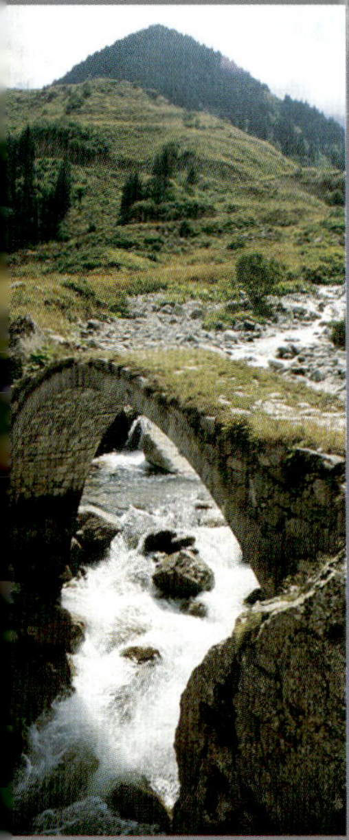

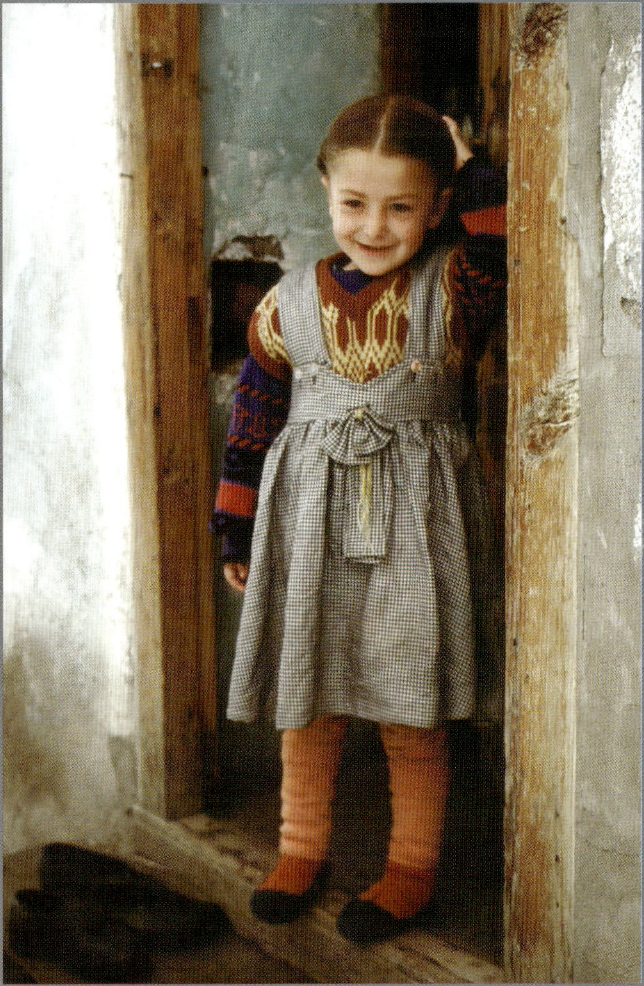

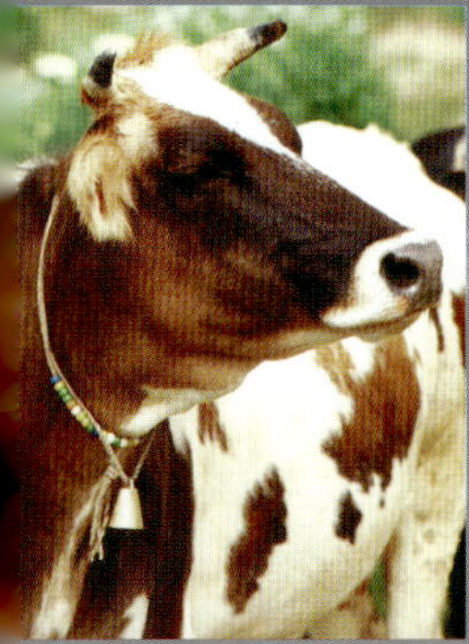

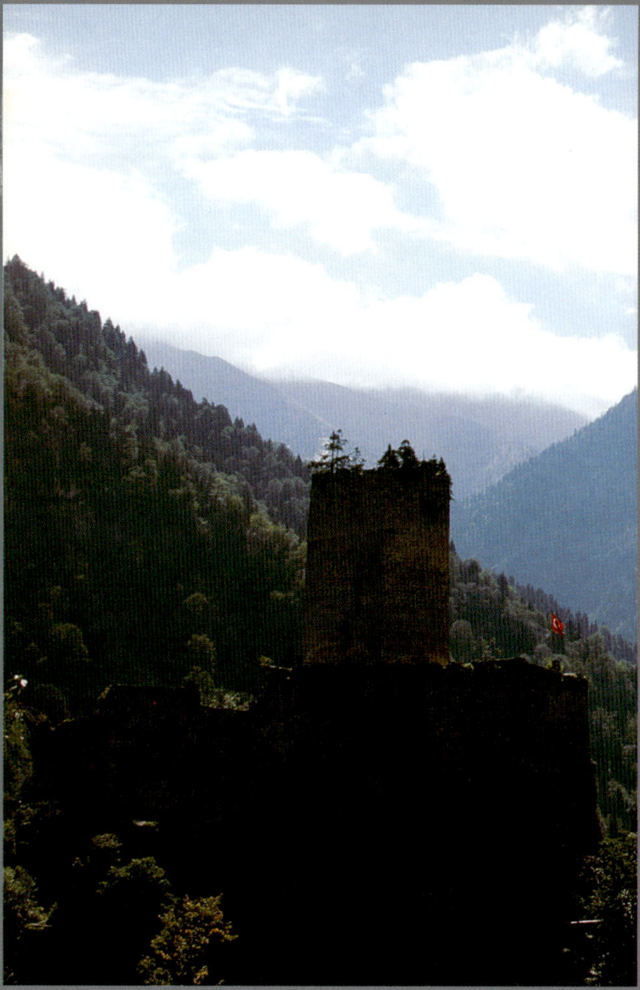

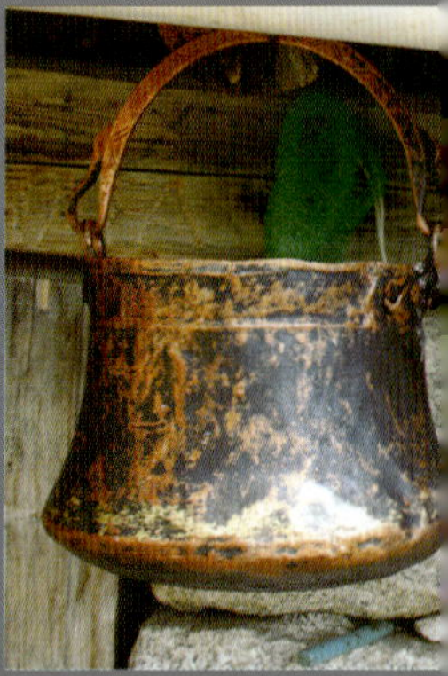

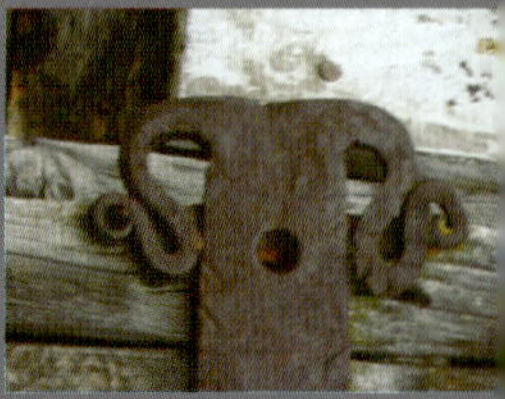

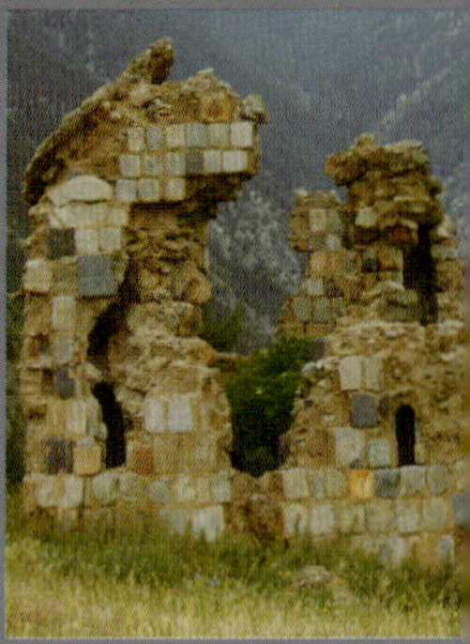

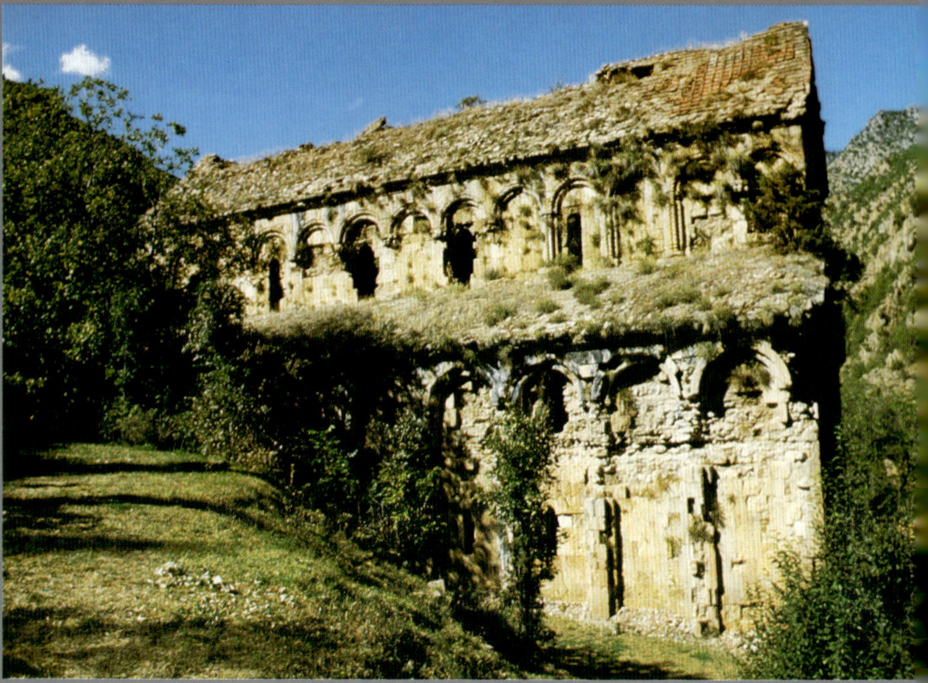

167

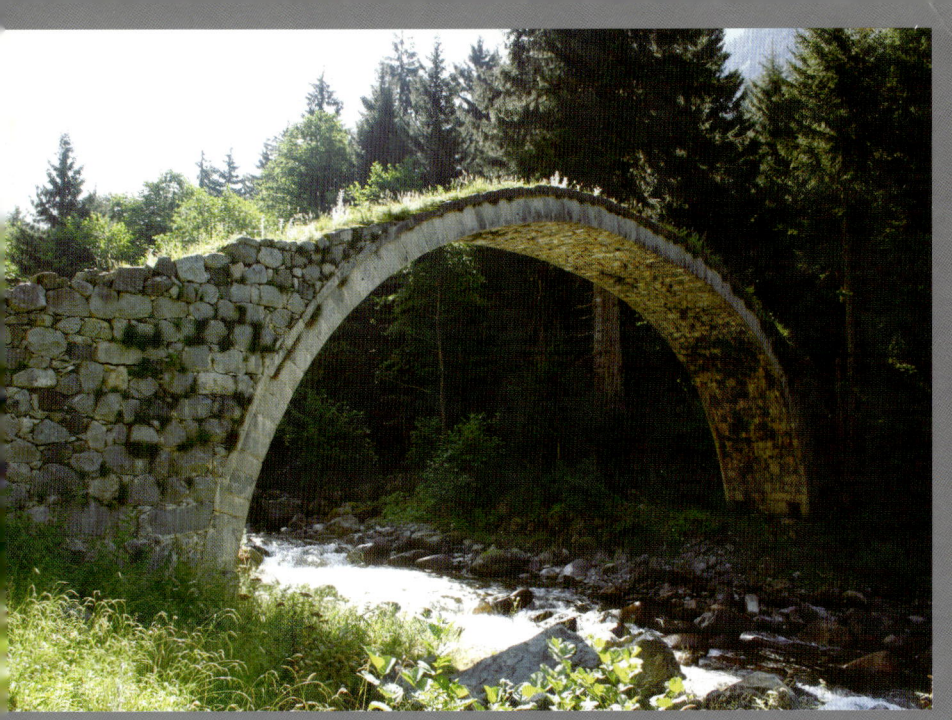

168

169

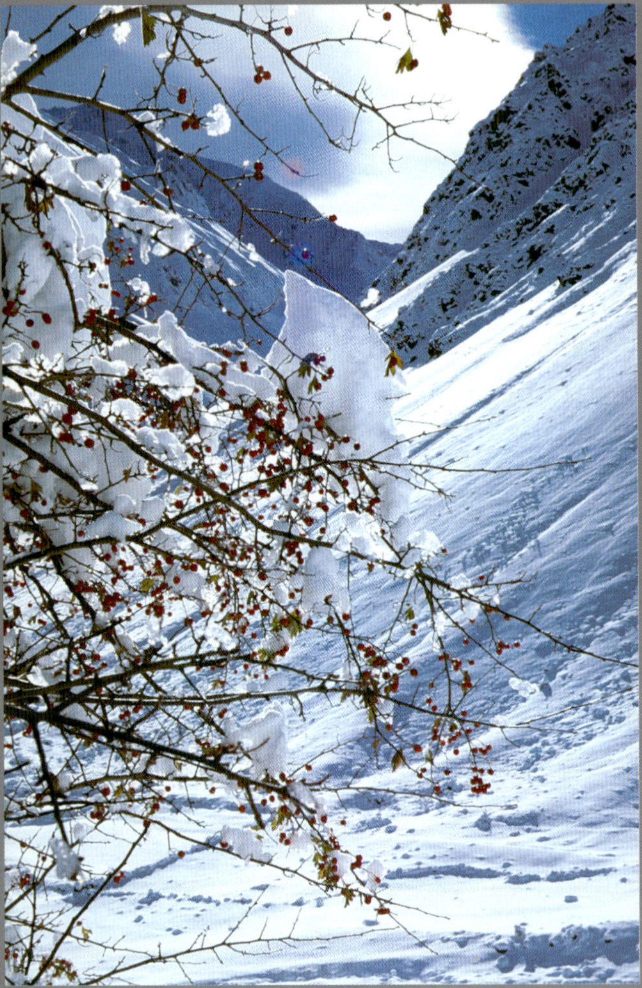
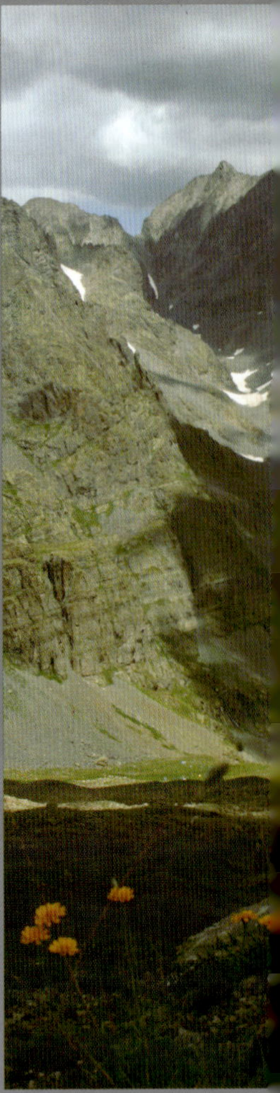
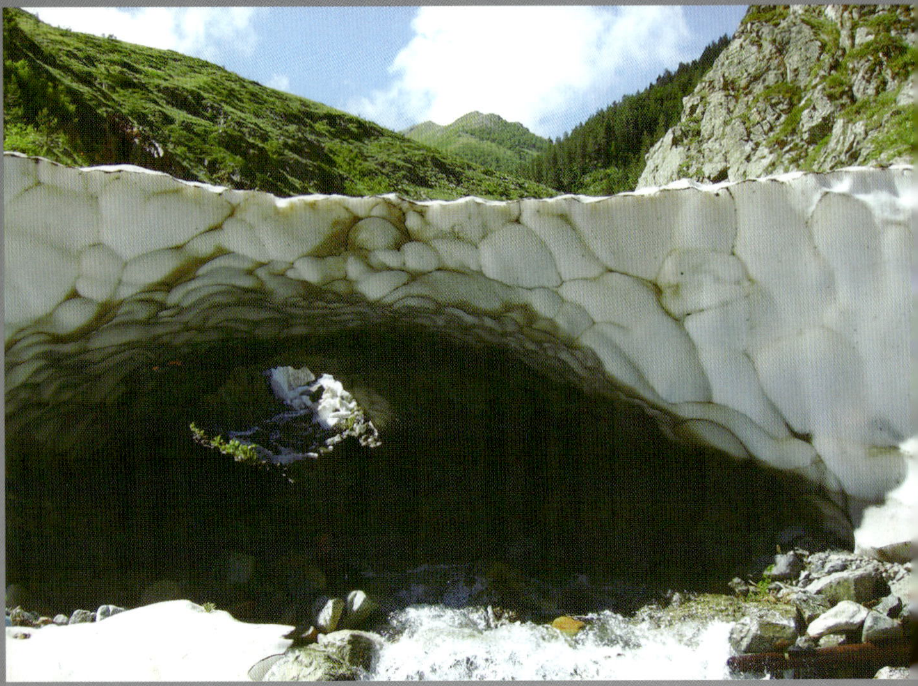

171

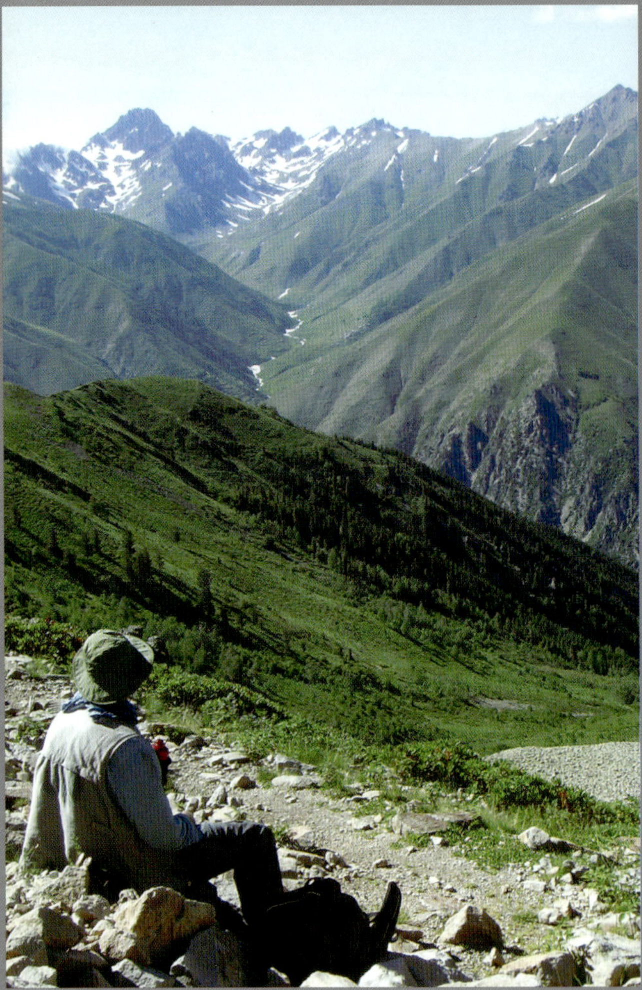
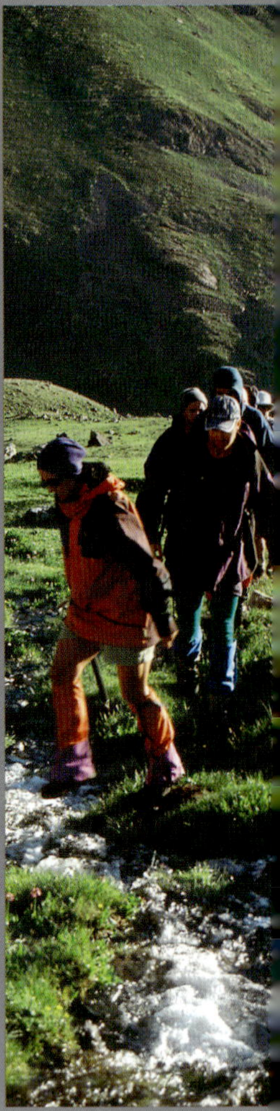
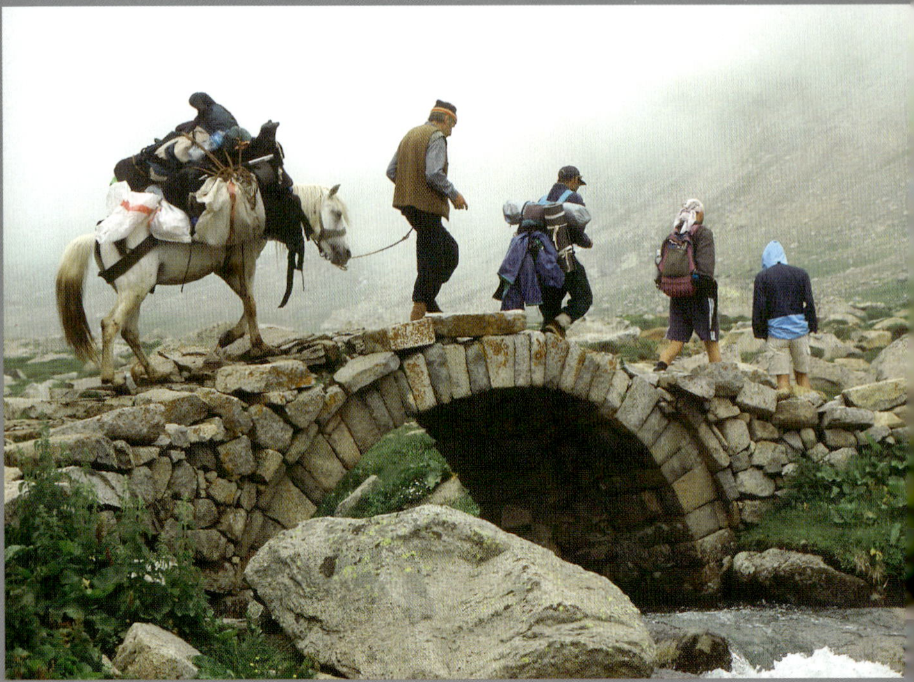

173

174

175

TREKKING TOURS IN TAURUS MOUNTAINS

TREKKING IN KACKAR & KARCAL MOUNTAINS

MT. ARARAT EXPEDITIONS

LYCIAN WAY TOURS

SKI MOUNTAINEERING EXPEDITIONS IN TURKEY

EXPLORER
OUTDOOR SPECIALIST | **TURKEY**

Cinnah Caddesi No: 40 / 16 Çankaya, Ankara / Turkey | Tel: +90 (312) 438 00 95 | Fax: +90 (312) 438 00 96
www.explorer.com.tr